GATEWAY *to* FREEDOM

ALSO BY ERIC FONER

American History Now (editor, with Lisa McGirr, 2011)

The Fiery Trial: Abraham Lincoln and American Slavery (2010)

Our Lincoln: New Perspectives on Lincoln and His World (editor, 2008)

Herbert Aptheker on Race and Democracy: A Reader (editor, with Manning Marable, 2006)

Forever Free: The Story of Emancipation and Reconstruction (2005)

Voices of Freedom: A Documentary History (editor, 2004)

Give Me Liberty! An American History (2004)

Who Owns History? Rethinking the Past in a Changing World (2002)

The Story of American Freedom (1998)

America's Reconstruction: People and Politics after the Civil War (with Olivia Mahoney, 1995)

Thomas Paine (editor, 1995)

Freedom's Lawmakers: A Directory of Black Reconstruction Officeholders (editor, 1993; rev. ed. 1996)

The Reader's Companion to American History (editor, with John A. Garraty, 1991)

The New American History (editor, 1990; rev. ed. 1997)

A House Divided: America in the Age of Lincoln (with Olivia Mahoney, 1990)

A Short History of Reconstruction (1990)

Reconstruction: America's Unfinished Revolution 1863–1877 (1988)

Nothing but Freedom: Emancipation and Its Legacy (1983)

Politics and Ideology in the Age of the Civil War (1980)

Tom Paine and Revolutionary America (1976)

Nat Turner (editor, 1971)

America's Black Past: A Reader in Afro-American History (editor, 1971)

Free Soil, Free Labor, Free Men: The Ideology of the Republican Party Before the Civil War (1970)

GATEWAY *to* FREEDOM

The HIDDEN HISTORY *of the* UNDERGROUND RAILROAD

ERIC FONER

W. W. NORTON & COMPANY
New York | London

Printed in the United States of America
First Edition

For information about permission to reproduce selections from this book,
write to Permissions, W. W. Norton & Company, Inc.,
500 Fifth Avenue, New York, NY 10110

For information about special discounts for bulk purchases, please contact
W. W. Norton Special Sales at specialsales@wwnorton.com or 800-233-4830

Manufacturing by Quad Graphics, Fairfield
Book design by Chris Welch Design
Production manager: Julia Druskin

ISBN: 978-0-393-24407-6

W. W. Norton & Company, Inc.
500 Fifth Avenue, New York, N.Y. 10110
www.wwnorton.com

W. W. Norton & Company Ltd.
Castle House, 75/76 Wells Street, London W1T 3QT

1 2 3 4 5 6 7 8 9 0

To my students

CONTENTS

LIST OF MAPS AND ILLUSTRATIONS

Maps

Illustrations

FOLLOWING PAGE 78:

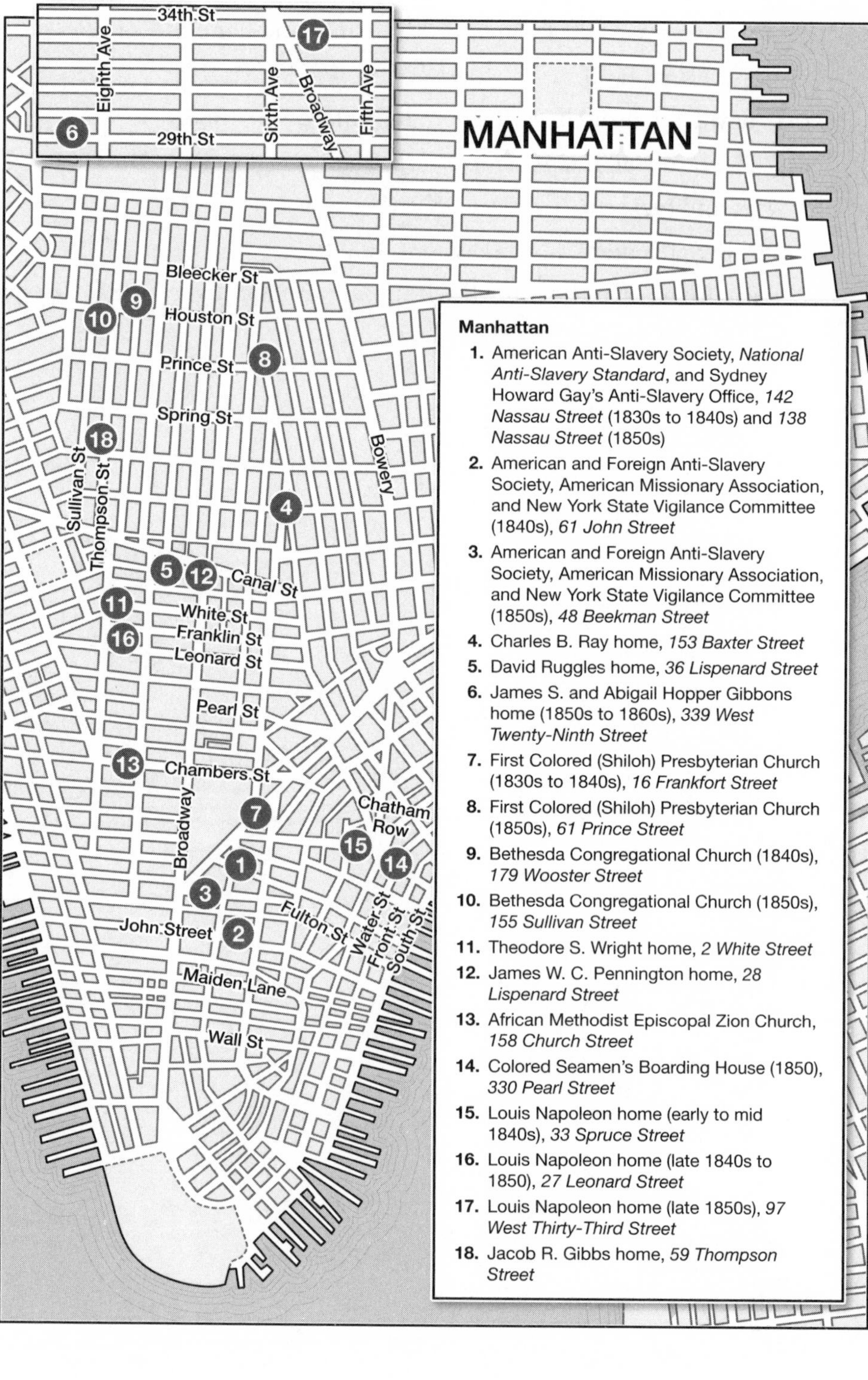
34th St
Eighth Ave
Sixth Ave
Broadway
Fifth Ave
29th St
MANHATTAN
Bleecker St
Houston St
Prince St
Spring St
Bowery
Sullivan St
Thompson St
Canal St
White St
Franklin St
Leonard St
Pearl St
Chambers St
Broadway
Chatham Row
Fulton St
Water St
Front St
South St
John Street
Maiden Lane
Wall St
Manhattan
1. American Anti-Slavery Society, *National Anti-Slavery Standard*, and Sydney Howard Gay's Anti-Slavery Office, *142 Nassau Street* (1830s to 1840s) and *138 Nassau Street* (1850s)
2. American and Foreign Anti-Slavery Society, American Missionary Association, and New York State Vigilance Committee (1840s), *61 John Street*
3. American and Foreign Anti-Slavery Society, American Missionary Association, and New York State Vigilance Committee (1850s), *48 Beekman Street*
4. Charles B. Ray home, *153 Baxter Street*
5. David Ruggles home, *36 Lispenard Street*
6. James S. and Abigail Hopper Gibbons home (1850s to 1860s), *339 West Twenty-Ninth Street*
7. First Colored (Shiloh) Presbyterian Church (1830s to 1840s), *16 Frankfort Street*
8. First Colored (Shiloh) Presbyterian Church (1850s), *61 Prince Street*
9. Bethesda Congregational Church (1840s), *179 Wooster Street*
10. Bethesda Congregational Church (1850s), *155 Sullivan Street*
11. Theodore S. Wright home, *2 White Street*
12. James W. C. Pennington home, *28 Lispenard Street*
13. African Methodist Episcopal Zion Church, *158 Church Street*
14. Colored Seamen's Boarding House (1850), *330 Pearl Street*
15. Louis Napoleon home (early to mid 1840s), *33 Spruce Street*
16. Louis Napoleon home (late 1840s to 1850), *27 Leonard Street*
17. Louis Napoleon home (late 1850s), *97 West Thirty-Third Street*
18. Jacob R. Gibbs home, *59 Thompson Street*

Gateway to Freedom

UNDERGROUND RAILROAD SITES IN NEW YORK CITY AND BROOKLYN

GATEWAY
to
FREEDOM

1

INTRODUCTION: RETHINKING THE UNDERGROUND RAILROAD

The nineteenth century's most celebrated black American first tasted freedom on September 4, 1838, when he arrived in New York City as a nineteen-year-old fugitive slave. Frederick Bailey had long hoped to escape from bondage. As a youth in Maryland he gazed out at the ships on Chesapeake Bay, seeing them as "freedom's swift-winged angels." He secretly taught himself to read and write, understanding, he later wrote, that knowledge was "the pathway from slavery to freedom." In 1836, he and four friends devised a plan to abscond by canoe onto the bay and somehow make their way north. But the plan was discovered, and before their departure the five were arrested, jailed, and returned to their owners.[1]

Two years later, while working as a caulker in a Baltimore shipyard, Bailey again plotted his escape, this time with the assistance of Anna Murray, a free black woman he planned to marry. She provided the money for a rail ticket, and Bailey borrowed papers from a retired black sailor identifying him as a free man. Dressed in nautical attire, he boarded a train, hoping to reach New York City. Maryland law required black passengers on the Philadelphia, Wilmington, and Baltimore line (which opened only a year before Bailey's escape) to apply for tickets before eight o'clock in the morning on the day of travel so that their free papers could be examined and, if necessary, investigated. But the measure remained largely unenforced. Bailey used a printed timetable to arrive at the station at the moment of the train's departure and purchased his ticket on board to avoid scrutiny.

Despite the short distance—less than 200 miles—the trip proved arduous and complicated. Thirty-five miles north of Baltimore the passengers had to disembark to cross the Susquehanna River by ferry. At Wilmington, they boarded a steamboat for Philadelphia. There, Bailey later recalled, "I enquired of a colored man how I could get on to New York." The man directed him to a depot where Bailey took a ferry to Camden, New Jersey, then the Camden and Amboy Railroad to South Amboy, then another ferry across the Hudson River to a dock at the foot of Chambers Street. Less than twenty-four hours after leaving Baltimore, he disembarked on free soil. "A new world burst upon my agitated vision," he would later write.[2]

In spite of his exhilaration, Bailey was frightened and alone, and he had no real plan about what to do next. He encountered Jake, a fugitive slave he had known in Maryland, who warned him that although they were in a free state, slave catchers roamed the city's streets. Shortly thereafter, a "warm-hearted and generous" black sailor directed him to the home of David Ruggles at 36 Lispenard Street, not far from the docks. Ruggles was secretary and prime mover of the New York Committee of Vigilance, founded three years earlier to combat an epidemic of kidnapping. Many years before Solomon Northup drew attention to this problem in his widely read memoir, *Twelve Years a Slave*, free blacks, frequently young children, were abducted on New York's streets for sale into southern slavery.[3] The committee also provided fugitives from the South with shelter, transportation, and if they were apprehended, legal representation. By 1838, Ruggles was the leader of a network with connections to antislavery activists in Baltimore, Philadelphia, New England, and upstate New York. He regularly scoured the wharfs, on the lookout for fugitive slaves. Ruggles took Bailey into his home and advised him to change his name to help avoid recapture. Frederick Bailey now became Frederick Johnson. Ruggles then gave him his first introduction to antislavery activities and mailed a letter to Anna Murray, urging her to come to New York at once. A few days later the couple married in Ruggles's parlor. The Reverend James W. C. Pennington performed the ceremony.[4]

Like Bailey, Pennington (born James Pembroke) was a fugitive slave. He had escaped in 1827, at the age of twenty-one, from Washington County, Maryland, just south of the Mason-Dixon Line, leaving behind his parents and ten brothers and sisters. Pembroke's journey to freedom proved far more harrowing than Bailey's. He started out on foot, but with "no knowledge of distance or direction," he ended up heading southeast, toward Baltimore, not north. He received advice from a number of people, white and black, about how to avoid slave catchers, but at one point a group of men seized him, hoping to claim the $200 reward his owner had advertised for his return. Pembroke managed to escape from his captors and eventually made his way to southern Pennsylvania, where a Quaker couple, William and Phoebe Wright, sheltered him for six months, paid him for work as a farm laborer, and taught him to read and write. Pennington moved on to New York City in 1828. He found a job in Brooklyn, attended classes in the evening, and became a teacher in a black school on Long Island. By the time he officiated at the Baileys' wedding, Pennington had become pastor of a local Congregational church.[5]

Unlike Pennington, Frederick Bailey did not remain in New York. He considered himself "comparatively safe," but Ruggles appreciated the precarious situation of fugitives in the city. Soon after their wedding he gave the couple five dollars (more than a week's wages for a manual laborer at the time) and told them to head to New Bedford, Massachusetts, where another black abolitionist would receive them. A major port city, New Bedford was the world's whaling capital. Its shipyards and oceangoing vessels provided employment to many free blacks and escaped slaves. Indeed, because of its strong abolitionist movement and thriving black community long accustomed to sheltering runaways, the city was known as the "fugitive's Gibraltar" (or, as a Virginia newspaper put it, "a den of negro thieves and fugitive protectors"). In the fall of 1838, having discovered that in New Bedford, Johnson families were "so numerous as to cause some confusion in distinguishing one from another," Frederick Bailey changed his name one last time. Henceforth, he would be known as Frederick Douglass.[6]

I

It is impossible to say how many slaves escaped to freedom in the decades before the Civil War. Contemporary sources are often of little help. For very different reasons, both abolitionists and slave-owners had a vested interest in exaggerating the numbers—the former to emphasize the black desire for freedom and their own efforts "like noble heroes . . . for suffering and oppressed humanity," the latter as evidence of a northern conspiracy to undermine the peculiar institution. Estimates—guesses, really—suggest somewhere between 1,000 and 5,000 per year between 1830 and 1860. This was hardly enough to affect the growth of the slave population (which approached four million in 1860), but sufficient to become a cause of alarm in the slave states and of contention between North and South, not to mention significant monetary loss for affected slaveholders.[7]

There were enough escapes that the southern physician Samuel A. Cartwright claimed to have identified a malady previously unknown to medical science: “drapetomania,” a “disease causing Negroes to run away.” (Frederick Law Olmsted, the New York journalist and landscape architect who wrote popular accounts of his visits to the South in the 1850s, noted that white servants had long been known to abscond. Perhaps, he suggested sarcastically, blacks had caught this disease from them.) Each escape had its own character and faced its own dangers, but those of Douglass and Pennington were in some ways typical. Most fugitives, like them, were young men who escaped alone. Those with immediate families often sought to retrieve their wives and children after reaching the North. Some, like Douglass, planned for months; others, like Pennington, decided to run away because of an immediate grievance—in his case, his owner’s threat to whip his mother for insubordination.[8]

All fugitive slaves faced daunting odds and demonstrated remarkable courage. Slave patrols and armed private groups dedicated to apprehending fugitives could be found throughout the South. Their numbers were augmented following Nat Turner’s rebellion in Southampton County, Virginia, in 1831, which resulted in the death of over fifty whites. The authorities regularly searched ships, railroad cars, and highways for fugitives. In the slave states, to aid a runaway slave carried severe legal penalties. Most slaves had little knowledge of geography or how to locate sympathetic persons outside their immediate neighborhoods, although many seem to have been aware that there were people, black and white, willing to help them. They often envisaged dangers even greater than those that actually existed. In the first of his three autobiographies, published in 1845, Douglass recalled that he imagined watchmen everywhere—“at every ferry a guard, on every bridge a sentinel, and in every wood a patrol of slave hunters.” He memorably explained his anxiety by asking the reader to imagine himself in “a land given up to be a hunting-ground for slaveholders . . . where he is every moment subjected to the terrible liability of being seized upon by his fellowmen, as the hideous crocodile seizes upon his prey!"[9]

It is impossible to think of fugitive slaves without also thinking of the underground railroad. Douglass later referred to David Ruggles as the only "officer of the underground railroad" he encountered during his escape. The term, in fact, did not yet exist in 1838 when Douglass reached the North, and it remains unclear exactly when it originated. One account attributes its first use to an article in a Washington newspaper in 1839, quoting a young slave who said he hoped to escape on a railroad that "went underground all the way to Boston." Whatever its origin, the phrase soon became ubiquitous. In 1842, an Albany abolitionist newspaper reported that twenty-six fugitives had passed through the city, and that "all went by the 'underground railroad.' " By 1853, the *New York Times* could observe that "the 'underground railroad' " had "come into very general use to describe the organized arrangements made in various sections of the country, to aid fugitives from slavery." That same year, a North Carolina newspaper offered its own definition: "An association of abolitionists whose first business is to steal, or cause to be stolen, seduced or inveigled . . . slaves from southern plantations; . . . to steal him from an indulgent and provident master; to carry him to a cold, strange, and uncongenial country, and there leave him . . . to starve, freeze, and die, in glorious freedom." There was even a popular song entitled "The Underground Railroad"; one newspaper predicted it would "have a great 'run.' "[10]

During the 1850s, journalists throughout the country credited the underground railroad with far more organization and impact than it actually enjoyed. The southern press attributed escapes of all kinds—by land and sea, to the North, Canada, or southern cities—to the underground railroad. In 1860, the *New York Herald*, a fierce opponent of abolitionism, described the underground railroad as essentially a fund-raising racket that preyed on the misplaced sympathy of well-meaning whites. But, it continued, "the underground railroad is no myth. [It] stretches through every free state in the Union and has its agents and emissaries on the borders of every slave state."[11]

This book is a study of fugitive slaves and the underground railroad in New York City. The nation's major metropolis, New York before the Civil War consisted of Manhattan and the Bronx, with most of the population concentrated below Thirty-Fourth Street. The city was a crucial way station in the metropolitan corridor through which fugitive slaves made their way from the Upper South through Philadelphia and on to upstate New York, New England, and Canada. Since the underground railroad, by definition, can only be understood as an intercity, interregional enterprise, I also devote attention to other key sites in this northeastern network. I discuss as well the national debate and federal legislation relating to fugitive slaves, and how the fugitive issue played a crucial role in precipitating the Civil War.

Along with Douglass and Pennington, some of the most famous fugitives in American history, including Harriet Jacobs and Henry "Box" Brown, passed through New York City. So did Harriet Tubman, who made several forays into Maryland to rescue slaves and sometimes brought them through New York on their way to Canada. But efforts, public and clandestine, to aid runaways in New York have only recently begun to attract serious study. Most histories of the underground railroad devote little attention to activities there. Graham Hodges's recent biography of David Ruggles offers a pathbreaking history of the Vigilance Committee during the 1830s, but this part of his narrative, understandably, ends when Ruggles left New York in 1840. In the early 1840s, the *Colored American,* a black-owned newspaper published in the city, and Ruggles's own *Mirror of Liberty,* major sources of information about the committee and its activities on behalf of fugitives, ceased publication. For most of the remaining years of the antebellum era, details about the operations of the underground railroad in the city are fragmentary and hard to come by.

The reasons for this relative paucity of information are not difficult to understand. Unlike communities in upstate New York, New England, and parts of the Midwest, where the antislavery movement flourished, New York had close economic ties to the slave South and a pro-southern municipal government. Nominally, the city housed the national headquarters of the two major abolitionist organizations, the American Anti-Slavery Society and, after it divided in 1840, the American and Foreign Anti-Slavery Society. Both usually held their annual conventions in the city, often on the same days in May. But apart from that week, members of abolitionist societies were few and far between. Along with David Ruggles, this small cadre included the wealthy merchant Lewis Tappan, the black ministers Charles B. Ray and Theodore S. Wright, the abolitionist editor Sydney Howard Gay, and other men and women whose activities this book relates.

Throughout our history, white Americans have prided themselves on enjoying greater freedom than any other people in the world. For blacks the situation has always been more complicated. It took a very long time for the North as a whole, and New York City in particular, to emerge as sites of freedom as far as blacks were concerned. Not until 1827 did slavery in New York come to an end, and even after that, via the capture and return of fugitive slaves, southern and federal law protecting slavery reached into the city and all the free states. This was an era when hundreds of thousands of immigrants entered the United States through New York City, seeking economic opportunity or fleeing religious and political persecution. Despite the hardships they encountered, New York was truly a gateway to freedom for most of them. Many hundreds of fugitive slaves also passed through New York. But especially after the Fugitive Slave Act of 1850 went into effect, few could remain in the city without running a serious risk of being returned to bondage. For them, freedom had to be enjoyed somewhere else.

Even after slavery ended in New York, the South's peculiar institution remained central to the city's economic prosperity. New York's dominant Democratic party maintained close ties to the South, and some local officials were more than happy to cooperate in apprehending and returning fugitive slaves. Abraham Lincoln carried New York State in the election of 1860 thanks to a resounding majority in rural areas, but he received only a little over one-third of the vote in New York City. More than once, proslavery mobs ran amok, targeting abolitionist homes and gatherings and the residences and organizations of free blacks.[12] The Vigilance Committee held annual meetings at which it announced how many fugitives had been assisted in the previous year, but it faced a chronic shortage of funds and much of its work was conducted by a handful of individuals, in far greater secrecy than was common in parts of the North with more pervasive antislavery sentiment. "We dared not" hold meetings publicly, Anthony Lane, the treasurer of the Vigilance Committee in the 1840s and 1850s, later recalled, since fugitive slaves were frequently present and the owners or their agents "in the city, in hot pursuit."[13] The *National Anti-Slavery Standard*, published in New York, included notices about the escapes of slaves in other parts of the country, but very little about the underground railroad in its own city. A few fugitive slaves, including Frederick Douglass, wrote memoirs that offer important information about their experiences passing through New York City. But overall, the story of the underground railroad in New York is like a jigsaw puzzle many of whose pieces have been irretrievably lost, or a gripping detective story where the evidence is murky and incomplete.

Fortunately, however, Sydney Howard Gay, the editor of the

National Anti-Slavery Standard and a key underground railroad operative from the mid-1840s to the eve of the Civil War, kept a detailed record of the assistance he and an interracial group of coworkers provided to fugitives in 1855 and 1856.[14] Gay's outpost operated independently of the city's Vigilance Committee, although it sometimes cooperated with it. Until recently, few scholars were aware of the existence of Gay's manuscript, which contains accounts of the escapes of over 200 runaways who passed through New York and of how Gay and his associates undertook to help them. Gay's Record of Fugitives, discussed in chapter 7, has never before been analyzed in detail for the rare account it offers of the inner workings of the underground railroad in New York and its connections south and north of the city. Along with riveting stories that reveal the motives and experiences of fugitives, Gay's record makes clear that by the 1850s New York had become a key site in a well-organized system whereby escaping slaves who reached Philadelphia from Virginia, Maryland, Delaware, and the District of Columbia were forwarded to Gay's office and then dispatched to underground railroad operatives in Albany, Syracuse, Boston, and Canada.

After the passage of the Fugitive Slave Law of 1850, materials such as Gay's made individuals vulnerable to federal prosecution. Unfortunately for the historian, a number of persons active in the underground railroad burned their papers in 1850. Gay's Record of Fugitives was known only to a few intimates, but he certainly took a calculated risk in transcribing and preserving it.[15]

Overall, during the years from 1835, when the New York Committee of Vigilance was founded, to 1860, the eve of the Civil War, between 3,000 and 4,000 fugitive slaves may have received assistance while passing through the city.[16] These numbers, based largely on public claims, sometimes as part of fund raising by the Vigilance Committee, may well be exaggerated. But the precise figure is less important than the fact that throughout the antebellum era, slaves continued to escape, helped in New York and other northern communities by little-known men and women, operating against formidable odds.

II

To what extent a clandestine network of agents in northern communities, with outposts in the South, actually existed, has long been a point of dispute among historians. Soon after the Civil War, a number of abolitionists published their reminiscences, hoping to remind readers of their accomplishments and to reinforce the national commitment to protecting the freedom slaves had acquired during the Civil War. Several such works highlighted organized efforts to assist runaway slaves. Some went overboard with the railroad metaphor, portraying the underground railroad, in the words of one writer, as extending "across all the northern states" with "its side tracks, connections and switches; its stations and conductors . . . ; its system of cypher dispatches." Although these memoirs included much information about slaves' determination to be free, they tended to make white abolitionists the central actors of the story.[17]

One notable exception was William Still's *The Underground Railroad,* a compilation of material about fugitive slaves who passed through Philadelphia that was undertaken at the request of the Pennsylvania Anti-Slavery Society and published in several editions beginning in 1872. A black abolitionist, Still had been hired as a clerk in the society's office in 1847, and by the following decade he was directing the activities of the city's Vigilance Committee. He kept a journal, analogous to Gay's, with a detailed account of hundreds of fugitive slaves, many of whom appear in both documents. Fearing prosecution, Still at various times hid his records in a barn and a local cemetery. Drawing on his journal, Still's book contains a treasure trove of information, although the absence of any discernible principle of organization somewhat limits its usefulness. Still carefully placed the experiences of the fugitives at the center of the story while giving full credit to those who assisted them, and explained how he forwarded them to freedom. In the 1870s, Robert Smedley, a physician in southeastern Pennsylvania, conducted interviews with surviving abolitionists about the underground railroad. After his death his manuscript was finalized and published by the black abolitionist Robert Purvis and Marianna Gibbons, a member of a white abolitionist family. The book emphasized the key role of the region's rural Quaker families in assisting fugitives.[18]

The scholarly study of the underground railroad began in the 1890s, when Wilbur H. Siebert, a history professor at Ohio State University, developed what became a lifelong fascination with the subject. Siebert sent questionnaires to dozens of surviving abolitionists asking for their recollections about the operations of the underground railroad. He conducted interviews, scoured local newspapers, and retraced routes taken by fugitive slaves. Siebert lived to the age of ninety-five, and between 1896 and 1951 he published several volumes on the underground railroad, in addition to works on loyalists during the American Revolution and the history of Ohio. He laid the groundwork for all future study of the subject.

Siebert noted that the underground railroad should not be thought of as a formal institution with a membership, officers, and a treasury, and that efforts to assist fugitives ebbed and flowed throughout the decades preceding the Civil War. But overall, he presented a portrait of a highly organized system involving thousands of northern agents and a "great and intricate network" of stations leading to Canada. He reinforced this image with detailed maps (largely a product of his vivid imagination) that looked very much like contemporary railroad maps and purported to show the regular routes taken by escaping slaves. Siebert's general history of the underground railroad, published in 1898, identified no fewer than 3,211 "agents" by name, nearly all of them white men. The book said very little about activities in New York. Of these "there is scarcely any information," he wrote, and his exhaustive list of agents included only nine in the city. His account of other locales, however, was prone to exaggeration. In southeastern Pennsylvania, he wrote, "there seems to have been scarcely any limitation upon the number of persons . . . willing to assume agencies for the forwarding of slaves." Siebert tended to ignore replies to his questionnaires that did not fit his image, such as one from a Massachusetts abolitionist who emphasized the ad hoc nature of responses to the arrival of fugitives and noted, "We had no regular route and no regular station."[19]

Siebert's work powerfully influenced both scholarly and popular conceptions of the underground railroad. It remained largely unchallenged until 1961, when Larry Gara published *The Liberty Line,* a searing critique of Siebert's methods and conclusions as well as the work of other writers, such as Smedley. Gara acknowledged his own debt to the materials his predecessors had gathered, but he chided Siebert for accepting at face value the romanticized reminiscences of "old time abolitionists," lumping together individuals who occasionally aided a fugitive with those who devoted a great deal of time and energy to such assistance, and exaggerating the degree of organization of their efforts. Historians, Gara insisted, had offered legitimacy to a "popular legend" that emphasized the role of benevolent whites at the expense of escaping slaves and free black communities in the North. Gara did not deny that a small number of energetic individuals, such as William Still, systematically assisted fugitives, but he emphasized that slaves almost always escaped on their own initiative and received little help from abolitionists until they reached the North. The idea of a highly organized transportation system ferrying multitudes to freedom, Gara insisted, was a myth.[20]

The Liberty Line appeared just as the study of African American history began to enter the scholarly mainstream and with it an emphasis on the "agency" of ordinary black Americans. Gara's critique conformed to this perspective, and most historians quickly accepted his conclusions, a response that, unfortunately, led to a long period of scholarly neglect of the underground railroad. The term appears only twice in the index of the most comprehensive study of runaway slaves, by John Hope Franklin and Loren Schweninger, published in 1999. Instead, they emphasize that a far larger number of slave "absentees" ran off for a few days or weeks, hiding out in the vicinity and then returning to their homes, than ever reached the North.[21]

Recently, however, historians both within and outside the academy have begun to question the sweeping nature of Gara's revisionism. While acknowledging Siebert's exaggerations, they insist that the reminiscences he and others gathered cannot be entirely discounted. They have supplemented a rereading of these documents with in-depth local research and a close examination of pre–Civil War abolitionist correspondence and antislavery newspapers, white and black, and produced inventories of sites and people connected to fugitive slaves.[22] Biographies have appeared of such key underground railroad figures as David Ruggles, Robert Purvis, and Jermain W. Loguen, the "underground railroad king" of Syracuse. Scholars have also begun the difficult task of exploring covert systems of aid to fugitives within the slave states as well as lines of communication between slave communities. The most recent general account of the underground railroad, by the independent historian Fergus Bordewich, follows Gara in noting that the number of fugitives has been exaggerated, but it traces the emergence of local groups in the North that assisted runaway slaves. Far more, however, remains to be done in analyzing how vigilance networks functioned on the local level, and how they built connections with groups across the antebellum North.[23]

Meanwhile, independent of the scholarly debate, the underground railroad has enjoyed a resurgence as a focus of public history. A major museum, the National Underground Railroad Freedom Center, opened in Cincinnati in 2004. The National Park Service has developed a variety of valuable educational activities related to the subject (as well as a bicycle "adventure" along underground railroad routes), and numerous local groups have been engaged in identifying sites where fugitive slaves were hidden. While prone to exaggeration for reasons ranging from community pride to the desire to increase tourism, such work has deepened our understanding of how local activists assisted fugitive slaves. The popular appeal of the underground railroad is not difficult to understand, even apart from the inherent drama of escaping from bondage. At a time of renewed national attention to the history of slavery, the Civil War, and Reconstruction, subjects that remain in many ways contentious, the underground railroad represents a moment in our history when black and white Americans worked together in a just cause.[24]

The picture that emerges from recent studies is not of the highly organized system with tunnels, codes, and clearly defined routes and stations of popular lore, but of an interlocking series of local networks, each of whose fortunes rose and fell over time, but which together helped a substantial number of fugitives reach safety in the free states and Canada. Vigilance committees thrived and then fell into abeyance, only to be reconstituted after a few years. The "underground railroad" should be understood not as a single entity but as an umbrella term for local groups that employed numerous methods to assist fugitives, some public and entirely legal, some flagrant violations of the law. The underground railroad in New York City conforms to this pattern.

It was more than a coincidence that both Frederick Douglass and James W. C. Pennington originated in Maryland. For obvious reasons, escape from the states that bordered on free soil proved far easier than from the cotton kingdom of the Lower South. Runaways farther south tended to head to cities such as New Orleans and Mobile, where they hoped to lose themselves in the free black population, or to Indian nations, Mexico, or nearby British possessions like the Bahama islands. Some managed to establish settlements in remote areas, such as Virginia's Great Dismal Swamp.[25] The Canadian census of 1861 found that 80 percent of southern-born blacks in Canada, many of them fugitive slaves and their children, had been born in only three states—Maryland, Virginia, and Kentucky. These, along with Missouri, a prominent Kentuckian wrote on the eve of the Civil War, "have borne all the losses and annoyance." Delaware, where the institution was in rapid decline (on the eve of the Civil War, the state contained only 1,800 slaves), also experienced numerous escapes, including, in 1850, a slave who belonged to the son of Douglass's former owner.[26]

The largest number of fugitives discussed in the pages that follow originated in Maryland, a state particularly vulnerable to escapes because of its long land border with Pennsylvania. Interspersed among advertisements for the sale of horses, pianos, cough medicine, and false teeth, nearly every issue of the *Baltimore Sun*, the state's major newspaper, carried notices, headed "Ran Away," offering rewards for fugitive slaves from throughout the state. With the nation's largest free black community—25,442 men, women, and children in 1850, compared with fewer than 3,000 slaves—Baltimore was the "black capital" of the Upper South, a haven for fugitives from the countryside and a place where skilled slaves like Douglass could not only work on their own and live apart from their owners but also find free blacks willing to assist their quest for freedom. In most parts of Maryland, free blacks outnumbered slaves, and blacks traveling on their own were a common sight, making escape easier.[27]

Maryland also had numerous transportation routes, by sea, rail, and road, heading to the North. Indeed, while the words "fugitive slave" conjure up an image of escapes like Pennington's—on foot, through woods and fields—new modes of transportation that proliferated in the Jacksonian era not only catalyzed the expansion of market capitalism (and with it the rapid spread of cotton cultivation into the Deep South) but also offered new possibilities for flight. Many slaves escaped from Baltimore and other Upper South ports by stowing away on coastal vessels, finding employment on ships that needed crewmen, or locating captains who would take their money to transport them to freedom. Two years after Douglass reached New York, the *Colored American* took note of how the railroad had become "a means of emancipation":

> A few years since, when elopements from slavery were fewer than they now are, the poor slave . . . [who] would flee from his chains . . . had to wind his way by a circuitous route, on foot, sleeping by day, and walking by night, and after a week's time, he might, if not overtaken, as was frequently the case, reach New York. . . . Now so extensive are our railroads . . . that a poor fugitive may leave Baltimore in the morning, and the third night following, may find himself safely in Canada.

The editor hoped the "railroad mania" would continue until lines penetrated the "extreme South," offering greater opportunities for slaves there to escape to freedom. Of course, railroads, and from 1844, the telegraph, also made possible rapid travel and communication among slaveowners and slave catchers, facilitating the capture of fugitives.[28]

"I escaped," Pennington later wrote, "without the aid . . . of any human being. . . . Like a man, I have emancipated myself."[29] And by far the greatest credit for successful escapes goes to the fugitives themselves. Few, however, succeeded entirely on their own. Douglass's escape was facilitated by his fiancée in Baltimore and the black sailor who loaned his papers. Pennington received assistance while on the road in Maryland and shelter from the Wrights and other Quaker families in Pennsylvania. When he reached New York, however, no organization existed to assist fugitives; he really was on his own. Douglass was fortunate enough to arrive after the formation of the Vigilance Committee, one of whose purposes was to assist fugitives like himself.

Before the Fugitive Slave Act of 1850 made the return of runaways a federal responsibility, their rendition depended on owners or their agents locating and seizing their human property, or local officials in the North doing so. In some parts of the North, public opinion made this extremely difficult. But when they reached the free states, fugitives usually found themselves in the Lower North, where pro-southern sentiment was strong, abolitionism weak, and numerous judges, sheriffs, and policemen were more than willing to assist in their apprehension. This was why Ruggles dispatched Douglass and his wife to the safer environs of Massachusetts and other runaways to upstate New York and Canada.[30]

Most escapes could not have been successful without the support of black communities, free and slave, North and South. Long before there were organized networks to assist fugitives, individual slaves and free blacks offered hiding places and in other ways provided them with assistance in the South. In the North, black men and women whose names are lost to history offered aid to slaves seeking freedom: hotel employees informed slaves brought to New York City by their owners that they were legally free; stevedores assisted fugitives hidden on ships from southern ports; anonymous individuals who encountered fugitives on the streets offered them aid. Free blacks were the main activists in the vigilance committees modeled on New York's that sprang up in Philadelphia, Boston, Syracuse, and other cities. The leadership of these groups, organized at the local level but in frequent communication with counterparts elsewhere, was generally interracial, but the committees were "to a considerable extent, and in some places entirely sustained by the colored people," the white abolitionist Samuel May Jr. noted.[31]

At the time of the American Revolution, there had been few free blacks anywhere in the country. The growth of the free black population, North and South, in the first half of the nineteenth century proved crucial for the prospects of fugitive slaves. So did the rise of the abolitionist movement. Especially after the emergence of militant, interracial abolitionism in the early 1830s, sympathetic whites offered aid—material, legal, and monetary—to individual fugitives and to the black-dominated vigilance committees. The networks assisting fugitives offered a rare instance in antebellum America of interracial cooperation and a link between the lower-class urban blacks who provided most of the daily activism of vigilance committees and their more affluent white allies.

Nearly every prominent white abolitionist, as well as antislavery politicians like William H. Seward and Thaddeus Stevens, at one time or another assisted fugitive slaves; many sheltered them in their homes. So did just about every major black abolitionist.[32] Douglass, of course, became the era's greatest orator, editor, and writer in the cause of abolition and human rights. Pennington, while less well known, published *A Text Book of the Origin and History of the Colored People* (1841), a challenge to American racism, and participated in numerous efforts to achieve abolition and equal rights for northern blacks. Both provided aid to fugitives. Douglass concealed runaway slaves in his home in Rochester and forwarded them to Canada. "On one occasion," he later recalled, "I had eleven fugitives under my roof." Pennington also aided individual fugitives and helped to raise money in Great Britain for New York's Vigilance Committee.[33]

Urban vigilance committees and rural antislavery activists hid runaway slaves and sent them on their way, and on occasion violently rescued fugitives from the clutches of slave catchers. They also defended fugitives in court, published accounts of their experiences, and raised money to purchase their freedom and that of their families. The public activities of these groups had an important impact on the evolving sectional conflict. Vigilance committee lawyers played a crucial role in persuading northern courts to recognize the "freedom principle"—the doctrine that once a slave (other than a fugitive) left a jurisdiction where local law established slavery, he or she automatically became free. Underground railroad operatives were deeply involved in campaigns for equal citizenship for northern free blacks, including the right to vote, access to public education, and economic opportunity. "Vigilance" involved all these activities and more.

Abolitionists of all persuasions considered aid to fugitives a form of practical antislavery action. Indeed, "practical" became a favorite description of underground railroad activities. "This was practical abolition," David Ruggles declared, in describing the work of the New York Vigilance Committee in aiding escaped slaves, protecting free people from kidnappers, and combating the illegal slave trade. One Philadelphia abolitionist described William Still as "a sincere practical advocate of the cause of human rights."[34] "Practical" meant that vigilance committees devoted themselves not simply to the dramatic escapes that have come to characterize our image of the underground railroad, but to day-to-day activities like organizing committees, raising funds, and political and legal action. Many of these activities took place in full public view, not "underground."

While many individuals assisted a fugitive at one time or another, only a small number devoted themselves primarily to that task, and even the most energetic "station masters" engaged in many other activities, from editing or writing for abolitionist newspapers to lecturing, fund raising, and attending antislavery conventions. Rather than an independent institution, in other words, the underground railroad formed part of what Charles Sumner, the abolitionist senator from Massachusetts, called the "antislavery enterprise," the broad spectrum of individuals, outlooks, and activities devoted to bringing about the end of slavery.[35]

In the slave states and many parts of the free, assisting a fugitive slave carried considerable risk. The abolitionist Charles T. Torrey, a Yale-educated minister, died in the Maryland state penitentiary in 1846 after being convicted of helping fugitives escape from Washington, D.C. William Brodie, a black sailor from New York, was heavily fined by a Georgia court, and when unable to pay, he was sold into slavery. Thomas Garrett, who made no secret of his aid to fugitives in Delaware, had to pay a substantial fine after being sued by the owner of runaways. Such cases occurred in the North as well. An Ohio judge fined John Van Zandt, a farmer, $1,500 for assisting nine fugitives from Kentucky. His case went all the way to the U.S. Supreme Court, which in 1847 upheld his conviction. William Henry Johnson, a black hairdresser active in the underground railroad in Philadelphia, abandoned the city in 1859 for Norwich, Connecticut, "to escape imprisonment for having assisted fugitive slaves."[36]

Nonetheless, it is striking how few underground railroad activists north of the Mason-Dixon Line suffered legal consequences for their activities, which often were widely publicized. Northern officials seem to have had little interest in prosecuting those who assisted fugitive slaves. Indeed, rather than operating entirely in secret, the underground railroad was a quasi-public institution. In many northern communities the identity of those most closely involved in aiding fugitives was widely known. Underground railroad activists frequently reported their accomplishments in local newspapers. The Cleveland Vigilance Committee even had a banner, described in *Frederick Douglass' Paper*: "The divine Hercules with a club; the monster slavery prostrate at his feet; a woman in the distance, with her manacles broken; he points to the motto, 'LIBERTY.' " The *National Anti-Slavery Standard* felt compelled to warn vigilance committees about their "disposition to boast publicly of the success with which the slave hunter has been foiled," thereby revealing too much about their methods. The "frequent exposure through the public prints, of the modes of escape of fugitives, and of the expedients employed to prevent recapture," the paper observed, played into the hands of "pursuers" and made the task of the runaway "tenfold" more difficult.[37]

III

Running away, of course, constituted only one part of a spectrum of slave resistance that ranged from day-to-day contestation with owners and overseers to outright rebellion, but it had the strongest and most persistent political impact. Most fugitives, it seems safe to say, were thinking of immediate or long-standing grievances, not the national implications of their actions, when they embarked on their journeys to freedom. But the actions of fugitive slaves exemplified the political importance of slave resistance as a whole and raised questions central to antebellum politics, understood not simply as electoral campaigns but as the contest over slavery in the broad public sphere. At the most basic level, running away from slavery gave the lie to proslavery propaganda. His encounters with fugitives, William Still related, led him to realize how many slaves had "deeply thought on the subject of their freedom," were aware of the existence of Canada and "other places of retreat," and had begun to plan escapes "very early in life." Some had made provision in advance for their lives in freedom. Among a group of fugitives discovered on a ship heading north from Virginia in 1858, one was bound for New York to meet his wife and another had arranged with friends for a job at a Canadian hotel.[38]

Because escapes refuted the widely circulated idea of the contented slave, southern newspapers often exaggerated the role of northern agents in enticing slaves to run away. The Reverend Thornton Stringfellow, a Virginia cleric known for his proslavery sermons, even claimed that having been persuaded by outsiders to escape, fugitives were "constantly returning to their masters" because of the hardships they encountered in the North. Newspaper advertisements seeking the recapture of fugitives frequently described runaways as "cheerful" and "well-disposed," as if their escapes were inexplicable. But these notices inadvertently offered a record of abusive treatment—mentions of scars and other injuries that would help identify the runaway—that provided powerful material for abolitionist propaganda. One of the most successful antislavery tracts, Theodore Weld's *American Slavery As It Is*, relied on sources from the slave states, including numerous excerpts from fugitive slave advertisements, to condemn the institution. Weld congratulated the authors of these public announcements for their "commendable fidelity to truth" in candidly detailing the "mutilations" visible on fugitives' bodies.[39]

"There is a spirit among the slaves themselves," wrote James Miller McKim, a leading Philadelphia abolitionist and longtime member of that city's vigilance committee, "that is helping on the work of emancipation." For the abolitionist crusade, fugitive slaves provided an infusion of new leadership, a point of unity in a movement badly fractured between advocates and opponents of political action, among other divisions, and a challenge to rethink the traditional commitment to nonviolence. In the 1840s and 1850s, fugitive slaves, including Douglass, Pennington, Henry Highland Garnet, Henry Bibb, Henry Brown, and many others, emerged as eloquent abolitionist lecturers, writers, and editors. Their advent, the historian Benjamin Quarles has written, was "a godsend to the cause." Those who had experienced slavery, the country's most prominent abolitionist, William Lloyd Garrison, declared in 1850, were "the best qualified to address the public," and speeches by fugitive slaves attracted large audiences in the North and Great Britain. Fugitive slave narratives—accounts written by runaways of their ordeals and accomplishments—emerged in these years as a popular literary genre.[40]

Renditions of escaped slaves reinforced abolitionists' claim that the Slave Power reached into the North, and that slavery threatened all Americans' cherished civil liberties, particularly the right of a person accused of a crime to state his or her case before a jury (something explicitly denied to alleged runaways in the Fugitive Slave Act of 1850). In national politics, the actions of fugitives and their allies forced onto center stage explosive questions about the balance between federal and state authority, the extent to which the laws of slave states extended into the North, and the relationship of the federal government to slavery. These issues were debated and litigated at every level of society, from local petition drives and court cases to the halls of Congress and the chambers of the Supreme Court in Washington. The rendition of fugitives emerged as a source of contention at the very founding of the republic—it was discussed at the constitutional convention, and the first national measure to provide for their recapture became law in 1793, only four years after George Washington's inauguration. Later, the fugitive issue helped to launch the careers of major antislavery politicians, including Salmon P. Chase and William H. Seward, members of Lincoln's cabinet who had become widely known before the Civil War for their efforts on behalf of runaway slaves.

The status of fugitive slaves also became a significant point of contention in Anglo-American and Mexican-American diplomacy. After the War of Independence and War of 1812, the federal government made concerted efforts to retrieve slaves—numbering in the thousands—who had escaped to the British, or obtain monetary compensation for their owners. The unwillingness of the government in London to countenance the return of these slaves and those who subsequently escaped to Canada or British possessions in the Caribbean inspired innumerable complaints from Washington. Despite pressure from American administrations, Mexico, which abolished slavery in the 1820s, also refused to extradite fugitives to the United States. Treaties with Indians, however, frequently stipulated their responsibility to return escaped slaves. The federal government's active efforts to assist slaveholders who had lost fugitives reinforced the abolitionist contention that the Slave Power effectively determined national policy, just as the return of fugitives by northern officials revealed the complicity of the free states in the evil of slavery.[41]

So many slaves escaped from the Upper South, the *New York Times* suggested in 1855, that slavery there would soon be "so unprofitable that it will hardly be worth preserving." The rising number of fugitives from Maryland and Kentucky created apprehension in the cotton kingdom about the vulnerability of slavery on the border with the free states. It provided the immediate catalyst for the passage of the Fugitive Slave Law of 1850, which required citizens to assist in the capture of fugitives and overrode local laws and procedures that impeded their return. Effective enforcement of that law quickly became a major demand of the South as sectional tension escalated during the 1850s, and a source of deep resentment in much of the North. Ironically, when it came to fugitive slaves, the white South, usually vocal in defense of local rights, favored vigorous national action, while some northern states engaged in the nullification of federal law. Northern assistance to fugitive slaves and the unwillingness of local juries to convict persons who took part in widely publicized rescues influenced congressional debates over slavery and emerged as a key point of contention during the secession crisis. And the spectacle of thousands of black northerners fleeing to Canada after the enactment of the Fugitive Slave Law of 1850 offered a jarring counterpoint to the familiar image of the United States as an asylum for those denied liberty in other countries.[42]

"What measure of abolitionists," asked the *Friend of Man,* an antislavery newspaper, in 1840, "is regarded with more sympathy and favor, than efforts to assist the fugitives? Thousands will lend a helping hand *here,* who will do nothing else for the slave." Individual encounters with fugitive slaves and resistance to the Fugitive Slave Law forced ordinary northerners who had no connection with the abolitionist movement to confront the question of the relationship between individual conscience and legal obligation. Of course, many, probably most, northerners, even those who hated slavery, felt that respect for the law and constitution must override sympathy for fugitives. Typical was Abraham Lincoln, who wrote in 1855 that he hated "to see the poor creatures hunted down," but out of reverence for the rule of law, "I bite my lip and keep quiet." But in March 1861, Lincoln felt compelled to devote a portion of his first inaugural address to the question of fugitive slaves and to propose changes in federal law that would secure greater legal rights for accused runaways. None of this would have happened without the actions of the slaves who sought to escape to freedom and the northerners, black and white, male and female, who took part in organized efforts to assist them. All in all, the fugitive slave issue played a crucial role in bringing about the Civil War.[43]

Stripped of previous distortions, the story of the underground railroad remains one with an extraordinary cast of characters and remarkable tales of heroism, courage, and sheer luck. Decades after his own escape from slavery, recalling his long career as one of the country's foremost advocates of abolition and racial justice, Frederick Douglass reflected, "I never did more congenial, attractive, fascinating, and satisfactory work" than in assisting runaway slaves.[44]

As for the fugitives, those who encountered them could not but be moved by their stories, which, as one abolitionist put it, far exceeded "the fictitious sufferings and adventures of imaginary characters" conjured up by novelists. Fugitive slaves, wrote James Miller McKim, represented "some of the finest specimens of native talent the country provides," and their actions offered "ample proof" of everything abolitionists maintained about "the capacity of the colored man." In 1855, as the *National Anti-Slavery Standard*'s Philadelphia correspondent, McKim penned a dispatch expressing the hope that when slavery had met its "just doom," the story of fugitive slaves and those who aided them would inspire pride among all Americans:

> These wonderful events . . . now being enacted before the American people, will, one day, be justly appreciated. Now, deemed unworthy of the notice of any, save fanatical abolitionists, these acts of sublime heroism, of lofty self-sacrifice, of patient martyrdom, these beautiful Providences, these hair-breadth escapes and terrible dangers, will yet become the themes of the popular literature of this nation, and will excite the admiration, the reverence and the indignation of the generations yet to come.[45]

2

SLAVERY AND FREEDOM IN NEW YORK

The history of slavery, and of fugitive slaves, in New York City begins in the earliest days of colonial settlement. Under Dutch rule, from 1624 to 1664, the town of New Amsterdam was a tiny outpost of a seaborne empire that stretched across the globe. The Dutch dominated the Atlantic slave trade in the early seventeenth century, and they introduced slaves into their North American colony, New Netherland, as a matter of course. The numbers remained small, but in 1650 New Netherland's 500 slaves outnumbered those in Virginia and Maryland. The Dutch West India Company, which governed the colony, used slave labor to build fortifications and other buildings, and settlers employed them on family farms and for household and craft labor. Slavery was only loosely codified. Slaves sued and were sued in local courts, drilled in the militia, fought in Indian wars, and married in the Dutch Reformed Church. When the British seized the colony in 1664, New Amsterdam had a population of around 1,500, including 375 slaves.[1]

Under British rule, the city, now called New York, became an important trading center in a slave-based New World empire. In the eighteenth century, the British replaced the Dutch as the world's leading slave traders, and the city's unfree population steadily expanded. New York merchants became actively involved in the transatlantic slave trade as well as commerce with the plantations of the Caribbean. Slave auctions took place regularly at a market on Wall Street. Between 1700 and 1774, over 7,000 slaves were imported into New York, most of them destined for sale to surrounding rural areas. This figure was dwarfed by the more than 200,000 brought into the southern colonies in these years. But in 1734, New York's colonial governor lamented that the "too great importation of . . . Negroes and convicts" had discouraged the immigration of "honest, useful and laborious white people," who preferred to settle in neighboring colonies like Pennsylvania. By mid-century, slaves represented over one-fifth of the city's population of around 12,000. Ownership of slaves was widespread. Most worked as domestic laborers, on the docks, in artisan shops, or on small farms in the city's rural hinterland. In modern-day Brooklyn, then a collection of farms and small villages, one-third of the population in 1771 consisted of slaves.[2]

New Yorkers later prided themselves on the notion that in contrast to southern slavery, theirs had been a mild and relatively benevolent institution. But New York slavery could be no less brutal than in colonies to the south. "Hard usage" motivated two dozen slaves to stage an uprising in 1712 in which they set fires on the outskirts of the city and murdered the first whites to respond. There followed a series of sadistic public executions, with some conspirators burned to death or broken on the wheel. The colonial Assembly quickly enacted a draconian series of laws governing slavery. These measures established separate courts for slaves and restricted private manumissions by requiring masters to post substantial bonds to cover the cost of public assistance in the event that a freed slave required it. The discovery of a "Great Negro Plot" in 1741, whose contours remain a matter of dispute among historians, led to more executions and further tightening of the laws governing slavery.

As a result, few black New Yorkers achieved freedom through legal means before the era of the Revolution. Most censuses in colonial New York did not even count free blacks separately from slaves. On the eve of the War of Independence, the city's population of 19,000 included nearly 3,000 slaves, and some 20,000 slaves lived within fifty miles of Manhattan island, the largest concentration of unfree laborers north of the Mason-Dixon Line. One visitor to the city noted, "It rather hurts a European eye to see so many Negro slaves upon the streets."[3]

I

As long as slavery has existed, slaves have escaped to freedom. During the colonial era, long before any abolitionist networks offered assistance, New York City became both a site from which fugitives fled bondage and a destination for runaways from the surrounding countryside and other colonies. Black farmsteads on the northern edge of New Amsterdam were notorious for sheltering fugitives. Offering refuge to the slaves of one's rivals became a common practice in imperial relations, facilitating runaways' quest for freedom. Connecticut and Maryland, the British colonies nearest to New Netherland, encouraged Dutch slaves to escape and refused to return them. In 1650, Governor Petrus Stuyvesant threatened to offer freedom to Maryland slaves unless that colony stopped sheltering runaways from the Dutch outpost.[4]

As the slave population increased under British rule, so did the number of escapes from the city. Since nearby colonies, controlled by the British, no longer offered safe refuge, slaves often escaped to upstate Indian nations or French Canada. As early as 1679, New York's colonial Assembly imposed a fine of twenty-five pounds—a considerable sum at the time—for harboring fugitives. In 1702, taking note of the alarming practice of slaves "confederating together in running away," it banned gatherings of more than three slaves. Three years later the lawmakers mandated the death penalty for any slave found without permission more than forty miles north of Albany. Another law, seeking to reduce fugitives' mobility, made it illegal for a slave to gallop on horseback. Meanwhile, even as some slaves attempted to escape from New York City, others fled there on foot or arrived hidden on ships. Many found employment on the docks or on the innumerable vessels that entered and left the port. The city's newspapers carried frequent notices warning captains not to hire runaways. Especially during the eighteenth century's imperial wars, however, such admonitions were routinely ignored, due to the pressing need for sailors on naval vessels and privateers.[5]

New York City's colonial newspapers published advertisements for runaways of various kinds—not only slaves, but also indentured servants, apprentices, soldiers, and criminals—and the number increased steadily over the course of the eighteenth century. One study of several hundred fugitive-slave notices in the city's press found that 255 of the runaways originated in New York City, 259 in nearby New Jersey, 159 in rural New York, and 25 as far away as Virginia and the West Indies. These advertisements conveyed considerable information about the fugitives to assist in their apprehension. One, for example, from the *New-York Gazette* in 1761 offered a reward of five pounds for the return of the slave Mark Edward:

> A well set fellow, near six feet high, talks good English, plays well on a fiddle, calls himself a free fellow, goes commonly with his head shaved, hath two crowns on the top of his head, small black specks or moles in his eyes. . . . Had on when he went away, a good pair of leather breeches, a blue broadcloth jacket, a red jacket under it without sleeves, a good beaver hat.

The vast majority of colonial runaways were young adult men. Because of the small size of slaveholdings, numerous married slaves lived apart from one another, and many fugitives were said to have absconded to join family members. Individuals, white and black, on occasion assisted fugitives, but no organizations existed to do so and most runaways appear to have eventually been recaptured.[6]

Although justices of the peace and other officials sometimes pursued runaway slaves, no law in colonial New York dealt explicitly with their recapture—this generally relied on action by the owner himself, through newspaper ads, letters, and the physical seizure of the fugitive. Such owners were exercising the common-law right of "recaption," which authorized the reappropriation of stolen property, or lost property capable of locomotion—a stray horse, for example, or a fugitive slave—without any legal process, so long as it was done in an orderly manner and without injury to third parties. (The right also extended to the recapture of runaway indentured servants, apprentices, children, and wives, but, given the subordinate position of women under the common law, not to an aggrieved wife hunting down an absconding husband.) Since the law presumed blacks to be slaves, accused fugitives had a difficult task proving that they were free.[7]

Throughout the colonies, the American Revolution disrupted the system of slavery and seemed to place its future in jeopardy. Nowhere was this more true than in New York City. Before the imperial crisis that led to American independence, chattel slavery had not been a matter of public debate, although colonists spoke frequently of the danger of being reduced to metaphorical slavery because of British taxation. By the early 1770s, however, a number of Methodist and Quaker congregations in the city encouraged members to manumit their slaves. Quakers were particularly prominent in antislavery activity in the late colonial period. Their belief that all human beings, regardless of race, possessed an "inward light," allowing God to speak personally to each individual, led increasing numbers of Quakers to condemn slavery as an affront to God's will. Most Quakers, however, disliked political agitation and saw abolition as a process that should take place gradually, with as little social disruption as possible.[8]

During the American Revolution, slavery in New York City experienced profound shocks, from very different directions. One was the rise of a revolutionary ideology centered on individual liberty, which convinced a number of patriot leaders of slavery's incompatibility with the ideals of the nation they were struggling to create. After an initial reluctance to enlist slaves as soldiers, moreover, New York's legislature allowed owners to send slaves as replacements for military service, with the reward of freedom. In 1777, the Continental Congress opened the ranks of the revolutionary army to black men, promising freedom to slaves who enrolled. By the end of the war, an estimated 6,000 black men had served in state militias and the Continental Army and Navy. Most were slaves who gained their freedom in this manner, including an unknown number from New York City.[9]

Of more import to New York's slaves, however, were the actions of British officials who offered freedom to the slaves of patriots in order to weaken the revolutionary cause. The first emancipation proclamation in American history preceded Abraham Lincoln's by nearly ninety years. Its author was the Earl of Dunmore, the royal governor of colonial Virginia, who in November 1775 promised freedom to "all indentured servants, negroes, or others" belonging to rebels if they enlisted in his army. Several hundred Virginia slaves joined Dunmore's Ethiopian Regiment, their uniforms, according to legend, emblazoned with the words "Liberty to Slaves." Unfortunately for their compatriots in bondage, American forces soon drove the governor out of the colony. With the remnants of his army, including its black unit, Dunmore arrived at Staten Island in August 1776. A month later, George Washington's forces retreated from Manhattan. As British forces occupied New York, many of the inhabitants fled, and a fire destroyed a considerable part of the city.[10]

The British did not leave New York City until the War of Independence had ended. During the occupation the city became "an island of freedom in a sea of slavery," a haven for fugitive slaves from rural New York, New Jersey, and Connecticut, as well as for hundreds of black refugees who had fled to British lines in Virginia, the Carolinas, and Georgia. The influx reached the point that, for a time, city officials directed Hudson River ferryboats to stop transporting runaway slaves to the city. The fugitives, along with New York slaves who remained when their owners departed, found employment reconstructing the damaged parts of the city and working for the British army as servants, cooks, and laundresses and in other capacities. For the first time in their lives, they received wages and were effectively treated as free, although their ultimate fate remained uncertain. When the British evacuated Philadelphia in 1778, more black refugees arrived, and still more followed in 1781 and 1782 after the British defeat at Yorktown.[11]

Of course, some black New Yorkers identified with the cause of independence. Black men had taken part in the crowd actions of the 1760s and 1770s that protested British measures such as the Stamp Act, including the group that tore down of a statue of George III in 1775. But once the British occupied the city, New York's slaves and black refugees from other colonies concluded that their freedom depended on Britain winning the war. This belief was reinforced in June 1779 when Sir Henry Clinton, the commander of British forces in North America, issued the Philipsburg Proclamation, which greatly extended Dunmore's original order by promising freedom to all slaves, except those owned by loyalists, who fled to

British lines and embraced the royal cause. "Whoever sells them," he added, "shall be prosecuted with the utmost severity." According to the Pennsylvania cleric Henry Mühlenberg, the idea that "slaves will gain their freedom" in the event of a British victory quickly became "universal amongst all the Negroes in America."[12]

When the War of Independence ended, 60,000 loyalists, including some 4,000 blacks—those formerly enslaved in the city, others who had fled there during the conflict, and slaves brought by loyalist owners—were behind British lines in New York City. One who left a record of his experiences was Boston King, a slave in the South Carolina low country who fled to Charles Town in 1780 when the British invaded the colony. Thanks to them, he later recalled, "I began to feel the happiness of liberty, of which I knew nothing before." King soon made his way to New York City, where, he wrote, the restoration of peace "diffused universal joy among all parties, except us, who had escaped from slavery." Rumors spread that fugitive slaves "were to be delivered up to their masters, . . . fill[ing] us all with inexpressible anguish and terror." Slaveowners appeared in the city, hoping to retrieve their slaves. The Treaty of Paris of 1783 specified that British forces must return to Americans property seized during the war, but Sir Guy Carleton, who had succeeded Clinton as British commander, insisted that this provision did not apply to slaves who had been promised their freedom.[13]

The British had offered liberty to slaves for strategic reasons, not abolitionist sentiments. "Practice determined policy," writes the historian Christopher Brown, but, he adds, "policy, over time, drifted toward becoming a matter of principle." When Carleton met with George Washington in May 1783 to implement the peace treaty, the American commander asked about "obtaining the delivery of Negroes and other property." Washington, in fact, hoped the British would keep a lookout for "some of my own slaves" who had run off during the war. He expressed surprise when Carleton replied that to deprive the slaves of the freedom they had been promised would be a "dishonourable violation of the public faith."

On Carleton's orders, when British ships sailed out of New York harbor in 1783, they carried not only tens of thousands of white soldiers, sailors, and loyalists, but over 3,000 blacks, most of whom had been freed in accordance with British proclamations. Carleton kept careful records of most of them and provided Washington with a "Book of Negroes," listing 1,136 black men, 914 women, and 750 children who left New York City with his forces. The largest number originated in the South, but about 300 were from New York State. They ended up in Nova Scotia, England, and Sierra Leone, a colony established by British abolitionists on the west coast of Africa later in the decade. Thanks to Carleton, Boston King secured his freedom. So did Henry and Deborah Squash, a married couple who had been the property of George Washington. For years, the British decision to remove American slaves and their refusal to compensate the owners remained a sore point in Anglo-American relations.[14]

The question of fugitive slaves also proved contentious within the new republic. During and after the War of Independence, several northern states launched the process of abolition. Vermont, at the time a self-proclaimed independent republic with few if any slaves, was first to act, in 1777 prohibiting slavery in its constitution. Massachusetts and New Hampshire, where slavery ended via court decisions, quickly followed, along with Pennsylvania, Connecticut, and Rhode Island, which enacted laws for gradual emancipation. These measures generally provided for the return of fugitive slaves, although Massachusetts offered them asylum.[15]

The Articles of Confederation, the national frame of government from 1781 to 1789, contained no provision relating specifically to runaway slaves, although it did require the return of individuals charged with "treason, felony, or other high misdemeanor."

The first national law relating to fugitive slaves was the Northwest Ordinance of July 1787, which prohibited slavery in federal territories north of the Ohio River but also provided that slaves escaping to the region from places where the institution remained legal "may be lawfully reclaimed." The following month, as the constitutional convention neared its conclusion, Pierce Butler and Charles C. Pinckney of South Carolina proposed a similar provision. With little discussion, the delegates unanimously approved what became Article IV, Section 2:

> No person held to service or labour in one state, under the laws thereof, escaping into another, shall, in consequence of any law or regulation therein, be discharged from such service or labour, but shall be delivered up on claim of the party to whom such service may be due.[16]

Along with the clause counting three-fifths of the slave population in apportioning congressional representation among the states and the one delaying the abolition of the international slave trade to the United States for at least twenty years, the fugitive slave clause exemplified how the Constitution protected the institution of slavery. As Pinckney boasted to the South Carolina House of Representatives during its debate on ratification, "We have obtained a right to recover our slaves in whatever part of America they may take refuge, which is a right we had not before." A delegate to the Virginia ratifying convention agreed: the Constitution offered "better security than any that now exists." This should be considered something of an exaggeration, as the return of fugitives across state lines was hardly unknown. Some critics charged that the purpose of the clause was to destroy the "asylum of Massachusetts."[17]

The fugitive slave clause represented a significant achievement for slaveowners. In the *Somerset* decision of 1772, Lord Mansfield, the chief justice of England, had freed a slave who sued for his liberty after being brought by his owner from Boston to London. The idea that slavery was "so odious" that a person automatically became free when he or she left a jurisdiction where local law recognized the institution quickly entered the English common law and was embraced by antislavery Americans as the "freedom principle." But the U.S. Constitution established as a national rule that slaves did not gain their liberty by escaping to free locales, and assumed that the states would cooperate in their return. The fugitive slave clause strongly reinforced the "extraterritoriality" of state laws establishing slavery—their reach into states where the institution did not exist. Nonetheless, as the antebellum era would demonstrate, its ambiguous language left it open to multiple interpretations. On key questions the Constitution remained silent: whether the responsibility for "delivering up" runaway slaves rested with the state or federal governments, and what kind of legal procedures should be required for their rendition. A dispute over these questions soon ensued between Pennsylvania and Virginia, leading in 1793 to the passage of the first national law on the subject of fugitive slaves.[18]

Pennsylvania's gradual emancipation law of 1780 freed the children of slaves born after March 1 of that year and required owners to register living slaves or they would automatically become free. It also recognized the right of out-of-state owners to recover fugitives. A Pennsylvania slave named John Davis gained his freedom because his owner, a Virginian, failed to register him. Nonetheless, the owner brought Davis from Pennsylvania to Virginia. Davis escaped, and the owner hired three Virginians to pursue him. They seized Davis in Pennsylvania and removed him from the state. Thomas Mifflin, Pennsylvania's governor, requested the extradition of the three men as kidnappers. Virginia's governor refused, and Mifflin asked George Washington, now president, to have Congress clarify how fugitive slaves were to be recovered. The result was the Fugitive Slave Act of 1793, which remained the only federal law on the subject until 1850.[19]

The brief 1793 enactment consisted of four sections, the first two of which dealt with fugitives from justice. The portion relating to slaves provided that an owner or his agent could seize a runaway and bring him or her before any judge or magistrate with "proof" (the nature unspecified—it could be a written document or simply the word of the claimant) of slave status, whereupon the official would issue a certificate of removal. Any person who interfered with the process became liable to a lawsuit by the owner.

The law made rendition essentially a private matter, identifying little role for the state or federal governments. It put the onus on the owner to track down and apprehend the fugitive, frequently a difficult and expensive process. On the other hand, it offered no procedural protections allowing free blacks to avoid being seized as slaves—there was no mention of the accused fugitive having the right to a lawyer or a jury trial, or even to speak on his own behalf. Nothing in its language, however, barred states from establishing their own, more equitable procedures to deal with accused fugitives, and as time went on, more and more northern states would do so. But the law firmly established slavery's extraterritoriality. A state could abolish slavery but not its obligation to respect the laws of other states establishing the institution. Indeed, as Samuel Nelson, a justice of New York's Supreme Court and later a member of the U.S. Supreme Court majority in the *Dred Scott* decision, noted in 1834, because of the Fugitive Slave Act of 1793, "slavery may be said still to exist in a state" even after it had been abolished.[20]

Meanwhile, as other northern states moved toward abolition, slavery in New York persisted. In 1777, when New York's Provincial Congress drafted a state constitution, Gouverneur Morris, a patriot who would later be a signer of the federal Constitution and ambassador to France, proposed that the state document include a provision for gradual emancipation, "so that in future ages, every human being who breathes the air of this state, shall enjoy the privileges of a freeman." Nothing came of the idea, but with the establishment of American independence, the issue became more pressing. Should slavery be strengthened, given the disruptions that had occurred, or should it be abolished? New York City's Common Council embraced the former approach, enacting a law in 1784 "regulating Negro and mulatto slaves." The following year, the question of slavery's future came before the state legislature, where it became embroiled in a debate over the rights of free blacks. The House passed a bill for gradual abolition, coupled with a prohibition on free blacks voting, holding office, or serving on juries. The Senate at first refused to agree to these restrictions, which had no counterpart in the abolition laws of other northern states, but eventually accepted the ban on black suffrage. The state's Council of Revision then vetoed the bill on the grounds that it violated the revolutionaries' own principle of no taxation without representation.

Despite this impasse, antislavery sentiment had grown strong enough that the legislature in 1785 moved to loosen the laws regulating private manumission. In the colonial era, such measures had been meant to discourage the practice by demanding that the owner post a large monetary bond. The new law dropped this provision, simply requiring a certificate from the overseers of the poor that the slave was capable of supporting himself or herself (thus prohibiting owners from relieving themselves of responsibility for slaves who could not perform labor, such as small children and elderly and infirm adults). By the time slavery ended in New York, the majority of slaves who became free had done so via manumission.[21]

At the same time, the first organized efforts to abolish slavery in New York made their appearance. In 1785, a group of eighteen leading citizens founded the New York Manumission Society. A majority were Quakers, but the society also included some of the city's most prominent patriots of other denominations, including Governor George Clinton, Mayor James Duane, and Alexander Hamilton. John Jay served as the organization's president until he left the city in 1789 to become chief justice of the United States. As suggested by its full name—the New York Society for Promoting the Manumission of Slaves, and Protecting Such of Them as Have Been or May be Liberated—the group assumed the role of guardian of the state's slaves and freed blacks. Compared to later abolitionist organizations, the Manumission Society was genteel, conservative, and paternalistic. It denied membership to blacks and devoted considerable effort to warning them against "running into practices of immorality or sinking into habits of idleness," such as hosting "fiddling, dancing," and other "noisy entertainments" in their homes. Its constitution forthrightly condemned "the odious practice of enslaving our fellow-men." But it claimed that because blacks were afflicted with poverty and "hostile prejudices," and "habituated to submission," abolition must come gradually and whites must take the lead in securing it: "the unhappy Africans are the least able to assert their rights."[22]

The Manumission Society eventually grew to a few hundred members, including merchants, bankers, shipowners, and lawyers. Many were themselves slaveholders, including half the signatories on the society's first legislative petition, in 1786. John Jay himself owned five slaves while he headed the organization. (Jay later explained that he purchased slaves in order to free them, after "their faithful services shall have afforded a reasonable retribution.") Nonetheless, the society's members were the only whites actively campaigning for an end to slavery. They lobbied the legislature, but also did much more. Over the course of its life (it survived until 1848), the Manumission Society offered legal assistance to blacks seeking freedom, worked strenuously to oppose the kidnapping of free blacks and slave catching in the city, brought to court captains engaged illegally in the African slave trade, and sponsored antislavery lectures and literature. It encouraged individuals to manumit their slaves and monitored the fulfillment of promises to do so. It attempted, unsuccessfully, to persuade the city's newspapers to stop printing advertisements for slave auctions and fugitive slaves, which promoted the image of blacks as property rather than persons. And as one of its first actions, it established the African Free School, which became the backbone of black education in the city. Eventually, seven such schools were created, from which emerged leading nineteenth-century black abolitionists, including James McCune Smith and Henry Highland Garnet.

The Manumission Society operated within the law. It did not countenance direct action against those seeking to retrieve fugitives in the city. Although it offered legal assistance to accused runaways, many members pledged to abide by the Fugitive Slave Act of 1793. Nonetheless, the society's activities encountered strong resistance in a city where slavery remained widespread. For their part, blacks quickly realized that despite its elitism, the society was willing to listen to and act on their grievances. They did not hesitate to seek its help.[23]

In 1788, the Manumission Society persuaded the legislature to enact a law barring the importation of slaves into the state and their removal for sale elsewhere. However, the first federal census, in 1790, revealed that although the Revolution had led to an increase in the free black population, slavery remained well entrenched in New York. Slaves still far outnumbered free African Americans. The state's population of 340,000 included over 21,000 slaves, along with 4,600 free blacks. The city recorded a black population of 3,100, two-thirds of them slaves. Twenty percent of the city's households, including merchants, shopkeepers, artisans, and sea captains, owned at least one slave. In the immediate rural hinterland, including today's Brooklyn, the proportion of slaves to the overall population stood at four in ten—the same as in Virginia.[24]

Even though New York City's free black population more than tripled during the 1790s, reaching 3,500 by 1800, the number of slaves also grew, to nearly 2,900. The buying and selling of slaves continued—a majority of the slaveholders in 1800 had not owned a slave a decade earlier. Bills for abolition came before the legislature several times, but without result. Resistance was strongest among slaveholding Dutch farmers in Brooklyn and elsewhere. "The respect due to *property*," a French visitor noted in 1796, constituted the greatest obstacle to abolition. In that year, following John Jay's election as governor, a legislative committee proposed a plan for gradual emancipation, with owners to be compensated by the state. But most legislators did not wish to burden the government with this expense.[25]

Meanwhile, slaves took matters into their own hands. Now that Pennsylvania and the New England states had provided for abolition, the number of free blacks in those states was increasing, providing more places of refuge. At the same time, the city's growing population of free blacks, many of whom proved willing to harbor or otherwise assist runaways, made it an attractive destination for slaves from nearby rural areas. The number of fugitive slave ads in New York newspapers had declined sharply in the mid-1780s, possibly because slaves expected action to abolish the institution. When this was not forthcoming, the number rose dramatically. The growing frequency of running away during the 1790s helped to propel a reluctant legislature down the road to abolition. So did the declining economic importance of slavery as the white population expanded and employers of all kinds relied increasingly on free labor.[26]

In 1799, New York's legislature finally adopted a measure for gradual abolition, becoming the next-to-last northern state to do so (New Jersey delayed until 1804). The law sought to make abolition as orderly as possible. It applied to no living slave. It freed slave children born after July 4, 1799, but only after they had served "apprenticeships" of twenty-eight years for men and twenty-five for women (far longer than traditional apprenticeships, designed to teach a young person a craft), thus compensating owners for the future loss of their property. While the law guaranteed that slavery in New York would eventually come to an end, its death came slowly and not without efforts at evasion. For slaves alive when it was passed, hopes for freedom rested on their ability to escape—and running away soon became "epidemic"—or the voluntary actions of their owners. Immediately after its passage, the Manumission Society noted an alarming rise in the illegal export of blacks from the state. But after 1800, because of manumissions, the number of slaves in New York City fell precipitously. Nonetheless, 1,446 slaves remained in the city in 1810 and 518 as late as 1820.

In 1817, the legislature decreed that all slaves who had been living at the time of the 1799 act would be emancipated on July 4, 1827. On that day, nearly 3,000 persons still held as slaves in the state gained their freedom, and slavery in New York finally came to an end. But the 1817 law also allowed southern owners to bring slaves into the state for up to nine months without their becoming free. In 1841, the legislature repealed this provision and made it illegal to introduce a slave into the state. But many southern owners ignored the new law and local authorities did little to enforce it, so for years after abolition slaves could still be seen on the city's streets.[27]

While slavery no longer existed, New York City's prosperity increasingly depended on its relations with the slave South. As the cotton kingdom flourished, so did its economic connections with New York. By the 1830s, cotton had emerged as the nation's premier export crop, and New York merchants dominated the transatlantic trade in the "white gold." Dozens of boat companies sprang up in the 1820s and 1830s, their vessels gathering southern cotton from Charleston, Savannah, Mobile, New Orleans, and other southern ports and bringing it to New York for shipment to Europe. New York banks helped to finance the crop as well as planters' acquisition of land and slaves; New York insurance companies offered policies that compensated owners upon the death of a slave; New York clothing manufacturers such as Brooks Brothers provided garments to clothe the slaves. New York printers produced stylized images of fugitives for use in notices circulated in the South by owners of runaway slaves. On the eve of the Civil War, J. D. B. De Bow, editor of the era's premier southern monthly, wrote that New York City was "almost as dependent upon Southern slavery as Charleston." The city's businessmen advertised in *De Bow's Review,* which was actually published in New York. The economy of Brooklyn, which by mid-century had grown to become the nation's third largest city, was also closely tied to slavery. Warehouses along its waterfront were filled with the products of slave labor—cotton, tobacco, and especially sugar from Louisiana and Cuba. In the 1850s, sugar refining was Brooklyn's largest industry.[28]

Southern businessmen and tourists became a ubiquitous presence in New York City. One journalist estimated that no fewer than 100,000 southerners, ranging from travelers seeking a cooler climate to planters and country merchants conducting business, visited New York City each summer. Local newspapers regularly praised southern society and carried advertisements by upscale shops directly addressed to southern visitors. Some companies, such as the investment bankers and merchants Brown Brothers and Co., which owned slave plantations in the South, emphasized that they had branches in southern cities. Major hotels, such as the Astor, Fifth Avenue, and Metropolitan, made special efforts to cater to southerners. Many owners brought slaves along on their visits. Hotels provided them with quarters, although they refused accommodations to free black guests.[29]

It was not unknown for a fugitive who had taken up residence in New York to read in a newspaper of his owner's arrival or even to encounter him on the street. Slave catchers from the South roamed the city; as late as 1840 a group of armed law enforcement officers from Virginia boarded a ship in New York harbor, searched it without a warrant, and removed a fugitive slave. The combination of what one abolitionist called the city's "selfish and pro-slavery spirit" and the presence of a rapidly growing free black community ready to take to the streets to try to protect fugitive slaves would make New York a key battleground in the national struggle over slavery.[30]

II

In the first three decades of the nineteenth century, as the institution of slavery in New York withered and died, the city witnessed the emergence of the North's largest free black community, a development that made it easier for fugitive slaves to blend into the city. By 1820, nearly 11,000 free blacks lived in New York, and by 1830 nearly 14,000. Very quickly an infrastructure of black institutions emerged—fraternal societies, literary clubs, and ten black churches, representing the major Protestant denominations. New York City replaced Philadelphia as the "capital" of free black America. It was the site of the nation's first newspaper owned and edited by African Americans, *Freedom's Journal*, established in 1827. Others followed during the next fifteen years: *The Rights of All*, *Weekly Advocate*, and *Colored American*.[31]

Despite this burgeoning community life, the living conditions of black New Yorkers deteriorated. Even as gradual abolition proceeded, racism became more entrenched in the city's culture. Before 1821, non-racial property restrictions determined which men could vote. But in that year, while eliminating property qualifications for whites, the state's constitutional convention imposed a prohibitive $250 requirement for blacks. By 1826, only sixteen black men in the city were able to cast a ballot. Blacks could not serve on juries or ride on the city's streetcars. The ferries that carried passengers between New York and Brooklyn barred blacks from the comfortable "ladies" cabin (in which white men and women were allowed to travel). Black institutions became frequent targets of racial hostility. In 1815, a mysterious fire destroyed the African Methodist Episcopal Zion Church at 158 Church Street, which housed the city's largest black congregation. The parishioners quickly raised the money to rebuild.

There was no black "ghetto" in New York City before the Civil War. African Americans could be found living in every ward. But as real estate prices rose in the first decades of the nineteenth century, blacks became concentrated in small apartments in back alleys and basements in poor neighborhoods. Many lived near the docks or in the Five Points (just north of today's City Hall), a multiethnic neighborhood notorious for crime, overcrowding, and poverty—so notorious, in fact, that it became a tourist destination, attracting visitors as diverse as Charles Dickens, Davy Crockett, and Abraham Lincoln. Black men and women found themselves confined to the lowest rungs of the economic ladder, working as domestic servants and unskilled laborers. Ironically, many of the occupations to which blacks were restricted—mariners, dock workers, cooks and waiters at hotels, servants in the homes of wealthy merchants—positioned them to assist fugitive slaves who arrived hidden on ships, or slaves who accompanied their owners on visits to New York and wished to claim their freedom.[32]

Only a tiny number of black New Yorkers were able to achieve middle-class or professional status or launch independent businesses. These, in general, were the men who founded the educational and benevolent societies. Mostly ministers and small shopkeepers, the black elite constituted less a privileged economic class than a self-proclaimed "aristocracy of character," eager to prove themselves and their people entitled to all the rights of American citizens. Given their tiny numbers and limited economic prospects, they had frequent contact with the far larger number of lower-class black New Yorkers. Nonetheless, the elite disdained the taverns, dance halls, and gambling establishments frequented by the lower classes of all racial and ethnic backgrounds, and promoted a strategy of racial uplift based on self-improvement, temperance, education, and mutual relief.[33]

Members of the black elite shared the moral uplift outlook of the Manumission Society, and many worked closely with it. They campaigned incessantly for equal rights, but also felt that one way to achieve recognition from white society was for lower-class blacks to behave in ways that did not reinforce racial stereotypes. African Americans' responses to the final end of slavery on July 4, 1827, reflected these tensions. A gathering that March decided to celebrate abolition on July 5 so as not to annoy "white citizens," who had become accustomed to holding their own festivities on Independence Day. Another faction, however, insisted on blacks' right to a share of public space. In the end, a low-key black event took place on July 4, followed by a black parade along Broadway the next day, with bands, banners, and a public dinner.[34]

Although reliable statistics do not exist, it is clear that New York City in the 1820s remained a destination for fugitive slaves, or a way station as they traveled to upstate New York, New England, and Canada. In 1826, a local newspaper complained bitterly of the "increase of Negroes in this place," lamenting that the city had become "the point of refuge to all the runaways in the Union." Most fugitives arrived on their own, without any public recognition. On occasion, however, their exploits were dramatic enough to warrant coverage in the local press, such as in July 1829, when six black men and one woman leaped ashore from an arriving vessel and with "light hearts and nimble feet" disappeared into the city. Sometimes, free blacks took to the streets in spontaneous efforts, generally unsuccessful, to prevent the removal of slaves from the city or the recapture of fugitives. In 1801, twenty-three black New Yorkers were jailed for forcibly attempting to stop a white émigré from the revolution in Saint-Domingue from taking a group of slaves to Virginia. The Manumission Society, which had been seeking to prevent the removal, prohibited under the 1788 state law, condemned the riot. In 1819, 1826, and 1832, angry blacks tried to prevent the departure of fugitives seized by slave catchers. In 1833, a "large collection of blacks" rioted in the Five Points, having "taken umbrage at one of their own color" for providing information that led to the capture of fugitive slaves. Some of those involved in these events engaged in violent altercations with the police.[35]

The Manumission Society had a special committee that offered legal assistance to fugitives. Nonetheless, the situation of runaways in New York remained fraught with danger. A Virginia lawyer residing in the city, F. H. Pettis, in 1838 advertised his services for those seeking "to arrest and secure fugitive slaves," promising "he or she will soon be had." (Three years later, to the delight of the *Colored American,* Pettis found himself before a judge, charged with having "obtained $125 worth of eatables" at a restaurant run by a black New Yorker and not paying the bill.) "Forgetful that they are in a free state," slaveowners entered black churches during Sabbath services looking for runaways, and broke into blacks' homes and carried them off without any legal proceeding. *Freedom's Journal* advised fugitive slaves to leave the city for "some sequestered country village" or Canada, as "there are many from the South now in daily search of them." "When I arrived in New York," Moses Roper, a fugitive from Florida who made his way to the city on a coastal vessel in 1834, later recalled, "I thought I was free; but I learned I was not and could be taken there." Roper decided to leave for Albany, New England, and eventually London. In New York, the abolitionist Sarah Grimké wrote in 1837, fugitives were "hunted like a partridge on the mountain."[36]

But the situation of black New Yorkers legally entitled to freedom also proved precarious. As northern slavery ended, an epidemic followed of kidnapping of free blacks, especially children, for sale to the South. New York was hardly alone. Philadelphia, less than two dozen miles from the border with slavery, witnessed frequent abductions. An investigation in 1826 revealed the existence of an interracial gang based in Delaware that had lured nearly fifty black men, women, and children onto ships in Philadelphia and transported them to be sold in the South. As late as 1844, the abolitionist weekly *Pennsylvania Freeman,* in an article entitled "Kidnappers," complained, "Our state is infested with them." Even Boston, far from the South, was not immune to the kidnapping of black residents.[37]

Kidnapping was a problem of long standing for black New Yorkers. In 1784, city authorities rescued a group of free blacks whom "man-stealers" had forced onto a ship, "destined either for Charleston or the Bay of Honduras." The Manumission Society's first statement of purposes, in 1785, mentioned prominently "the violent attempts lately made to seize and export for sale, several free Negroes" in the city. Due in part to pressure from the society, New York passed a stringent law against kidnapping in 1808. In 1821, the society expressed the hope that in the "not far distant" future the practice would be "unknown among us." Instead, it seemed to increase, partly because the end of the slave trade from Africa in 1808 and the spread of cotton cultivation led to a rapid rise in the price of slaves. In the 1820s, a gang known as the Blackbirders operated in the Five Points, seizing both fugitives and free blacks living there. *Freedom's Journal* regularly complained about the "acts of kidnapping, not less cruel than those committed on the Coast of Africa," that took place in New York City.[38]

The Fugitive Slave Act of 1793 established a procedure by which kidnappers could behave in an ostensibly legal manner, by obtaining certificates of removal from unscrupulous public officials. A group of Philadelphia free blacks in 1799 petitioned Congress to take action on the matter, but the committee to which the House referred the issue never submitted a report. Eventually, several northern states enacted laws to offer procedural protection to individuals claimed as fugitive slaves. Pennsylvania, the only northern state to border on three slave states, led the way in 1820 with An Act to Prevent Kidnapping, which limited the authority to issue certificates of removal to state judges, instead of local officials, and offered those accused of being fugitives the opportunity to prove their free status. The law also authorized a prison term of up to twenty-one years for removing a black person from the state without legal process. Six years later, in response to complaints from Maryland that the law had made the rendition of fugitives too difficult, Pennsylvania expanded the number of officials able to issue a certificate. But it also mandated that only a constable, not the owner, could seize an alleged runaway, and required proof in addition to the word of the claimant before a person was deemed a slave. However, the law denied the alleged fugitive the right to a trial by jury, for which blacks had been agitating.

New York followed in 1828 with a similar law prohibiting the private seizure of a fugitive and outlining a recovery process involving state or local courts. In a backdoor manner, it offered an alleged fugitive the opportunity to have his or her status determined by a jury. The accused fugitive could file a writ de homine replegiando (a writ to release a man from prison or from the custody of a private individual). Under this writ, unlike a writ of habeas corpus, a jury, not a judge, adjucates the claim to freedom. But many officials refused to recognize the legitimacy of such a writ. Some actively conspired to send free blacks into slavery.[39]

Most outrageous were the activities of Richard Riker, the city recorder, who presided over the Court of Special Sessions, New York City's main criminal court. An attorney and important figure in the local Democratic party, Riker held the office, with brief interruptions, from 1815 until 1838. With a group of accomplices including city constable Tobias Boudinot and the "pimp for slaveholders" Daniel D. Nash, Riker played a pivotal role in what abolitionists called the Kidnapping Club. In accordance with the Fugitive Slave Act, members of the club would bring a black person before Riker, who would quickly issue a certificate of removal before the accused had a chance to bring witnesses to testify that he was actually free. Boudinot boasted that he could "arrest and send any black to the South."[40]

If kidnapping posed a threat to the freedom of individual black New Yorkers, the rise of the colonization movement placed in jeopardy the entire community's status and future. The gradual abolition laws of the northern states, including New York's, said nothing about removing free blacks from the country; it was assumed that they would remain in the United States as a laboring class. But the rapid growth of the free black population in the early republic alarmed believers in a white America. Founded in 1816, the American Colonization Society directed its efforts toward removing from the country blacks already free, but the long-term goal of many members was to abolish slavery and expel the entire black population. In the 1820s, most organized antislavery activity among white Americans took place under this rubric. Upper South planters and political leaders dominated the society, but advocates of colonization were also active in New York City.[41]

The colonization movement made significant progress in the 1820s when it obtained funds from Congress and established Liberia on the west coast of Africa as a refuge for blacks from the United States. Some African Americans shared the society's perspective. John Russwurm, for a time an editor of *Freedom's Journal,* decided in 1829 to move from New York to Liberia, where he worked as a journalist and public official until his death in 1851. Russwurm and other black supporters of colonization believed that racism was so deeply embedded in American life that blacks could never enjoy genuine freedom except by emigrating.[42]

Most black Americans, however, rejected both voluntary emigration and government-sponsored efforts to encourage or coerce them to leave the country. They viewed the rise of the colonization movement with alarm. Beginning with a mass meeting in Philadelphia in January 1817, a month after the founding of the American Colonization Society, northern blacks repudiated the idea. In New York, a new antislavery, anti-colonization black leadership emerged in the 1820s, led by three clergymen: Peter Williams Jr., the pastor of St. Philip's Episcopal Church on Centre Street, not far from the Five Points; Samuel Cornish, minister of the First Colored (later Shiloh) Presbyterian Church; and Theodore S. Wright, who later succeeded Cornish in his pulpit. The fact that many members of the New York Manumission Society were attracted to colonization soured the organization's relations with leading black New Yorkers. *Freedom's Journal* was founded at a meeting of the city's black leaders seeking a way to oppose the colonization movement. "Too long," declared its opening editorial, "others have spoken for us"—a thinly veiled reference to the Manumission Society. The group later forced Russwurm to resign as editor when he embraced colonization.[43]

Asserting their own Americanness, free blacks articulated a vision of the United States as a land of equality before the law, where rights did not depend on color, ancestry, or racial designation. "This Country is Our Only Home," declared one editorial in the *Colored American*. "It is our duty and privilege to claim an equal place among the *American people*." Through the attack on colonization, the modern idea of equality as something that knows no racial boundaries was born.[44]

The black mobilization against colonization became a key catalyst for the rise of a new, militant abolitionism in the 1830s. Compared to previous antislavery organizations that promoted gradual emancipation and, frequently, colonization, the new abolitionism was different: it was immediatist, interracial, and committed to making the United States a biracial nation of equals. In New York City, as elsewhere, the new abolitionist movement arose from the joining of two impulses: black anti-colonization and white evangelicism. The spread of revivalist religion promoted the idea that both individuals and society could be purged of sin. In this spirit, many white abolitionists concluded that slavery and racism could be banished from the United States. Many who had previously been sympathetic to the Colonization Society now denounced it for exacerbating racial prejudice in America.[45]

The first abolitionist organization to reflect the new approach was the New-England Anti-Slavery Society, founded in January 1832. In 1833, the New York City Anti-Slavery Society followed. That December, a convention in Philadelphia founded the American Anti-Slavery Society (AASS). Its constitution demanded the immediate abolition of slavery without the "extirpation" of the black population, and the removal of prejudice and unequal laws against them. It repudiated the use of "all carnal weapons," including physical force, and pledged to rely on "moral suasion"—that is, appealing to the conscience of slaveholders and the nation—to bring about the end of slavery. The new abolitionists' forthright rejection of colonization made the movement far more appealing to free blacks than the genteel reformism of the Manumission Society.[46]

From the beginning, interracial cooperation was a hallmark of the new abolitionism. Several black New Yorkers, including Cornish, Wright, and Williams, served on the AASS's initial executive committee. The New York City Anti-Slavery Society openly sought black membership—there was "no way to destroy the prejudice," it declared, but "to invite our colored brethren to a participation with us." White abolitionists welcomed black leaders at meetings, published their writings and speeches in antislavery newspapers, served on committees and took part in public events with them, and worked individually to help uplift black New Yorkers.[47]

Between the formation of the AASS in 1833 and the end of the decade, over 200,000 northerners joined local groups dedicated to the abolition of slavery and equal rights for black Americans. New York City was crucial to the society's early growth. The organization established its national headquarters at 142 Nassau Street. Virtually the entire initial executive committee consisted of New Yorkers, and much of the organization's early funding came from the city. But the diffusion of abolitionist ideas faced many obstacles. The first meeting of the New York City Anti-Slavery Society, on October 2, 1833, was dispersed by a mob stirred up by the Colonization Society. The New York State Anti-Slavery Society (founded in 1834) made far greater progress upstate than in the city.[48]

Two groups dominated among New York City's white abolitionists: moral reformers strongly influenced by evangelical religion, and radical Quakers. Of the former, none played a more crucial role over the next thirty years than the Tappan brothers, Arthur (the first president of the AASS) and Lewis. Born in Northampton, Massachusetts, in the 1780s, the Tappans had moved to New York in the 1820s and prospered as silk merchants. They financed antislavery activity in New York as well as many other benevolent enterprises, including the American Bible Society, the Magdalen Society (an effort to uplift prostitutes), and the construction of the Broadway

Tabernacle to host the sermons of the era's greatest evangelist, Charles Grandison Finney.

Employing his formidable business skills, Lewis Tappan oversaw the AASS publications board, which in 1836 launched a massive campaign of printing and distributing antislavery materials. He also served as superintendent of a Sabbath school "mostly composed of colored children." In 1833, two years after William Lloyd Garrison's *Liberator* made its appearance in Boston as a voice of immediate abolitionism, Arthur Tappan funded the publication of an abolitionist weekly, the *Emancipator*, in New York. He also paid for Garrison's trip to England to establish relations with British abolitionists. In 1835, the parish of East Feliciana, Louisiana, offered a reward of $50,000 (an unheard-of sum in those days) for "delivery . . . of the notorious abolitionist, Arthur Tappan, of New York."[49]

Black New Yorkers, as we have seen, had long acted individually to assist fugitive slaves, taking them into their homes and keeping a lookout for stowaways who arrived on the docks. The white abolitionists in the Manumission Society had long doubted the "propriety" of acting in ways that violated the law. But the militant abolitionism that emerged in the 1830s included individuals who would play important roles in what came to be called the underground railroad. Lewis Tappan owned a horse that regularly carried fugitives from his "agent" at Havre de Grace, Maryland, to Pennsylvania. In January 1838, a runaway slave from Alabama arrived at Tappan's home on New Year's Day and was sent to England, at Tappan's expense. Arthur Tappan also aided fugitives with "his purse, advice and sympathy."[50]

William Jay, the son of John Jay, who "early imbibed my father's hostility to slavery," divided his time between residences in New York City and Bedford, Westchester County, where he long served as a judge. More conservative than the Tappans, he warned against needlessly alienating white public opinion by admitting black members to local antislavery societies and having them speak at antislavery meetings. Nonetheless, Jay contributed money and offered refuge to fugitives. Early in the 1830s, Judge Jay wrote to another abolitionist that he would "withhold his obedience" to state laws outlining procedures for the return of fugitives, and "refuse all applications that may be made to me" to execute them. "I shall ever deem it both a duty and a pleasure," he added, "to facilitate the escape of any fugitive slave." These were remarkable affirmations by a sitting judge. The British abolitionist Joseph Sturge, who visited the United States in 1841, reported that Jay spoke openly of "the runaway slaves who called at his house." Jay died in 1858. His will included a bequest of $1,000 "to be applied . . . in promoting the safety and comfort of fugitive slaves."[51]

Isaac T. Hopper, his daughter Abigail Hopper Gibbons, and her husband James S. Gibbons, all of whom moved to the city from Pennsylvania in the late 1820s and 1830s, exemplified the Quaker presence in New York abolitionism. A generation older than the new breed of militant abolitionists, Hopper served as a mentor to New Yorkers who became involved in the underground railroad. Born in Woodbury, New Jersey, in 1771, he had established himself as a tailor in Philadelphia at the age of sixteen. He soon joined the Pennsylvania Abolition Society. Hopper's history of assisting runaways and kidnap victims began in the 1790s, and fugitive slaves frequently stayed at his home in Philadelphia. In 1804, Hopper persuaded a local court to free a slave brought to that city by Pierce Butler of South Carolina, author of the Constitution's fugitive slave clause. Junius C. Morel, a black journalist and abolitionist who had been born a slave in North Carolina and moved to the North with the permission of his white father, described Hopper, whom he had encountered in Philadelphia, as "the first white man that I ever saw, who pitied the colored man."

Hopper left Pennsylvania for New York in 1829 after being "disowned" by his Quaker congregation, which disapproved of public antislavery agitation, especially in cooperation with non-Quakers. He joined the New York Manumission Society, took fugitives into his home at 110 Second Avenue, established a bookstore to sell Quaker and antislavery publications, and became a founding member of both the AASS and the New York City Anti-Slavery Society. In 1840, Hopper began publishing "Tales of Oppression" in the *National Anti-Slavery Standard,* a series of dramatic accounts of the fugitive slaves he had assisted in Philadelphia. Hopper's daughter and son-in-law moved frequently in lower Manhattan, before purchasing a house at 339 West Twenty-Ninth Street in the 1850s. Wherever they were living, their home served as a refuge for fugitives, as well as the place William Lloyd Garrison stayed when he visited New York. Another radical Quaker, Barney Corse, a wealthy leather merchant and member of the Manumission Society, worked with Hopper to combat kidnappers and provided funds to defend blacks accused of being fugitives. Hopper and Corse exemplified the link between the antislavery activism that descended from the revolutionary era and the radical abolitionism of the 1830s, and between earlier efforts to assist runaway slaves and the underground railroad.[52]

Black New Yorkers responded enthusiastically to these white abolitionists' demand for greater rights for blacks in the North, and their principled rejection of colonization. They appreciated the risks white abolitionists incurred because of their commitment to the cause and their financial contributions, which few if any blacks could match. When the *Colored American* issued an appeal for funds in 1837, it called upon others to emulate "our Tappans, our Jays, and our Smiths, who have been blessed with the disposition as well as the means to give." (A wealthy upstate reformer, Gerrit Smith for three decades dispensed much of his fortune aiding the abolitionist cause.) To be sure, black New York leaders sometimes accused white allies of sharing the prejudices of their society, and insisted on the necessity of holding all-black conventions and maintaining separate uplift societies. Never before, however, had black and white Americans worked so closely for common goals.[53]

As abolitionists stepped up their activities, the prospects of retaliation also escalated. Throughout the 1830s, northern mobs (well over 100 by one count) broke up abolitionists' meetings and destroyed their printing presses. As in other parts of the North, colonizationists instigated and participated in anti-abolitionist violence in New York City. The *Courier and Enquirer*, at the time the most influential newspaper in the United States, was edited by James Watson Webb, a leading colonizationist. It excoriated abolitionists for promoting "amalgamation" (interracial marriage) and endangering the Union, on which the city's prosperity rested. In May 1834, Lewis Tappan organized a week of public meetings to promote abolition and denounce colonization. The following month, Tappan, who opposed the common practice of relegating black worshipers to "Negro pews," invited the Reverend Samuel Cornish to sit alongside him during services at a Presbyterian church. A number of parishioners vocally objected, whereupon the minister made tolerance the subject of his sermon.[54]

Tolerance, however, was in short supply in New York City in 1834. That July, a full-fledged riot broke out, with mobs attacking black homes, churches, and businesses, as well as the residences of leading white abolitionists. The crowd demolished St. Stephen's Church and burned Lewis Tappan's home on Rose Street (just east of City Hall) to the ground. With some 7,000 persons taking part, this was the largest and most destructive riot in the city until the uprising against the Civil War draft three decades later. The violence lasted for several days, ending only when the militia arrived. Many New Yorkers blamed the abolitionists for the riot. The Episcopal bishop of New York ordered Peter Williams Jr. to resign from the executive committee of the AASS, which he proceeded to do, although he remained a member until his death in 1840.[55]

The violence temporarily shook the abolitionist movement. Arthur Tappan issued a "Disclaimer," which insisted that the organization had "no desire to encourage intermarriages between white and colored persons" or "resistance to the laws." An "Address to the People of Color" by the AASS executive committee quickly followed. It condemned the outrages committed against the black community and praised African Americans for their "peaceful endurance," but it also chastised them for intemperance, "profaning" the Sabbath, and frittering away their money on lottery tickets. After a bit of a hiatus, however, the AASS renewed its activities in the city and gathered new recruits. Alarmed by the assaults on his home and business, Lewis Tappan moved to Pierrepont Street in Brooklyn Heights, but redoubled his commitment to the antislavery cause. William Jay now accepted appointment to the AASS executive committee. In 1835, he was elected president of the New York State Anti-Slavery Society.[56]

Not long after the riots, Elizur Wright Jr., the editor of the *Emancipator*, began publishing "Chronicles of Kidnapping," a series of essays exposing how the Fugitive Slave Act of 1793 operated in New York City. The articles told the stories of black persons who had been shipped south by city officials without a hearing and of accused fugitives who had spent months in prison before their cases were adjudicated. In one instance, a North Carolina slaveowner, Dr. Rufus Haywood of Raleigh, staged a midnight raid on the home of one Lockley. Despite protests that he was a free man, Lockley, his wife, and their twelve-year-old daughter were imprisoned as fugitives, and after a series of hearings before Recorder Richard Riker, they were taken south by Haywood. Peter Martin, who had lived in the city for four years with his wife and child, was arrested at his employer's store, held in a "coffin-like cell" for months, and returned to slavery in Virginia. Martin's case ended more happily than most, as his employer raised the money to purchase his freedom. A month after his return to slavery, Martin was back at his old job in New York.[57]

In what Wright called a "vile and despicable outrage," a Virginia slaveowner, Richard Haxall, a member of the family that owned one of Virginia's largest flour mills, accompanied by a city policeman, dragged out of an African Free School seven-year-old Henry Scott, whose father had brought him from Virginia to New York. Haxall claimed that Henry had been the property of his late father and that ownership had passed to his mother. He failed, however, to produce a will. Nonetheless, Recorder Riker lodged the boy in jail. Through the efforts of African Americans, including his classmates, and white abolitionists, Scott's plight was widely publicized and aroused considerable sympathy. He was released from prison and taken to live with Elizur Wright and his family.[58]

Such efforts on behalf of kidnap victims and fugitives were ad hoc and sporadic. As early as 1828, *Freedom's Journal* had called for the creation of an organization "for the preventing of kidnapping and man-stealing." Precedents existed; the editors mentioned the Protecting Society of Philadelphia, a short-lived adjunct of the Pennsylvania Abolition Society. Not until 1835, however, did such a group come into existence in New York. The leading spirit in its creation and in its activities for the first five years was David Ruggles. Born in Connecticut in 1810, one of eight children of a free black family, Ruggles did not belong to New York's black elite. He had been educated at a Sabbath School for the poor, and came to the city at the age of fifteen. Ruggles worked for a time as a mariner, then opened a grocery store at 1 Cortlandt Street, on the corner of Broadway. He quickly became involved in the black community's institutional life, joining the Garrison Literary and Benevolent

Society and the Phoenix Literary Society. But his main activity was abolitionism. Soon after its founding in 1831, he became an agent of Garrison's *Liberator*. When the *Emancipator* was established, Ruggles became that paper's general agent; he was the only individual to work for both publications simultaneously. Ruggles solicited subscribers in the city, Pennsylvania, New Jersey, and upstate New York, making contacts that would prove invaluable when he turned his attention to aiding fugitive slaves.[59]

It was Ruggles who in November 1835 called a mass meeting to respond to the epidemic of kidnapping. The meeting created the Committee of Vigilance for the Protection of the People of Color. It appointed an interracial executive committee "to aid the people of color, legally, to obtain their rights." With the advent of the Vigilance Committee, a new chapter opened in the battle over fugitive slaves in New York City.[60]

3

ORIGINS OF THE UNDERGROUND RAILROAD: THE NEW YORK VIGILANCE COMMITTEE

I

The New York Vigilance Committee began its life in 1835 with large ambitions and a very small membership. Initially, it consisted of only five persons: David Ruggles; William Johnston, an English-born abolitionist and grain merchant who served for several years as treasurer; George R. Barker, a white businessman and another lifelong abolitionist; James W. Higgins, a black grocer; and Robert Brown, a white attorney. Soon, the black ministers Theodore S. Wright, Samuel Cornish, and Charles B. Ray joined the executive committee, along with Thomas Van Rensselaer, who had escaped from slavery in New York's Mohawk Valley in 1819. (Van Rensselaer's owner "sent messengers in all directions, and traveled himself as far as Canada" in an unsuccessful effort to retrieve him.) Sometime in the 1820s, Van Rensselaer made his way to New York City, where he opened a restaurant, became superintendent of a Sabbath School, and in 1834 presided over a gathering of over 2,000 people to celebrate emancipation in the British West Indies.[1]

In a number of incarnations, the Vigilance Committee survived until the eve of the Civil War. Over the course of its life, it propelled the plight of fugitives to the forefront of abolitionist consciousness in New York and won support from many outside the movement's ranks. It forced the interconnected issues of kidnapping and fugitive slaves into the larger public sphere. The committee's active leaders generally consisted of only a dozen or so individuals, most of whom lived near each other in lower Manhattan. Yet the group and its supporters took part in a remarkable range of activities. In effect, the committee combined the moral suasion of the American Anti-Slavery Society, the legal strategy of the Manumission Society, and the direct-action tradition of the city's black population.

In the years following its founding, the Vigilance Committee held monthly meetings to raise money, report on its activities, and spread its antislavery message. It petitioned the legislature to expand the rights of free blacks and accused fugitives. It employed lawyers who went to court attempting to block kidnappers, prevent the return of fugitive slaves, suppress the illegal slave trade, and secure the freedom of slaves brought to the city by southern or foreign owners.

In addition to these public and entirely legal pursuits, the Vigilance Committee, as Ruggles announced in a report on the group's activities in December 1836, "did not scruple to help fugitive slaves to places of safety," a task, he noted, "almost wholly neglected" before the organization's formation. Assisting fugitives was "but one branch" of the committee's work and "not even the major part." Most of its attention was devoted to kidnapping cases. But in the year since its formation, Ruggles claimed, the committee had "saved" 300 persons "from being carried back into slavery." At another meeting, William Johnston noted that "multitudes of fugitive slaves" came through the city. Before the formation of the Vigilance Committee, they arrived "friendless, poor, ignorant and unprotected," and in "nine cases out of ten, they were retaken." Now, for the first time, organized assistance was available to aid them "in escaping to a land of freedom." "This," Ruggles declared, was "practical abolition."[2]

Despite the committee's interracial leadership, most of those who attended its meetings and took part in its activities were black New Yorkers. Kidnapping posed a threat to every black family. The committee's first annual public meeting, in May 1837, was "crowded to overflowing, mostly with colored people," but also attracted a "goodly number" of white delegates to the annual gathering of the AASS, which took place simultaneously in the city. Ruggles's annual report, declared the white abolitionist Henry C. Wright, was "a pamphlet that should go into every house in the land." It not only exposed the activities of kidnappers but also offered a lengthy account of the numerous forms of inequality to which blacks in New York City were subjected, including the "pro-slavery feeling" that barred them from education, employment, and equal treatment in the courts. The report praised the work of the AASS but suggested that its focus on abolition had led it to neglect "minor evils" (compared to slavery) at home. Invoking Ruggles's favorite phrase, it urged its readers to act "in every case of oppression and wrong . . . and thus . . . prove ourselves practical abolitionists."[3]

The Vigilance Committee quickly established an innovative system to raise funds: an "effective committee" of 100 persons, male and female, each of whom would collect money—as little as a penny a month—from ten or more friends. Among other things, the funds would pay Ruggles's annual salary of $400 and his expenses as the group's full-time secretary and general agent. Taken together, the effective committee and its donors represented by far the largest group of New Yorkers engaged in antislavery work in the mid-1830s.[4]

Throughout its life, however, the Vigilance Committee found itself chronically short of funds. Ruggles published monthly reports of receipts, most of them donations of under one dollar from ordinary black New Yorkers. Black churches and fraternal organizations, such as the Ladies' Literary Society, also raised money.

Indeed, although men dominated the group's leadership, black women did much of the fund raising—the "ladies," as Ruggles put it, "who collect from their friends one penny a week." Members of the executive committee also made donations, including Ruggles himself, who gave fifty dollars in 1837. The largest individual contributions came from prominent white abolitionists, including William Jay, the Tappan brothers, and Gerrit Smith. At the 1837 annual meeting, Johnston acknowledged that the committee's work had been "cramped and impeded by our poverty. The work demands thousands where we have tens." A year later, Ruggles reported that in the previous month, twenty-six fugitives had come to the committee's attention, but because of lack of funds, they could be offered nothing more than "I wish you well, with faint prospects before them." Nonetheless, in the first decade of its existence, the Vigilance Committee later claimed, it assisted around 2,000 fugitive slaves to gain their freedom.[5]

Much of the Vigilance Committee's success in its first few years can be attributed to the indefatigable Ruggles, "the most active man in the city," one abolitionist newspaper called him. Operating in New York City presented daunting challenges. The committee essentially worked out of Ruggles's home at 36 Lispenard Street (a building that remains standing today). It found it difficult to locate "a permanent place" for its monthly meetings and generally had to rely on black churches to provide space. Nonetheless, early in 1838 Ruggles issued a report on no fewer than 173 cases he had dealt with since the committee's founding, including investigations and assistance to kidnap victims and fugitive slaves.[6]

Ruggles boarded incoming ships looking for slaves. In one instance, he and other committee members rescued three Africans illegally brought into the port. He introduced them at a Vigilance Committee meeting, noting that more Africans had been shipped to New York by illegal slave traders in the previous year than the Colonization Society had "succeeded in exporting from this state to Africa." The slave traders against whom Ruggles brought charges included Nathaniel Gordon, who in 1862 would become the only American executed for participation in the slave trade from Africa. In 1838, Ruggles alerted the district attorney to Gordon's crimes, and a judge ordered him held on $5,000 bail. But a grand jury refused to issue an indictment.[7]

In 1838, Ruggles learned that two years earlier, a South Carolina family had brought three slaves to work in their summer home in Brooklyn. Ruggles entered the home and confronted the owner, explaining New York law and the time limit on slave transit: "They are as free as I am; after remaining here nine months, they have a right to demand wages for every hour's service they have performed." Ruggles refused to leave when ordered to do so, and eventually departed with one of the slaves; the other two evidently remained in slavery. The press reported the incident, one newspaper calling Ruggles "an insolent black fellow." In 1838, a free black New Yorker informed Ruggles that the captain of a coastal vessel had tricked his son and two other black sailors into leaving their ship in New Orleans, where they were sold into slavery. Ruggles gathered evidence from other sailors and secured the captain's arrest. The committee succeeded in persuading the purchaser in the South to send the three home.[8]

Apart from all this, Ruggles was constantly writing, producing his own antislavery and anti-colonization tracts and publicizing the Vigilance Committee's monthly meetings in the *Emancipator, Colored American,* and his own periodical, the *Mirror of Liberty.* The first magazine edited by a black American, the *Mirror* published five issues between 1838 and 1841. In 1838, Ruggles established a reading room where New Yorkers who paid a small annual fee could "have access to the principal daily and leading anti-slavery papers." He filled the antislavery press, black and white, with notices warning about the practices of the kidnappers who "infested" the city—some of whom he identified by name—and offering detailed descriptions of their victims. The notices bore an eerie resemblance to fugitive slave ads. One read:

> Francis Maria Shields, a girl of about 12 years of age, is missed by her guardians and acquaintances. . . . She is middling size, dark brown complexion, short hair, with a scar over her right eyebrow. Her dress was a purple and white frock, white straw hat, lined with pink, and trimmed with straw colored ribbon, mixed stockings, and boots. Any person who will give such information as will lead to the restoration of said girl to her guardian and friends, shall be rewarded.[9]

Ruggles and the committee enlisted a group of antislavery lawyers to take cases of kidnapping to court and to contest the rendition of alleged fugitives. This was not an easy task in a city where many public officials openly sympathized with slaveholders and some connived in kidnapping. A speaker at one of the committee's public meetings in 1838 denounced "the pusillanimous and disgraceful conduct" of judges, district attorneys, and other officials in kidnapping cases. Despite federal statutes outlawing the Atlantic slave trade, New York City judges treated foreign ships entering the harbor as if they were from the South, enjoying the right to bring slaves for the transit period of up to nine months. In 1838, Ruggles attempted to secure a writ of habeas corpus for a young "apprentice" (a temporary status of recently freed West Indian slaves) who had been brought on a ship to New York and was in danger of being transported to South Carolina to be sold. Two judges refused to hear the plea, one claiming illness, the second "as he wanted his dinner." By the time a third judge agreed to issue the writ, the ship and youth had departed. Meanwhile, Recorder Richard Riker and his

Kidnapping Club continued their notorious activities. In March 1837, John Price, who had lived in the city for several years with his wife, was arrested by Tobias Boudinot, taken to Riker, and after a summary hearing remanded to a Maryland slaveowner who claimed him as a fugitive. That December, Riker sent to slavery Alfred Canada, charged with being a fugitive from North Carolina, without allowing him the opportunity to have a lawyer or introduce witnesses.[10]

Horace Dresser, the Vigilance Committee's leading attorney, argued most of the cases before the recorder. A graduate of Union College, Dresser later became famous as the author of works on legal and historical subjects, including *Battle Record of the American Rebellion* as well as a manual of tax law. When he died in 1877, the *New York Times* recalled that "at a time when it was exceedingly unpopular," Dresser had been "the very first lawyer to plead the cause of the slave in the New York courts"—an exaggeration, given the earlier efforts of the Manumission Society. In the 1830s, however, Dresser was indeed "called upon in all slave cases," as the *Colored American* put it. His "services are abundant," it added, but his "remuneration is comparatively nothing at all." Against formidable odds, Dresser occasionally won a legal victory. He was able to obtain writs of habeas corpus to bring to court and liberate individuals held in captivity by kidnappers. Generally, however, there was little Dresser or his associate Robert Sedgwick could do, given the attitude of local officials and the duty to return fugitives established in federal and state law. In one instance, Dresser learned that an alleged runaway was about to be taken before the recorder. He rushed to the office only to see Riker rule in favor of the claimant and remark, "I am glad the man has got his nigger again."[11]

With the legal obligation to return fugitives clear, Dresser's arguments generally revolved around identification—was the accused actually the person referred to orally by the alleged owner and his witnesses or in a document from a slave state? In 1836, Abraham Goslee, who claimed to be a free man from Maryland but was charged with being a slave who had escaped the previous year, was brought before the recorder. Sedgwick presented three black witnesses who stated that they had known Goslee in the city before the date of his supposed escape, as well as an affidavit from the clerk of Somerset County Court in Maryland affirming Goslee's free status. Nonetheless, Riker pronounced Goslee a slave and ordered him dispatched to Maryland. The police arrested four black men after the hearing for loudly calling for Goslee to be rescued.[12]

A case that produced "tremendous excitement," and success for the committee, involved thirty-year-old William Dixon, arrested in April 1837 by the kidnappers Tobias Boudinot and Daniel D. Nash and a policeman from Baltimore. Dixon was brought before Recorder Riker and charged with being Jake, a slave who had absconded from Walter P. Allender in 1832. Dixon, who earned his living as a whitewasher, denied being Allender's slave or ever having lived in Baltimore. The case lasted, on and off, for four months while both sides rounded up witnesses. Allender brought over a dozen persons from Baltimore who identified Dixon as his slave. Horace Dresser produced several witnesses, white and black, who testified that Dixon had lived in New York and Boston well before 1832. The *New-York Commercial Advertiser,* a newspaper not known for sympathy with abolitionists, pronounced the testimony of Dixon's witnesses "very strong in his favor." Some of the witnesses perjured themselves, for Dixon was indeed the fugitive Jake.[13]

Continuing a pattern that would persist until the Civil War whenever an alleged fugitive appeared before a judge, large crowds of black New Yorkers, estimated by various newspapers at from several hundred to nearly 2,000, gathered at the courthouse in lower Manhattan during the proceedings. Hundreds of blacks who could not gain admission paraded on Broadway, wearing hats bedecked with mottos such as "No Slavery" and "Down with Kidnapping." At one point, after the recorder decided to send Dixon south, "a rush was made instantly from all quarters." The crowd seized Dixon and hurried him away, but the police soon recaptured him. During the affray, Judge John M. Bloodgood arrived on the scene. Bloodgood remarked that had he known in advance of the riot, he would have "brought his percussion caps with him," as he "would have liked to have sent a few of those damn niggers to hell."[14]

The Vigilance Committee appealed Riker's order to the New York Supreme Court by filing a writ de homine replegiando, seeking a jury trial, and when denied, the committee appealed to the state's highest tribunal, the Court for the Trial of Impeachments and the Correction of Errors. On both sides, costs mounted. Allender, according to the *Mirror of Liberty*, expended $1,500 on the case and became "quite fatigued with the trouble and expense." The Vigilance Committee spent $700 and Dixon himself incurred "heavy liabilities . . . in defending his liberty." The case never reached a final judgment. Dixon was released on bail and left for Canada. Allender, probably worn out by the time-consuming and expensive proceedings, returned to Maryland. Dixon soon reappeared in New York and continued to enjoy his freedom. In May 1838, he addressed the committee's second anniversary meeting. Five months later, when Frederick Douglass arrived in New York from Maryland, he encountered Dixon, whom he knew as "Allender's Jake," on the streets. Dixon warned him of the danger of recapture and told him to leave the city. Oddly, if Douglass's recollection is correct, Dixon did not mention that Douglass might receive help from the Vigilance Committee. Fortunately for Douglass, another individual directed him to David Ruggles.[15]

Another case that attracted considerable attention originated when John McPherson, a Maryland slaveowner, encountered Henry Metscher on a New York street in October 1837 and claimed that he was Nat, who had escaped four years earlier. Nash and Boudinot arrested Metscher on the pretext of having committed an assault. Perhaps mindful of the near riot a few months earlier, three judges declined to hear the case, but McPherson finally located one who examined documents from Maryland indicating that a slave named Nat owned by McPherson had run away in 1833. The judge ruled that Metscher was the same individual, which he strenuously denied. Dresser presented evidence that Metscher had lived in New Jersey before Nat's escape, and asked for permission to present witnesses affirming this, but the judge ordered Metscher sent to Maryland. Nash and Boudinot removed him from the city. All these cases intensified demands, which extended well beyond the abolitionist movement, for the state to allow a jury, not a single official, to determine the status of an accused fugitive. "It is a momentous question," declared the *New York Evening Post*, "whether the liberty of a man can be decided by any other tribunal than . . . a jury."[16]

As these and other cases involving the Committee of Vigilance demonstrate, once authorities brought an individual to court as an alleged fugitive, he was almost certain to be remanded to slavery. As a result, Ruggles devoted considerable effort to helping fugitives avoid apprehension. The committee's clandestine assistance to fugitive slaves is much more difficult to document than its highly visible public and legal actions. In the 1830s, the committee's reports offered long accounts of kidnapping cases but no specifics about aid to fugitives. It is clear, however, that Ruggles's home became a destination for many runaway slaves, whom he dispatched to upstate New York or New England, often to the homes of abolitionists he had encountered during his days as traveling agent for the antislavery press.

In addition to Frederick Douglass, a few other fugitives recorded their experiences with Ruggles. William Green escaped from Maryland to New York, and a friend directed him to Ruggles. "He was very active in procuring material aid for and in giving us good advice," Green later wrote. James L. Smith, who absconded from Virginia to Philadelphia in 1838, was sent on to New York City with a letter addressed to Ruggles. After a few days in Ruggles's home, he departed for Hartford, with an introduction to an abolitionist there. Smith later became a minister and antislavery lecturer in Massachusetts. Operating before the widespread advent of railroads in the Northeast, Ruggles seems to have dispatched most of the fugitives by coastal vessel or Hudson River steamboat. (Before the completion of a rail link in 1851, the latter was the major mode of transportation between New York City and Albany.)[17]

Although those who challenged kidnappers and assisted fugitive slaves were rarely prosecuted, anyone involved in such activities exposed himself to danger. In 1838, Ruggles was arrested and "committed to a felon's dungeon," having been charged with harboring a criminal and encouraging a slave to escape. This unusual case arose when John P. Darg, a slave trader from New Orleans, arrived in New York, bringing along a slave, Thomas Hughes. Hughes sought refuge at the home of the Quaker abolitionist Isaac T. Hopper. It turned out that before escaping, Hughes had stolen $7,000 from Darg. Hopper and Barney Corse offered to retrieve the money if Darg emancipated Hughes. They proceeded to recover the funds with the assistance of James S. Gibbons of the AASS. Darg then had them all—plus Ruggles, who had nothing to do with these events—indicted for complicity in theft. To delay Ruggles's release, the court set his bail at $5,000. The case never came to trial, and Hughes, after serving two years in prison for robbery, agreed to return to New Orleans with Darg as a free man, although he later turned up again in New York.[18]

Ruggles spoke and acted in a far more confrontational manner than other leaders of the Vigilance Committee and abolitionists more generally. In 1836, when George Jones, a free resident of New York, was arrested, ruled to be a fugitive on the testimony of several notorious kidnappers, and "dragged to slavery," Ruggles declared that blacks could no longer "depend on the interposition of the Manumission or Anti-Slavery Societies. . . . We must look to our own safety, . . . remembering that 'self-defence is the first law of nature.' " But the ideal of respectability to which many black leaders adhered clashed with the call for direct action. After the attempted rescue of William Dixon, Samuel Cornish published a stern rebuke in the *Colored American* to the participants in what he called a "disgraceful riot":

> Brethren, my heart is grieved at your conduct yesterday, and on all occasions of fugitive trials. We have an intelligent and efficient Vigilance Committee, who have eminent lawyers in their employ. . . . We have perfect confidence in the men whose business is to conduct these matters. And we must here enter our solemn protest, against your going to the courts at all . . . on the occasion of fugitive trials. . . . You . . . degrade yourselves, and all others in the least connected with you. . . . We ask the pardon and clemency of our municipal authorities, . . . in behalf of the ignorant part of our colored citizens.

Cornish especially reprimanded "those females" who "degraded themselves" by taking part in the altercation. He urged their husbands "to keep them at home."[19]

Cornish was a leading member of the Vigilance Committee. His editorials reveal the gap between the "aristocracy of character" and ordinary black New Yorkers, who, as he noted, frequently gathered in large numbers at fugitive trials, and whose militancy Ruggles's actions reflected. By the late 1830s, William Lloyd Garrison, whose *Liberator*, published weekly in Boston, had become the major voice of radical abolitionism, was preaching "non-resistance." This quasi-anarchist philosophy rejected all use of force and all institutions, including governments, that employed it. Many of the committee's leaders accepted the idea that "moral suasion" was the proper way to combat slavery. In December 1837, at a protest meeting shortly after the return to slavery of Henry Metscher, Ruggles reported a series of resolutions, one of which seemed to countenance violence: "we cannot recommend non-resistance to persons who are denied the protection of equitable law." A spirited debate followed. Theodore S. Wright, Charles B. Ray, and William P. Johnson, all members of the Vigilance Committee's executive committee, objected on the grounds that the resolution violated the "peace principles" of the AASS. Ruggles replied "with much warmth" that a person seized by a kidnapper "ought not only to use words implying resistance, but should resist even unto death." The meeting rejected his resolution.[20]

These differences undoubtedly contributed to the final breach between Ruggles and other leaders of the Vigilance Committee. In 1838, the *Colored American* printed a statement, provided by Ruggles, that John Russell, a black man, had forced three native Africans onto a ship heading to New Orleans. Lawyers brought a libel suit in Russell's name against the newspaper's editor, Samuel Cornish; the publisher, Philip A. Bell; and the printer. Russell won a judgment of $600. Cornish insisted that the Vigilance Committee should take responsibility for payment. The committee's leaders replied that Ruggles had acted alone and bore the responsibility. Ruggles contended that he had written the statement in his capacity as the committee's secretary. "We have been shamefully used in the libel case, from first to last, by somebody," Cornish complained. "If we believe the Vigilance Committee by Mr. Ruggles, and if we believe Mr. Ruggles by the Vigilance Committee."[21]

By 1839, Ruggles and the committee leadership were publishing conflicting accounts of these events and holding public meetings to denounce each other. The charges against Ruggles expanded; Cornish, Charles B. Ray, Theodore S. Wright, and others claimed that he had not kept proper financial records and had used Vigilance Committee money for private purposes. Cornish, who had once praised Ruggles effusively, now denounced him for "wilful misrepresentations and base falsehoods." Lewis Tappan, who along with his brother Arthur had contributed money to help pay the libel judgment, complained that Ruggles, "like most every colored man I have ever known," kept no regular financial records. Compared to Tappan's meticulous double-entry bookkeeping, this was undoubtedly correct. "Auditors" appointed by the Vigilance Committee, including Tappan and Horace Dresser, concluded that Ruggles owed the organization $326.17. For his part, Ruggles sued the committee for back wages. The controversy disturbed many abolitionists. The *Emancipator* published statements by both sides but declared, "We have formed no opinion on the merits of the unfortunate dispute." With his health deteriorating and finances exhausted, Ruggles resigned from the Vigilance Committee in 1839. He tried to revive the *Mirror of Liberty*, which had been suspended because of these difficulties, but its final issue appeared in 1841. Most of it was devoted to a long letter by Ruggles accusing Cornish, Wright, Ray, Philip A. Bell, and Lewis Tappan of engaging in a malicious conspiracy against him. He thanked James S. Gibbons and Isaac T. Hopper, among others, for their support. The Vigilance Committee, Ruggles claimed, had "apostatized."[22]

In 1840, Ruggles left New York. The following year, a conductor violently evicted him from a segregated railroad car in New Bedford after he refused to vacate his seat. Ruggles sued the company, but a local judge ruled that corporations enjoyed the right to exclude "vagabonds, wranglers," and other undesirables, including blacks, from their trains. Even the city known as the fugitive's Gibraltar evidently harbored racial prejudice. Soon afterward, Ruggles moved to a utopian community in Northampton, Massachusetts, where he established a water-cure medical practice. He died there in 1849. The Vigilance Committee survived the debacle and continued its work.[23]

Theodore S. Wright, who headed the Vigilance Committee in the 1840s, observed that in contrast to the highly public activities of abolitionist societies, the organization "deemed it prudent" to keep many of its actions secret. As a result, the committee's labors often went "unnoticed and almost unknown." Moreover, most of its work "devolves upon two or three individuals," who were "quite exhausted" by the "incessant demands on their time." This problem would plague the committee throughout its existence. Nonetheless, between 1835 and 1840, the period of Ruggles's leadership, the New York Vigilance Committee could boast of significant accomplishments. In the face of internal dissension, legal setbacks, and chronic funding problems, it claimed to have assisted more than 800 fugitives, "who are now enjoying the blessing of liberty." Largely composed of black New Yorkers, it had won the support and respect of the nation's leading white abolitionists. Speakers at its annual and monthly meetings included antislavery luminaries from as far away as Boston, upstate New York, and Canada.[24]

Before the advent of the Vigilance Committee, the *Emancipator* noted, the plight of fugitives had been a matter "too little thought of by the professed friends of the colored man." Many abolitionists, another antislavery newspaper remarked, had been "hesitant or timid" when it came to aiding runaway slaves: "had it not been for the activities of the colored people themselves in this department of labor, . . . it may be doubted whether much would have been accomplished." But in 1839, the New York State Anti-Slavery Society declared that "the assistance of the fugitive slave, and the defense of those arrested as such, are the . . . duty of abolitionists."

Even the staid Manumission Society regularly donated money to the Vigilance Committee.[25]

The committee's activities had also effected a subtle change in public attitudes. The "tide of public opinion," the committee declared in 1838, had forced kidnappers to change tactics. They now took victims directly to a judge for a secret hearing to avoid proceedings in open court, where sentiment would be against them. During the governorship of the antislavery Whig William H. Seward, the committee achieved several of its legislative aims. In 1840, new laws mandated a jury trial to determine the fate of alleged fugitives, required the claimant to post a bond to cover court costs in event the jury decided the accused was not a runaway slave, and prohibited local judges from issuing arrest warrants for fugitives. The following year, Seward signed a repeal of the 1817 law allowing slaves to be brought to the state "in transit" for up to nine months. Henceforth, the freedom principle applied in New York: any slave entering the state except a fugitive automatically became free. Soon after the law's passage, a constable tried to apprehend a Georgia slave who had escaped after being brought by her owner into the city, only to be driven away by an "angry multitude of blacks." The legislature also authorized the governor to appoint an agent to bring proceedings, at state expense, against kidnappers. And Seward rejected southern requests for the extradition of persons accused of aiding slaves to escape. All these developments increased the difficulty of retrieving fugitives and sent a message that kidnapping would no longer be tolerated. By 1842, the Vigilance Committee reported that the "disgraceful scenes" of kidnapping in the city had "gradually died away."[26]

New York and neighboring Brooklyn, to be sure, remained closely tied to southern slavery, and the new laws were not always enforced. In 1842, Edward Sexton, a fugitive slave from Mobile, was arrested in Brooklyn and brought before a judge without being

THE RUNAWAY. A familiar image of a fugitive slave, this "stereotype cut" was produced in New York City for use in reward handbills distributed by owners of runaways, an illustration of the close commercial ties between New York and the antebellum South. (*Anti-Slavery Record*, July 1837)

VIEW OF SOUTH STREET FROM MAIDEN LANE, a watercolor by the English-born artist William James Bennett from around 1827, depicts the bustling docks along the East River in lower Manhattan. New York maintained a flourishing trade with the South, and many fugitive slaves arrived hidden on coastal vessels. McKibbin and Gayley, whose shop is pictured at the right, are identified in the city directory as grocers. (Print Collection, Miriam and Ira D. Wallach Division of Art, Prints and Photographs, New York Public Library)

THE MAYOR AND POLICE OF NORFOLK SEARCHING CAPT. FOUNTAIN'S SCHOONER. This engraving, from William Still's book *The Underground Railroad,* depicts an episode in the 1850s. Albert Fountain, who transported numerous slaves to freedom on his vessel *City of Richmond,* is shown taking an axe to the boards of the deck to convince city officials that no slaves were on board. They departed without discovering twenty-one fugitives hidden below. (William Still, *The Underground Railroad*)

THE COLORED STEVEDORE, a pre–Civil War etching of one of the numerous African Americans who worked on New York City's docks. Many kept a lookout for fugitive slaves and put them in contact with persons who could assist them. (Department of Prints, Photographs, and Architectural Collections, New-York Historical Society)

THE COLORED STEVEDORE.—A REMINISCENCE.

A NORTHERN FREEMAN ENSLAVED BY NORTHERN HANDS. This engraving from an abolitionist publication in 1839 depicts the kidnapping of Peter John Lee, a free black resident of Westchester County, who was transported to the South and sold into slavery. Two of the men pictured, Tobias Boudinot, on the left, and Daniel D. Nash, on the right, were part of a Kidnapping Club that preyed on black residents of New York City. Combating kidnapping was a major aim of the New York Vigilance Committee, established in 1835.

(*American Anti-Slavery Almanac*, 1839)

THE DISAPPOINTED ABOLITIONISTS. This satirical lithograph from 1838 depicts three New Yorkers actively involved in assisting fugitive slaves in the 1830s. From the left, Isaac T. Hopper, a radical Quaker and longtime abolitionist; David Ruggles, founder of the New York Vigilance Committee; and Barney Corse of the New York Manumission Society. The image was inspired by a lawsuit against the three initiated by a slaveowner, John P. Darg, discussed in chapter three. (Collection of the author)

THE REV. THEODORE S. WRIGHT, head of the New York Vigilance Committee in the 1840s until his death in 1847. (Randolph Linsly Simpson African-American Collection, Beinecke Rare Book and Manuscript Library, Yale University)

LEWIS TAPPAN, New York City's most prominent white abolitionist. A wealthy merchant and the leading spirit of the American and Foreign Anti-Slavery Society, Tappan actively assisted fugitive slaves. (Portraits of American Abolitionists, Massachusetts Historical Society)

CHARLES B. RAY, minister of Bethesda Congregational Church and the leader of the New York State Vigilance Committee in the 1850s. (I. Garland Penn, *The Afro-American Press and Its Editors*)

SYDNEY HOWARD GAY, editor of the *National Anti-Slavery Standard* and chief operative of an underground railroad outpost located at the newspaper's office. (Portraits of American Abolitionists, Massachusetts Historical Society)

JOHN JAY II, grandson of the first chief justice of the United States and one of the few New York City lawyers willing to defend accused fugitive slaves in court. (Portraits of American Abolitionists, Massachusetts Historical Society)

JAMES S. GIBBONS, ABIGAIL HOPPER GIBBONS, AND FAMILY. This photograph from 1854 depicts a Quaker abolitionist couple active in the underground railroad in New York City, and their children. (Courtesy of Friends Historical Library of Swarthmore College)

accorded a jury trial as provided in the law of 1840. He admitted being an escaped slave and was returned to Alabama. Although state law barred local judges from issuing arrest warrants for fugitives, a police officer involved in this case remarked that he "had himself assisted in arresting several negroes under such warrants, who were delivered to the claimants and taken off." When a recently arrived fugitive slave worshiped openly in a black church, the *Colored American* warned that it was not "prudent . . . to be so public."

Yet sometimes, the unexpected happened. Even before the legislature revoked the right of slave transit, Robert H. Morris, who had succeeded the notorious Richard Riker as city recorder after the latter's retirement in 1838, freed a slave woman brought to the city on a vessel from Puerto Rico. The owner of the elegant Mansion House Hotel on Broadway, a member of the Whig party not known for antislavery views, secretly notified the committee when slaves who accompanied their owners wished to escape, although only "in cases where he supposed the owners were cruel." In 1842, a fugitive slave who approached a member of the night watch for assistance was "given a meal and shelter, clothing" and sent to the Vigilance Committee.[27]

The committee's influence extended beyond New York's borders. In 1837, Philadelphia abolitionists established their own Vigilant Committee, modeled on New York's. Two years later, the black abolitionist Robert Purvis, an admirer of David Ruggles, became its president. Philadelphia's committee began life as an interracial organization, but by 1840 it was composed entirely of blacks. Like its New York counterpart it operated openly and secretly at the same time, fighting legal cases on behalf of apprehended fugitives but also sheltering runaways and sending them farther north, generally to the Vigilance Committee in New York City. Committees in upstate New York soon followed. Stephen Myers, a black abolitionist and editor of the short-lived *Northern Star*, published in

1842 and 1843, became the key figure in the Albany Committee of Vigilance, described by Ruggles as "the most efficient organization in the State of New York, in the business of aiding the way-worn and weather-beaten refugee" from slavery.[28]

At its annual meeting of 1838, the AASS had urged abolitionists "to appoint committees of vigilance, whose duty it shall be to assist fugitives from slavery, in making their escape, or in legal vindication of their rights." By 1842, the *National Anti-Slavery Standard* could report the existence of such organizations "in most of our cities and large towns." New York City had taken the lead, but a broader infrastructure was now in place, a network of local individuals and groups, in frequent contact with one another, committed to assisting fugitive slaves. In the 1840s, their efforts would expand, and collectively they would become known as the underground railroad.[29]

II

Even as internecine warfare broke out in the New York Vigilance Committee, the national abolitionist movement fell to pieces. Trouble had been brewing for years over a number of issues pitting Garrisonians, centered in Boston, against the New York leaders of the AASS. William Lloyd Garrison's vehement attacks on American churches for complicity in slavery and his calls for abolitionists to withdraw from all institutions connected in any way with the South's peculiar institution offended many devout foes of slavery. The Tappans believed the movement must be conducted by men "of evangelical piety," a category that excluded the decidedly non-evangelical "Universalists or Unitarians" prominent in Boston. Garrison insisted that abolitionists could not in good conscience participate in a political system whose constitution protected slavery. Most New York abolitionists came to see politics as a promising arena for attacking the institution. The issue of women's rights proved even more contentious. Agitation on behalf of the slave had awakened some women to their own inequality. By the late 1830s, these women and male allies, including Garrison, were insisting on the right of women to speak in public and hold positions in abolitionist organizations.[30]

Garrison spoke for a minority of abolitionists, but Tappan and his followers believed his increasing radicalism alienated potential recruits to the antislavery cause. The division came to a head at the AASS's annual meeting in New York in May 1840. When the gathering elected the prominent abolitionist lecturer and fund-raiser Abby Kelley to the AASS business committee, Lewis Tappan rose and invited those who had voted in the minority to withdraw to another building to form their own abolitionist organization.[31]

Nearly all New York abolitionists, including the entire AASS executive committee except for Garrison's friend James S. Gibbons, followed the Tappans into the new American and Foreign Anti-Slavery Society. The American and Foreign took control of the *Emancipator,* in order to "keep it out of the hands of Mr. Garrison and his friends." The newspaper did not thrive and soon moved to Boston. A month after the split, the AASS established its own newspaper in New York City, the *National Anti-Slavery Standard.* A third group, which held aloof from both national organizations, soon emerged as the Liberty party, the first antislavery political party. Although New York City remained the site of the AASS headquarters and its annual meeting, the organization would henceforth be centered in New England, with pockets of support in Pennsylvania and Ohio. After 1840, as the two national societies limped along, the center of gravity in abolitionism shifted to a sprawling patchwork of local groups and, increasingly, to political action. In retrospect, the heated exchanges among people deeply committed to the same goal of ending slavery and improving the condition of free blacks exemplify what Sigmund Freud later called "the narcissism of small differences."[32] The task of assisting fugitive slaves, however, would remain a frequent point of cooperation among persons otherwise loath to work with one another.

Among New York City's black abolitionists, who admired both Garrisonians and Tappanites, the breakup of the AASS caused consternation. One participant in a large meeting two weeks after the split called it "a solemn crisis for the people of color." Initially, many declared their intention to remain neutral. Soon, however, most black leaders cast their lot with the local white abolitionists they had worked with on a daily basis—the American and Foreign in New York City, the AASS in Boston. Garrison remained immensely popular with ordinary black New Yorkers; James McCune Smith, a black physician, remarked that it was hard to know who loved the other more, Garrison the colored people, or the colored people Garrison. But because of their close ties with the Tappans, the presence of so many ministers among them, and their desire to engage in electoral politics, the city's black antislavery leaders almost unanimously went with the new organization. Henceforth, the New York Vigilance Committee would be almost interchangeable with the American and Foreign Anti-Slavery Society.[33]

During the 1840s, local vigilance committees became more numerous and more adept at communicating with one another—"increasingly efficient," according to a writer in the *Liberator*, "particularly on the Philadelphia and New York route." The term "underground railroad" came into widespread use to describe activities on behalf of fugitive slaves. As counterparts proliferated in other cities, New York, in the words of Charles B. Ray, the Vigilance Committee's corresponding secretary, served as "a kind of receiving depot" at which fugitives arrived from Washington, Baltimore, and Philadelphia and were dispatched to Albany and other towns in upstate New York, New Bedford, Boston, and Canada.[34]

In the 1840s, the New York Vigilance Committee continued to hold small monthly meetings and larger annual gatherings to report on its activities in aid of what it called "self-emancipated slaves." It made no apologies for flouting the law and the property rights of owners—slaves, it declared, had "a right to flee from bondage." The numbers seeking assistance, the committee reported in 1842, "increase every year." But money remained a problem. The annual report for 1840 could not be published for lack of funds—a serious setback, since the committee's leadership believed it would have "exhibited to the world . . . the good already accomplished" and inspired new contributions. In 1841, William Johnston, the treasurer, reported a debt of $1,150, "which presses heavily on the committee, and greatly retards its progress." He appealed to the "friends of human rights" for contributions, asserting that the number of fugitives the committee had assisted since its inception now surpassed 1,000. That year, the New York Colored Female Vigilance Committee was formed as an auxiliary to the all-male executive committee. It organized fund-raising events, including a penny-a-week system of contributions similar to the one that had helped finance the committee at its inception. Theodore S. Wright, the Vigilance Committee's president, expressed frustration that his group found itself in "increasing debt" while large amounts of money had been raised to aid the Africans who rebelled on the Spanish slave ship *Amistad* in 1839 and two years later gained their freedom in the United States. "What," he wondered, "was there in that case that does not occur in the case of every fugitive from southern slavery?"[35]

In 1842, convinced that secrecy about its activities impeded fund raising, the Vigilance Committee managed to publish another annual report. For the first time, it offered details about some of the individuals it had assisted, without identifying them by name. The stories offered glimpses of the cruel treatment that inspired slaves to run away, their means of escape, the fugitives' courage and tenacity, and the network of which the committee was a part. They also made clear that the Vigilance Committee's reputation reached far beyond New York and that many persons knew how to put fugitives in contact with the organization.

One fugitive slave, born in the French West Indies, had been sold to a planter near Baton Rouge who whipped him frequently. After one unsuccessful escape attempt, he made his way north on foot on a six-month journey, suffering "incredible hardships" before reaching New York. In the city he asked for help in "broken English," was brought to a member of the committee, and forwarded to Canada. A fugitive from Richmond hid on a ship carrying lumber to New York. He had been given the name of a man who could offer help, who in turn directed him to the committee. A runaway from the eastern shore of Maryland fought off slave catchers and managed to get to Philadelphia, from which that city's Vigilance Committee forwarded him to New York. A slave on an Alabama cotton plantation ran away after frequent whippings but was tracked down by bloodhounds. On his next attempt he took his owner's horse, outran the dogs, and ended up in Charleston, where friends paid a crew member to hide him on a ship bound for New York. There, a "colored servant" sent him to the Vigilance Committee. A female slave who secured passage on a ship to New York was directed to the committee by one of the sailors.[36]

In its 1842 annual report, the Vigilance Committee described itself as "a perfect anti-slavery institution . . . although connected with no organized anti-slavery society." In fact, however, after the abolitionist split of 1840 a remarkable degree of overlap existed between the committee and the American and Foreign Anti-Slavery Society, the group led by the Tappan brothers. The American and Foreign, commonly known among abolitionists as the "new organization," held an annual meeting in New York City, published occasional books and pamphlets, and acted as a liaison with British evangelical abolitionists. Overall, however, it failed to flourish. Unlike the AASS, it had no traveling agents and few local affiliates, and it never developed an effective newspaper. William Lloyd Garrison exaggerated only slightly when he commented in 1846 that the American and Foreign existed "in the person of Lewis Tappan."[37]

Tappan, moreover, while a man of formidable energy, had other claims on his time and fortune. By the mid-1840s, he decided to aid the Liberty party "in every way in which I can." In addition, Tappan in 1846 helped to bring into being the American Missionary Association, an interracial organization of antislavery churchmen, including virtually every prominent black minister in New York. The association set up schools and religious missions in Africa, in the Caribbean, and among fugitive slaves in Canada. It even sent missionaries into the Upper South, hoping to "inculcate an anti-slavery gospel." It also sought to win antislavery converts among evangelical Christians and to counteract the Garrisonians' strident attack on the churches for their complicity with slavery. Tappan became its treasurer and henceforth devoted much of his activity to the organization.[38]

Despite the numerous demands on his time and pocketbook, Tappan, along with other members of the American and Foreign Anti-Slavery Society in New York City, continued to devote themselves to assisting fugitive slaves. Tappan frequently attended the Vigilance Committee's monthly meetings, contributed money, raised donations from his contacts in Great Britain, and worked with Charles B. Ray to help fugitives in the city escape capture. When the Vigilance Committee issued an appeal for funds in 1844, it asked that contributions be sent to William Johnston, Ray, or Tappan, all members of the American and Foreign's executive committee. The Irish abolitionist Richard Webb noted that the American and Foreign existed as an organization only for "three hours of a single day"—during its annual meeting each May. "The rest of the year," he added, "it is the [New York] Vigilance Committee."[39]

The committee's key leaders exemplified this linkage. The group's president until his death in 1847, Theodore S. Wright, was the first black graduate of an American religious seminary (the Princeton Theological Institute) and minister of the First Colored (later Shiloh) Presbyterian Church on Frankfort Street. The son of a free black barber in Providence, Rhode Island, Wright had moved with his family to New York City as a youth and was educated in the African Free School. In the 1830s, he joined the AASS, became active in the Vigilance Committee, and helped found the Phoenix Literary Society, which promoted intellectual self-improvement in the black community. Wright was a founding member of the American and Foreign and, later, the American Missionary Association, and was also actively involved in the Liberty party.[40]

Charles B. Ray, who succeeded David Ruggles as the Vigilance Committee's secretary and its key activist in assisting fugitives, maintained contact with underground railroad activists south and north of New York. Born in Falmouth, Massachusetts, in 1807 to a mother who was herself a runaway slave, Ray was educated in the town's integrated public schools. In 1832, after being forced to withdraw from Wesleyan Seminary in Massachusetts because white students objected to his presence, Ray moved to New York City, opened a boot and shoe store, and soon became involved in the Vigilance Committee. Ray edited the *Colored American* from 1838 until its demise in 1841. Four years later he became pastor of New York's predominantly white Bethesda Congregational Church on Wooster Street; Lewis Tappan spoke at his investiture. Ray served on the executive committee of the American Missionary Association, which paid him an annual salary of $600 to work as a missionary among poor black New Yorkers. Like Wright, Ray for several years was a member of the executive committee of the American and Foreign and an early supporter of the Liberty party.

The homes of both men (Ray's at 153 Baxter Street, Wright's at 28 John Street) and their churches (both of which moved a number of times as the city expanded northward) provided hiding places for runaway slaves and hosted Vigilance Committee meetings. "Many a midnight hour," Ray later wrote of fugitives, "have I, with others, walked the streets, their leader and guide." On occasion, he traveled to Albany to ensure that fugitive slaves sent from New York arrived safely and were forwarded to Canada.[41]

Another Vigilance Committee operative connected with the American Missionary Association and the American and Foreign (at least to the extent that they employed him in 1849 to paint their offices on John Street) was Jacob R. Gibbs. Born a slave in Maryland around 1807, Gibbs purchased his freedom as a young man and established a thriving house-painting business in Baltimore. He was frequently hired to paint the mansions of nearby planters. "Long before there was an underground railroad," according to a later reminiscence by one of his associates, Gibbs helped slaves in the city and surrounding countryside to escape, distributing forged free papers from a collection he had assembled. In 1840, Gibbs joined a group of over 200 blacks who emigrated from Baltimore to Trinidad and British Guiana, where slavery had recently been abolished. From the latter, he sent back glowing reports of opportunities for black newcomers. But he soon returned to the United States, married, and resumed his clandestine activities.

In the early 1840s, Gibbs operated as the Baltimore agent of Charles T. Torrey, a New England–born abolitionist who moved to Washington, D.C., in 1841, lived in the home of a free black family, and with an interracial group of coworkers began shuttling slaves to the North. Gibbs sometimes accompanied the fugitives from Baltimore to Philadelphia, from which they proceeded to New York, Albany, and Canada. Some commentators credited Torrey with inventing the underground railroad as an organized system with outposts on both sides of the Mason-Dixon Line. Torrey's luck ran out in June 1844, when he was arrested in Baltimore. He died in the Maryland State Penitentiary two years later at the age of thirty-three. In the wake of Torrey's arrest, Gibbs prudently moved to New York City with his family. He quickly emerged as a "leading spirit" of the Vigilance Committee, meeting fugitive slaves at the docks and arranging lodging for them. A few years later he purchased a home in New Haven, but he maintained a place in New York where he hid escaped slaves.[42]

The death of Theodore S. Wright in 1847 led to the committee's reorganization as the New York State Vigilance Committee, with Isaac T. Hopper as president. The choice of the elderly Hopper (he turned seventy-six that year) represented less an expectation of energetic leadership than a mark of the esteem he enjoyed among abolitionists of all persuasions because of a long career aiding fugitive slaves. He had "more experience in such cases than any other man in America," David Ruggles had noted. However, Hopper, who was associated with the Garrisonians, not the American and Foreign, served only briefly. In 1848, Gerrit Smith, among whose numerous activities was leadership of the state's Liberty party, succeeded him as president. Unlike its predecessor, the revamped committee publicized its network of upstate connections. They included Luther Lee of Syracuse, the editor of the *True Wesleyan*, which sought to link Methodist theology with abolitionism, and Noadiah Moore, a farmer and businessman active in the Liberty party whose home near Lake Champlain, only seven miles south of the Canadian border, sheltered fugitives sent from New York City. Most of the committee's money now came from upstate cities and towns such as Auburn, Syracuse, and Niagara Falls, the heartland of New York abolitionism. But the organization's affairs continued to be conducted by an executive committee in New York City. By the time Smith assumed the presidency, a new way of describing those who assisted fugitives had come into general use. The New York State Vigilance Committee, declared the *Baltimore Sun* at the time of its first anniversary meeting in 1848, "is the celebrated underground railroad."[43]

"Any person who approves of the objects of the Committee," the reorganized group's constitution declared, "may become a member." But the state committee's leadership continued its "great and glorious" predecessor's close association with non-Garrisonian antislavery organizations. Charles B. Ray remained as corresponding secretary, and close associates of the Tappans held other key offices, including Simeon S. Jocelyn, the president of the American Missionary Association, as vice president, and William Harned, a Philadelphia-born Quaker and the Missionary Association's corresponding secretary as treasurer. In 1848, 1849, and 1850, Jocelyn presided over the Vigilance Committee's annual meetings, "composed mostly of colored people." When the committee issued an appeal for funds in 1849, it listed Harned's address as treasurer as 61 John Street, the same building that housed the American and Foreign Anti-Slavery Society and the American Missionary Association. This site became a gathering point for runaway slaves. Tappan later recalled a day when he went to his office there and found eighteen fugitives who had been sent from Pennsylvania and New Jersey. "The agent of the Underground Rail Road," he related, arranged for their transportation to Albany and Canada.[44]

The reorganized committee forthrightly declared its intention to "receive, with open arms, the panting fugitive." But it continued to encounter financial problems. A fund appeal in 1849 noted that while the wealthy Gerrit Smith had donated $500, in general the "friends of the slave" had failed to respond "promptly and generously" to previous solicitations. (Smith's gift came with strings attached: if, he made it clear, members of the committee voted for mainstream politicians and not the candidates of the Liberty party, he would not give again.) Nonetheless, by 1850, three years after its founding, the New York State Vigilance Committee claimed to have provided 1,000 fugitives with shelter, board, and transportation. Unfortunately, the committee offered no details as to whom it assisted or how. But such affirmations outraged defenders of slavery. One pamphlet outlining the South's grievances as sectional tensions worsened asked, "Are these people aware how deeply they have criminalized themselves in these avowals [of] . . . their felonious thieveries?"[45]

The Vigilance Committee, sometimes in conjunction with the American and Foreign, also devoted considerable effort to bringing court cases in the South claiming freedom for persons illegally held as slaves. One such litigation involved a free black woman who had been kidnapped in Baltimore and sold to an owner in Wilmington, North Carolina, where she lived for many years as a slave. Her brother finally succeeded in purchasing her freedom. The committee launched a lawsuit in North Carolina, obtained an affidavit from the Clerk of the Court of Anne Arundel County, Maryland, attesting to the woman's free birth, and won the release from bondage of her eight children and six grandchildren.[46]

The New York State Vigilance Committee, a British antislavery group noted, "is almost synonymous with the American and Foreign Anti-Slavery Society."[47] For this very reason, another group devoted to assisting fugitives emerged in the city, this one centered around followers of William Lloyd Garrison. Its leading figure was Sydney Howard Gay, editor of the weekly *National Anti-Slavery Standard,* the official publication of the AASS. In the 1840s, the "anti-slavery office" that housed the newspaper became a second outpost of the underground railroad in New York City.

4

A PATCHWORK SYSTEM: THE UNDERGROUND RAILROAD IN THE 1840S

I

Born in Hingham, Massachusetts, in 1814, Sydney Howard Gay came from a long line of distinguished New Englanders. One ancestor arrived in Massachusetts with John Winthrop; others included the Puritan luminaries John Cotton and Increase and Cotton Mather, as well as the revolutionary-era patriot James Otis. As time went on, the family suffered setbacks, most notably when Gay's grandfather, Martin Gay, was banished and his property confiscated for siding with the British during the War of Independence. Martin Gay's son Ebenezer, however, remained in Massachusetts, prospered as a banker, and fathered eleven children, among them Sydney. Ebenezer Gay departed early each morning for his office, before, he remarked, "hell is let loose."[1]

"My ancestry," Sydney Howard Gay wrote toward the end of his life, "is the best part of me." Painfully conscious of the challenge of living up to his distinguished lineage and suffering as a youth from bouts of ill health, Gay had difficulty finding a direction in life. He enrolled at Harvard in 1829 but withdrew after a year. In the 1830s, he traveled to China, hoping to establish himself as a merchant, but soon returned to Hingham. The crusade against slavery, he later wrote, "gave the first serious aim to my life." In 1838, "I announced myself" an abolitionist, "to the astonishment of all," as "I had never seen an anti-slavery paper . . . and had never heard but one anti-slavery lecture." Gay was soon writing articles for a Hingham newspaper denouncing the local minister for failing to attack slavery.

Gay became an antislavery lecturer, traveling in New England, New York, Pennsylvania, Indiana, and Ohio, sometimes accompanied by such prominent figures as Frederick Douglass and Abby Kelley, the latter a pioneer of abolitionism and feminism who challenged the nineteenth century's definition of woman's "place" by becoming an itinerant orator against slavery. Gay spread the Garrisonian abolitionist gospel, criticizing the "new organization" founded by the Tappans and comparing the Liberty party unfavorably with "the veriest pro-slavery priest in all Southland" because it favored abolitionists voting and holding office under a proslavery constitution. Abolitionist lecturing required personal courage. A mob broke up one meeting in an Indiana town, after which Gay's traveling companion, the black abolitionist Charles Lenox Remond, reported, "No harm was done but liberty was murdered." Gay dispatched articles to Garrison's *Liberator* about these tours. As a result of his labors, he believed, "the great principles of anti-slavery have become known, where before they were unknown."[2]

In 1845, Gay married Elizabeth Neall, the daughter of Daniel Neall, a wealthy Philadelphia Quaker and a vice president of the Pennsylvania Abolition Society. Five years earlier, Daniel Neall had attended a Quaker meeting in Delaware, where, according to a newspaper account, he addressed a meeting of black "gentlemen and ladies." A mob seized Neall that evening, applied a painful coat of tar and feathers, and carried him around the town of Smyrna on a rail. In keeping with Quaker principles, Neall did not resist; instead, he invited members of the mob to visit him in Philadelphia, where he would "gladly give them meat and drink." A few weeks later, two of them did arrive, to apologize for the assault. In her own right, Elizabeth Neall was a person of strong views and fierce independence, a committed abolitionist and proponent of women's rights. In 1840, at the age of seventeen, she flouted prevailing mores by traveling to London with four other women, but no male companion, to represent Pennsylvania at the World Anti-Slavery Convention. Received as "women-fanatics," they, along with other female delegates, were relegated to seats in the balcony (where Garrison joined them). Her engagement to Gay, a "worldly person" (that is, a non-Quaker) was initially opposed by her father and shocked many of her coreligionists. Like her husband, Elizabeth Neall Gay was a staunch Garrisonian who declared herself ready to "wage a war of extermination" against the "new organization."[3]

The Gays settled in New York City, where Sydney in 1844 became editor of the *National Anti-Slavery Standard*. He also served on the executive committee of the American Anti-Slavery Society and helped to organize the society's annual meeting in the city. Gay commuted daily from their home on Staten Island to the newspaper's office at 142 Nassau Street, not far from the headquarters of the rival American and Foreign Anti-Slavery Society. For a modest salary, Isaac T. Hopper managed the office, where he regaled Gay and others with tales drawn from his treasury of "anti-slavery lore."[4]

Quakers, of course, had been pioneers of antislavery thought in colonial America, and Quakers like Hopper and James and Abigail Gibbons formed an important part of the small Garrisonian contingent in New York City. Without them, Lewis Tappan wrote in 1844, "the Garrison party" would "soon become extinct." African Americans considered Quakers different from other whites. James Williams, who escaped from slavery in Alabama in 1837 and made his way on foot to Pennsylvania, was advised by a free black man there not to trust any white person "unless he wore a plain, straight collar on a round coat, and said 'thee and thou.' " By the 1830s, however, many Quakers recoiled from the militant language of the abolitionist agitation, fearing it unnecessarily produced strife within the larger society and among the Friends themselves.[5]

Some Quakers embraced racial egalitarianism. Abigail Hopper Gibbons joined the otherwise entirely black Manhattan Anti-Slavery Society in 1840 rather than the Ladies' New York City Anti-Slavery Society, which did not admit black members. Others adopted a patronizing attitude, rarely inviting blacks to join the Society of Friends and making those who chose to do so sit on separate benches. In 1839, the small group of abolitionist Quakers in New York City, including Hopper, James and Abigail Gibbons, and Barney Corse, formed the New York Association of Friends for the Relief of Those Held in Slavery and the Improvement of the Free People of Color. In 1840, the organization opened a school for black students at which Hopper, his wife, and James S. Gibbons taught. The Quaker abolitionists encountered a "hostile attitude" from their New York coreligionists, who, they claimed, shared the "popular prejudice against Anti Slavery operations." Many Friends, the group pointed out, were merchants "deeply involved" in buying and selling goods produced by slave labor. In 1842, Quakers attending the New York Monthly Meeting of the Society of Friends "disowned" Hopper and James S. Gibbons for, among other things, assisting with the publication of the *National Anti-Slavery Standard*. Lydia Maria Child, who taught at the black school the radical Quakers founded, later commented that most Quakers had seen their principles "buried in the mere shell of lifeless forms." But, she added, "when a Quaker *has* a soul, what large ones they have!" Gay relied on the small Quaker abolitionist cadre for support when he assumed the editorship of the *Standard*.[6]

Gay had taken on a daunting task. In 1840, when the Tappanites took control of the *Emancipator*, the AASS established the *National Anti-Slavery Standard* to spread the organization's principles. It began "without a subscriber, and without so much as a dollar in the treasury." Finding a permanent editor proved difficult. For a time, Nathaniel P. Rogers, who ran a New Hampshire abolitionist newspaper, served as editor from afar. In 1841, Lydia Maria Child replaced him, becoming the first woman to edit a political newspaper in the United States. Born in Medford, Massachusetts, in 1802, Child had achieved an international reputation as the editor of the *Juvenile Miscellany*, a periodical for children, and the prolific author of novels and popular nonfiction works for women, such as *The American Frugal House Wife*. When she and her husband, David Lee Child, became followers of William Lloyd Garrison in the 1830s, Mrs. Child turned her talents to abolitionist writing. Her tract *An Appeal in Favor of That Class of Americans Called Africans* (1833) was a powerful call for immediate abolition, a repudiation of racism, and an attack on the American Colonization Society. As the title suggests, Child insisted that blacks were as much Americans as whites and that their future lay in the United States. Her association with abolitionism destroyed Child's literary career, as her audience abandoned her. She assumed the editorship of the *Standard* both to spread the antislavery message and to support herself and her husband.

Under Child, the *Standard* flourished. She expanded its coverage beyond abolitionist news to include articles on foreign affairs and women's rights, as well as fiction, poetry, and sketches of the sights, institutions, and people of New York City. Her aim, she wrote, was to make the *Standard* "a good *family* anti-slavery newspaper." During Child's editorship the subscription list grew to 6,000, more than double that of Garrison's own *Liberator*.[7]

Rogers and Child could not resolve the tension between appealing to as many readers as possible and adhering to the Garrisonian party line, a minority outlook even in abolitionist circles. Rogers spent his editorship rehashing the schism of 1840. Child opted for a more inclusive approach, promising to "avoid all personality and controversy," so far as this could be done without a "compromise of principle." She criticized the American and Foreign for its "false" positions, but reprinted a "handsome and well-deserved tribute" to Lewis Tappan for his work for the *Amistad* captives. The Garrisonian leadership in Massachusetts complained that the paper lacked "fire." For her part, Child resented the "Boston clique's" assumption that they could "do my thinking for me." She suspected that her critics believed that the paper needed "a *man* at the helm." After two years, she resigned and was replaced by her husband. But he, too, soon departed, tired of interference from Boston. "There is not a saint beneath the sun," James S. Gibbons commented, "who would not sometimes grow impatient at the perpetual fault-finding of . . . we abolitionists. . . . We make the editor's chair as uncomfortable as possible."[8]

Clearly, when Gay became editor in 1844, he assumed a position fraught with difficulty. Moreover, New York City remained a hostile environment for abolitionists. Most of the *Standard*'s readers lived outside the city; in the metropolis itself, with a population of around half a million, the paper had 102 subscribers. "You don't know, you can't, in Boston," Gay wrote to the abolitionist Wendell Phillips in 1848, "just what my position is. . . . You are surrounded by a people growing in anti-slavery; I by a people who hate it." Even among the city's small band of abolitionists, Gay found himself isolated, since nearly all were affiliated with the "new organization" or the Liberty party. "As to abolitionists [meaning Garrisonians] in this blessed city," he wrote in 1844, "there are none to my knowledge, except [Oliver] Johnson [who worked on the paper] and . . . the colored office-boy." Even those close to the *Standard* strayed from the Garrisonian outlook, which eschewed involvement in politics.

James S. Gibbons, for example, announced his intention to vote for Henry Clay, the Whig presidential candidate, in 1844.[9]

Gay's lack of self-confidence compounded his problems. He worried that his work was not appreciated in Boston (Garrison had the annoying habit of omitting Gay's name as corresponding secretary when listing the officers of the AASS). Abolitionists there seem to have assigned Wendell Phillips the task of responding to Gay's stream of self-deprecatory letters and occasionally visiting New York to convey support and make sure he did not fall under the influence of Lewis Tappan. (On one visit, Phillips assured Gay that Garrison had denounced him "*only*" on "three or four" occasions.)[10]

Gay accepted the paper's role as "the exponent of the opinions and policies" of the AASS. As a result, he found himself defending positions, such as the idea of disunion as a way of separating northerners from the evil of slavery, that were unpopular even among many Garrisonians. The *Standard*'s circulation declined steadily, and Gay had to rely on infusions of money from Boston to keep the paper afloat. "The Standard is on its last legs," Gay wrote in 1846. Despite all this, the paper survived. For most of the years leading up to the Civil War, it remained the only abolitionist newspaper in New York City, and unlike his predecessors, Gay managed to persevere as editor for well over a decade.[11]

Long after the end of slavery, Gay recalled the Boston abolitionists as "the most charmed circle of cultivated men and women it has ever been my lot to know." But they could also act in distinctly uncultivated ways, especially in the 1840s, when, in the words of Lewis Tappan, "the warfare between the Old Organization . . . and the New Organization, including the Liberty Party" continued "unrelenting." Early in 1850, Samuel J. May, a Garrisonian abolitionist based in Syracuse, sponsored a meeting to broker peace between the factions. But the four-day gathering broke up in acrimony. The delegates could not even agree on a resolution endorsing cooperation among abolitionists. One thing on which the participants did concur, however, was that the Constitution's fugitive slave clause "ought never to have been adopted, and ought now not to be obeyed." Aiding fugitives was an activity in which warring abolitionists could and did cooperate. Later that year, the new Fugitive Slave Act would unite all abolitionists in opposition.[12]

Sydney Howard Gay's desire to assist fugitive slaves originated before his arrival in New York City. On his 1844 speaking tour, Gay wrote of his admiration for the antislavery men and women who welcomed runaways into their homes, and of the courage of the fugitives themselves. In Indiana, he encountered a group of twenty absconding slaves with armed slave catchers in hot pursuit. Although not an activity contemplated in the "infancy" of the abolitionist movement, he mused, assistance to fugitives had become "an efficient anti-slavery instrumentality," and eastern abolitionists ought to do more along these lines. Gay also appears to have been inspired by Charles T. Torrey, who, as noted in the previous chapter, helped slaves escape from Washington until his capture in 1844. In an editorial after Torrey's arrest, Gay opposed going into the South to help slaves escape, fearing that such actions might "produce civil war." In the same piece, however, Gay agreed that the constitutional obligation to return fugitives must not be obeyed, and wrote of personally assisting a "trembling slave" who had made his way "alone and unaided" to New York City. He also kept in touch with David Ruggles after the latter settled in Massachusetts. The *Standard*'s office on Nassau Street, like that of the Vigilance Committee on nearby John Street, became a key outpost of the underground railroad.[13]

Gay worked closely with Louis Napoleon, a black porter employed in his office who also made his living at various times as a furniture polisher and whitewasher. In the early 1840s, Napoleon lived at 33 Spruce Street, around the corner from Gay's office;

later in the decade he moved to 27 Leonard Street, not far from the ferry terminal where passengers (sometimes including fugitives) from Philadelphia and points farther south alighted. Napoleon left far less of a historical record than Gay or Tappan, and what information exists about him is fragmentary and contradictory. Some accounts describe him as having been born a slave in New York or Virginia and having remained in bondage until adulthood. The most reliable sources, however, give his date and place of birth as April 1, 1800, in New York. An article about his funeral in the *New York Sun*—headlined "Not the French Emperor but an Old Friend of the Fugitive Slaves"—identified Napoleon's father as Jewish and his mother as a slave at the time of his birth. Thus, he was born free under the gradual emancipation law enacted in 1799, but had to serve a long apprenticeship, which he did for a time at a tobacco warehouse in Manhattan.

By the 1830s, Napoleon had become actively involved in aiding fugitive slaves. He made trips to Maryland to help slaves escape, and scoured New York's docks searching for those who had concealed themselves on vessels and for slaves illegally brought to the city for shipment elsewhere. When he died, he was credited with having helped over 3,000 fugitives escape from bondage. Philip A. Bell, the publisher of the *Colored American* who later emigrated to California and established that state's first black newspaper, identified Napoleon and Vigilance Committee president Theodore S. Wright as the two "originators" of the underground railroad in New York City.[14]

Since the New York City Anti-Slavery Society had affiliated with the Tappanites, the city's band of Garrisonians in 1845 established the Manhattan Anti-Slavery Society. (This group should not be confused with an earlier body of the same name, composed of black women plus Abigail Hopper Gibbons.) The venerable Isaac T. Hopper served as president, Gay as corresponding secretary, and Mrs.

Gibbons sat on the Board of Managers. Among the Board's tasks was "to appoint a Vigilance Committee, of not less than ten members, whose special duty it shall be to extend aid to self-emancipated slaves." Given that a Vigilance Committee dominated by followers of Lewis Tappan already existed in New York City, it is hard to avoid the conclusion that the new group was intended as a Garrisonian alternative.[15]

The relationship between the two stations of the underground railroad in New York City might best be described as mostly friendly, occasionally unfriendly, competition. Abolitionists, Lewis Tappan later recalled, "vied with each other in devising means" to aid fugitive slaves and other blacks. From time to time, Gay cooperated with members of the other committee and even lent his name to its fund-raising appeals. A circular seeking contributions, issued by the New York State Vigilance Committee in 1849, stated that donations would be acknowledged in two newspapers, the *True Wesleyan* and *National Anti-Slavery Standard.* In 1849, Tappan himself sent a Miss Archer, "a slightly colored young lady from Jamaica," to Gay, so that he could assist her in securing a position as a teacher.[16]

That the feuding wings of New York City's abolitionist movement could mostly work in tandem in aiding fugitive slaves owed a great deal to the influence of Charles B. Ray, the key figure during the 1840s in the New York Vigilance Committee. Despite his close association with the Tappans and the Liberty party, Ray, in the words of Oliver Johnson, Gay's associate at the *Standard,* "did not in any degree share the hostility to Garrison manifested by many others," and tried to maintain cordial relations with all New York abolitionists. Ray's stance reflected that of most black abolitionists, who viewed sectarian divisions within the movement as a diversion from the goal of abolition. To be sure, many feuding white abolitionists, despite their heated exchanges, shared antislavery platforms. But blacks were especially put off by what Charles Lenox Remond called abolitionists' "open warfare" against one another. On his speaking tour of Great Britain in 1846, Frederick Douglass, at the time a full-fledged Garrisonian, insisted on meeting persons "of every antislavery creed." Criticized by members of the "Boston clique" for consorting with allies of Tappan, Douglass responded that he would speak against slavery "in any meeting when freedom of speech is allowed and where I may do anything towards exposing the bloody system." In 1849, Douglass addressed the annual meeting of the New York State Vigilance Committee despite its orientation toward the "new organization."[17]

The underground railroad depended for its effectiveness on political and personal networks. Gay's role as a national spokesman for Garrisonian abolitionism and his marriage to Elizabeth Neall provided him with direct connections to Pennsylvanians who sent fugitive slaves to New York. Philadelphia and its rural hinterland were among the few centers of Garrisonism outside New England, and home to a significant Quaker community, some of whose members, like Gay's in-laws, were active participants in the underground railroad. The region was the scene of violent confrontations between fugitives and slave catchers. In 1841, two police officers and a slaveowner arrested a female fugitive hiding in the house of a Quaker near Lancaster. A dozen blacks attacked the carriage. The officers shot and killed one of the group, but the slave was "rescued and carried off."[18]

Many members of Philadelphia's politically active free black community remained loyal to Garrison after the 1840 split, including Robert Purvis, head of the Philadelphia Vigilance Committee. Purvis and his wife Harriet, the daughter of James Forten, the most prominent black Philadelphian of the previous generation, maintained a close friendship with James and Abigail Gibbons and the Gays. Weakened, however, by lack of funds and charges of embezzlement (later disproved) against Dr. James G. Bias, a dentist and folk healer who tended to the medical needs of many fugitive slaves, Philadelphia's Vigilance Committee began to disintegrate in the early 1840s. It all but ceased operations in 1844 when Purvis moved his family from the city to a country estate. The committee would be reorganized and become active again in the early 1850s. In the interim, aid to fugitives passing through Philadelphia depended on the actions of individuals, especially James Miller McKim, the white Presbyterian minister who ran the office of the Pennsylvania Anti-Slavery Society and edited its weekly newspaper, the *Pennsylvania Freeman*.[19]

Two of the most celebrated fugitive slaves in American history arrived in New York City in the 1840s (albeit in very different ways) from Philadelphia. One was Harriet Jacobs, later the author of an autobiography published with the assistance of Lydia Maria Child. The book shocked mid-nineteenth-century readers by relating years of sexual abuse by Jacobs's owner and her decision to become the mistress of another white man for protection. Jacobs had absconded in 1835 from her owner's home in Edenton, North Carolina, and for seven years she hid in a small crawlspace above her free grandmother's kitchen in the town. In 1842, a "friendly captain" arranged for her transportation to Philadelphia, where Robert Purvis and the Vigilance Committee received her and sent her on to New York. The following year, she was reunited with her brother John S. Jacobs, who had escaped from his owner, a member of Congress from North Carolina, in 1838. John S. Jacobs settled in Boston, where, he wrote, "the hunted fugitive feels himself somewhat secure," and became a noted abolitionist lecturer.[20]

Gay had not yet moved to New York when Harriet Jacobs arrived, but by 1846 her brother was enlisting Gay's aid in countering her owner's efforts to capture her. John S. Jacobs also sought Gay's help in securing the release of a free-born friend being illegally held as a slave in North Carolina. By this time, Gay had established a reputation for assisting blacks in need. Jacobs wrote that he knew of no one else on "whom I could depend for prompt attention to the case." In 1854, Harriet Jacobs, then living in Boston, contributed two dollars to support the *National Anti-Slavery Standard.* Four years later, Gay wrote to Robert Purvis inquiring about her whereabouts, but Purvis replied that he had "lost . . . all trace of the woman." The light-skinned Purvis described Jacobs as "a beautiful creature, quadroon in color, *just enough* of Negro admixture to preserve real beauty from the . . . ugliness of whites in this country."[21]

Equally dramatic was the tale of Henry "Box" Brown, a skilled tobacco processor in Richmond whose wife and children, the property of a different owner, were suddenly sold to a Methodist minister in North Carolina to raise funds to satisfy a debt. With his family gone, Brown devised a plan to have himself shipped north in a crate. In March 1849, Samuel "Red Boot" Smith, a Massachusetts-born white shoemaker, packed Brown into a rectangular box "even too small for a coffin" (it measured only three feet long) and dispatched him by rail and steamboat to Philadelphia. Brown paid Smith, who had incurred considerable debts gambling, forty dollars for his assistance. Upon Brown's arrival, after a trip of more than 250 miles that took nearly twenty-four hours, McKim tapped on the crate, asking, "All right?" "All right, sir," came the reply. The lid was removed, and out stepped Brown, "with a face radiant with joy." "Good morning, gentlemen," he exclaimed, and launched into a "hymn of praise." McKim described the escape in an excited letter to Gay:[22]

> Here's a man who has been the hero of the most extraordinary achievement I ever heard of. . . . Nothing that was done on the barricades of Paris exceeded this in cool and deliberate intrepidity. . . . Nothing saved him from suffocating but the free use

> of water . . . and the constant fanning of himself with his hat. . . . He was twice put with his head downwards. . . . This nearly killed him.

McKim took Brown to his home "for a bath and some breakfast." A few days later he dispatched Brown (minus his box) to Gay's office in New York City, with instructions to forward him to Francis Jackson, the treasurer of the AASS, who hid Brown in his house in Boston. From there, Brown boarded a train to New Bedford, where his sister lived with "friends" (probably fugitives) from Richmond. Joseph Ricketson Jr., the most active white abolitionist in the city, awaited his arrival. "I received your valuable consignment of 200 pounds of humanity this evening," Ricketson reported to Gay. Ricketson put Brown up in his home and offered him a job.[23]

McKim urged Gay not to publicize Brown's exploit, fearing that it would compromise the shipping company and "prevent all others from escaping in the same way." But within a month, accounts of the escape had appeared in numerous newspapers, including the *National Anti-Slavery Standard*. Perhaps to deter inquiries into the operations of the underground railroad in the city, abolitionists did not mention that Brown had passed through New York, a fact also omitted from Brown's autobiography, published in 1849 (and mostly written by the white abolitionist Charles Stearns, whose turgid style seems inappropriate for an illiterate fugitive slave). Brown lived in Boston for a year. He regaled antislavery gatherings with the story of his escape and performed the hymn he had sung upon being released from his box. He took to the road with *Henry Box Brown's Mirror of Slavery*, a "moving panorama"—a popular form of entertainment using an enormous painting with numerous subdivisions. The individual scenes, which were accompanied by music and Brown's narration and singing, included images of Africa, the Middle Passage, various kinds of labor, and a final "grand tableau" of Universal Emancipation. After physically repelling an attempt to recapture him while he was in Providence to present his panorama, Brown departed in 1850 for England, where he became a fixture on the antislavery circuit. He never saw his wife and children again.[24]

Brown's story inspired other slaves to replicate his mode of escape, not always successfully. In 1856, a slave who tried to emulate Brown suffocated. The following year, however, a "female refugee" from Kentucky arrived "boxed up" in Canada, and another woman in a box was received by Jermain W. Loguen, who directed the underground railroad in Syracuse. In 1860, a crate roughly thrown onto a train platform in Indiana shattered, revealing a black man being shipped from Nashville to Cincinnati. In a striking illustration of the differences in the legal environment on two sides of the Mason-Dixon Line, McKim suffered no repercussions for his well-publicized role in the escape, but Red Boot Smith was arrested soon afterward for "boxing up" two more runaways, and was imprisoned in Virginia. Upon his release in 1856, Smith traveled to Philadelphia, where "colored citizens" held a meeting to honor him as a "martyr to the cause of freedom."[25]

Brown was one of many fugitives Gay directed to his Garrisonian associates in Boston. That city had one of the nation's most active abolitionist communities, which had long offered aid to runaways. In 1846, a slave known only as Joe escaped from a ship in Boston harbor and reached shore, but he was quickly captured by crew members. A large protest meeting, chaired by former president John Quincy Adams, followed at Faneuil Hall, and that gathering established a vigilance committee. The prominent reformer Samuel Gridley Howe became its chair; the abolitionist John W. Browne, the "general agent"; and its members included such luminaries as Theodore Parker and Wendell Phillips, along with black abolitionists Lewis Hayden (himself a fugitive slave) and William C. Nell.[26]

The Boston Vigilance Committee survived for only two years (it would be revived after the passage of the Fugitive Slave Law of 1850). While it lasted, John W. Browne communicated regularly with both Gay and Theodore S. Wright of the New York Vigilance Committee and received fugitives dispatched by both. As always, providing for them posed a financial challenge. On December 2, 1846, six fugitives arrived at Browne's office "sent to the care of our committee" by Wright in New York. Browne promised to find employment for them, but informed Gay that he hoped "the committees south of here" would "not send" so many to Boston. Two weeks later, nevertheless, Gay forwarded Joseph Johnson, a slave who worked on a ship based in New Bern, North Carolina. Johnson's opportunity to escape arose when the vessel, bound for Barbados, was "wrecked at sea" and another ship rescued the crew members and brought them to New York. Johnson decided he would prefer to "remain in a free state" and found his way to Gay. "We are afraid to keep him here," Gay explained, because the owner frequently visited the city. Browne gave Johnson "clothing and boots" and got him a job on a ship plying the route between Boston and New York. Shortly thereafter, in early January 1847, Gay sent two more men to Boston. One he had "kept here at considerable expense for some time"; the other had arrived on New Year's Day hidden on a ship from Norfolk.[27]

Both Gay and Browne feared that imposters were claiming to be fugitives in order to receive money. Browne sent to New York one man who said he had a wife and child in New Jersey and needed funds to purchase nine children still in slavery, but Browne wanted Gay to check on the man's story. Gay reported that the man arrived at his office drunk and could not be trusted. Gay, however, felt great solicitude for actual fugitives. He warned abolitionists in Massachusetts when slave catchers arrived in New York in pursuit of runaways he had directed there, and asked Browne to inform him regularly of the "safe arrival of the persons whom I sent to you. I feel some little anxiety when a fugitive goes from here to know whether he is drowned, caught by his master, or got safe to Boston."[28]

Gay sometimes used extraordinary means to help slaves achieve freedom. With Elias Smith, an antislavery lecturer from New England who worked on the *Standard,* and William H. Leonard, a black printer at the newspaper, Gay rescued from jail three slaves owned by the captain of the Brazilian vessel *Lembrança.* The ship had arrived in New York harbor in July 1847, and black stevedores notified William P. Powell, a black abolitionist who operated the Colored Seamen's Boarding House, that slaves were being held on board. While "a crowd of colored persons" gathered at the wharf, Powell dispatched Louis Napoleon to obtain a writ of habeas corpus. As a result, the slaves were brought to court and temporarily lodged in prison. John Jay II, a graduate of Columbia College and the son of the abolitionist William Jay and grandson of Chief Justice John Jay, appeared in court to represent the slaves. He demanded that they be freed in accordance with the state law barring slave transit. The captain insisted that a treaty between Brazil and the United States required each country to respect the property rights of citizens of the other.

After a series of hearings, a judge vacated the writ of habeas corpus and ordered the slaves returned to the ship. But by this time, as the *New York Tribune* put it, "the birds had flown." Reportedly, Gay and his companions, with the aid of an abolitionist incarcerated in the same prison for failing to pay a debt, had gotten the jailer intoxicated and removed the men, who were soon on their way to Boston. A month later they embarked for Haiti. The escape inspired a rare burst of humor in the *New York Evangelist.* The underground railroad, it quipped, "runs directly under the prison in New York, and . . . the slaves let themselves down through a stone trap-door into one of the cars." Shortly thereafter, another judge decided that the men could not be returned to Brazil in any case, since they had been brought to that country in violation of the international ban on the slave trade.[29]

II

As in the 1830s, both the New York Vigilance Committee and the group around Sydney Howard Gay tried their best to defend fugitive slaves through the legal system. In doing so, they made local courts the sites of political contests over slavery. The legal context for such initiatives changed dramatically in the 1840s with the U.S. Supreme Court's decision in *Prigg v. Pennsylvania,* its first relating to fugitive slaves.

The case arose from a dispute between Maryland and Pennsylvania that bore a striking resemblance to the controversy half a century earlier that led to enactment of the Fugitive Slave Law of 1793. Margaret Morgan, a slave in Maryland, had been allowed to live as if she were free. She married a free man from York County, Pennsylvania, just north of the Mason-Dixon Line, and in 1832 settled there with him, without objection from her owner (she was not, therefore, a fugitive slave). Five years later, after the owner's death, his niece hired a professional slave catcher, Edward Prigg, to retrieve Mrs. Morgan. In violation of Pennsylvania's 1826 law that outlined the legal procedure for the rendition of fugitives and made the removal of a black person from the state by force a felony, Prigg and three accomplices entered the Morgan home at night while the husband was away, seized Margaret Morgan and her six children, and brought them to Maryland. At least one of the children had been born in Pennsylvania and was thus free under state law. Pennsylvania indicted Prigg and his men for kidnapping and requested their extradition. The governor of Maryland refused. Nonetheless,

Prigg voluntarily returned to Pennsylvania to face trial and was convicted. The case then made its way to the U.S. Supreme Court.

In 1842, in *Prigg v. Pennsylvania,* the Court overturned Prigg's conviction, although the ruling was so complicated—with seven justices issuing opinions—that scholars to this day disagree about exactly what was decided. All nine justices affirmed the constitutionality of the Fugitive Slave Act of 1793, and all declared Pennsylvania's 1826 law on rendition and kidnapping an unconstitutional interference with the right to recover a fugitive. But on other important points, sharp differences emerged.

In the main opinion, Justice Joseph Story of Massachusetts declared that the Constitution's fugitive slave clause deserved special consideration because without it the Union "could not have been formed." Indeed, so "fundamental" was this provision that the framers could not have intended to leave enforcement in the hands of the states. Thus, Story concluded, Congress enjoyed the "exclusive" right to legislate regarding fugitive slaves. Story's description of the states' relationship to rendition was confusing and, in the opinion of some observers, self-contradictory. Describing national power as exclusive seemed to suggest that states had no role at all in rendition. They could not interfere with an owner's right to retrieve a fugitive, Story declared, but neither could they be "compelled to enforce" a national law on the subject—that was the responsibility of the federal government. State officials, to be sure, could assist in rendition "unless prohibited by state law," which seemed to invite the northern states to enact legislation barring public officials from participating in the recovery process. At the same time, Story reaffirmed the common law of recaption, an owner's "positive, unqualified right" to seize a slave (as Prigg had done) "in every state in the Union" with no legal process at all, so long as this was accomplished without a breach of the peace. Story entirely ignored the problem of kidnapping, or the fate of Mrs. Morgan and her children, which had given rise to the case in the first place. Three members of the court, including Chief Justice Roger B. Taney, vigorously disputed parts of Story's opinion. They insisted that the states possessed the authority to pass laws to assist slaveholders in recovering their human property.[30]

Ironies abounded in what the *New York Tribune*, founded a year earlier by the antislavery Whig journalist Horace Greeley, called "the most important decision which has proceeded from [the] bench for many years, perhaps ever." In upholding a right of the South, Story, a strong nationalist, offered a sweeping justification for federal authority over the states, something many southerners normally viewed with alarm. As the *Tribune* noted, "Vehement devotees of state rights" rejoiced over the decision, even though it denied a state "the right to protect its free citizens from being kidnapped and enslaved." The *Tribune* saw the ruling as a complete victory for slaveholders. The Court, it wrote, had declared the owner's right to secure the return of a fugitive "absolute and illimitable." The New York Vigilance Committee agreed, warning that by constitutionalizing the right of recaption, the decision would inspire a new wave of kidnapping. Because of its open-ended sanctioning of the seizure of fugitives and kidnapping of free blacks, one recent commentator has called *Prigg v. Pennsylvania* "the worst Supreme Court decision ever issued."[31]

Yet Story himself, on his return to Massachusetts after the Court's term ended, described the decision as "a triumph for freedom," since it eliminated any obligation on the part of free states to assist in the capture and return of fugitive slaves. Many northerners quickly interpreted *Prigg* as authorizing states to withdraw altogether from the unpleasant rendition process. Between 1842 and 1848, six free states enacted new personal liberty laws that barred public officials—judges, sheriffs, constables, and others—from taking jurisdiction in cases involving fugitives or offering assistance to those seeking their recapture, and prohibited the use of jails and other public buildings for their detention. The Massachusetts statute was known as the Latimer law, named after the fugitive slave George Latimer, who, with his pregnant wife Rebecca, reached Boston on a ship from Norfolk in 1842. After being recognized by an acquaintance of his owner, George Latimer was arrested and lodged in the city jail. A mob "persuaded" the jailer to release him, and the frightened owner, who had traveled to Boston, accepted $400 for Latimer's freedom. The following year, the legislature prohibited public officials from arresting alleged fugitives and judges from hearing such cases. New York did not enact a new measure, but its laws allowing alleged fugitives a jury trial and prohibiting magistrates from issuing warrants for their arrest remained on the books.[32]

Simultaneously, a series of laws and court decisions eliminated slave transit through the free states. Until the 1830s, northern states generally recognized the right of southern owners to bring slaves into their territory for a specified period of time. But beginning with a court decision in Massachusetts in 1836, state after state, including, as we have seen, New York in 1841, adopted the freedom principle that the moment a slave, other than a fugitive, set foot on free soil, he or she became free. The freedom principle made it possible for slaves traveling in the North with their owners to claim their liberty. Taken together, these legal developments placed new obstacles in the path of slaveholders seeking to retrieve fugitive slaves or retain ownership of slaves they brought into the North. At the annual meeting of the New York Vigilance Committee in 1846, a speaker commented on the "great change" that had taken place. The courts were now "respectful" to the committee's lawyers, and it was no longer necessary to "hurry" fugitives to Canada—they were "comparatively safe" in New York and New England. This would change dramatically in 1850.[33]

One New York jurist who proved remarkably sympathetic to fugitive slaves was John W. Edmonds, a circuit judge from 1845 to 1847 and subsequently a member of the state's Supreme Court. When Edmonds died in 1874, the *New York Times* reported that he was best known for his advocacy of "Spiritualism," having published several works on the subject in the 1850s. Before that, however, Edmonds was a protagonist in two highly publicized legal cases relating to fugitives. By this time, John Jay II had emerged as the city's leading lawyer in fugitive slave cases. As Gay noted, Jay provided his services without charge and "at great risk to his social and professional standing." Jay tried to remain aloof from abolitionists' internecine conflicts, refusing to "connect myself prominently" with the "old" or "new" organizations and taking up cases at the request of both outposts of the underground railroad. Jay's work did not go unnoticed by New York's pro-southern elite. In 1850, when he sought membership in a "fashionable club," Jay was "*black-balled*" on the grounds that he had "acted as counsel for a fugitive slave."[34]

One of Jay's cases before Judge Edmonds, which produced "much excitement" in the city, involved George Kirk, a twenty-two-year-old slave who hid on a ship sailing from Savannah to New York in October 1846. The captain discovered him at sea and placed him in chains, planning to return Kirk to his owner. When the ship docked in New York harbor, black stevedores engaged in unloading the vessel heard Kirk's cries for help. One of them reported his presence to Gay's office, whereupon Elias Smith and Louis Napoleon, who worked there, obtained a writ of habeas corpus from a local judge, requiring that Kirk be brought to court. (Napoleon played a role in this and other legal proceedings even though he was unable to read or write. The *New York Times* later described him as "a man of no education, but of considerable force of character.")[35] The ship captain declared that Kirk had admitted to being a fugitive, and added that for years "malicious and evil disposed persons" had organized systems of "robbery" to deprive slaveowners of their human property.

Gay engaged John Jay II and another attorney, Joseph L. White (who unlike Jay charged for his services), to defend Kirk. They argued that since the captain lacked a property interest in Kirk, he had no right to hold him or exercise the right of recaption. Moreover, Jay maintained, keeping a person in chains had a "contaminating influence" on the public culture of New York. Edmonds agreed, ruling that the rendition of a fugitive must take place according to legal procedures and that no person in New York could be imprisoned privately by another. He ordered Kirk discharged. Kirk was hustled off to Gay's office on Nassau Street, where "a large number of colored persons, male and female," gathered to protect him.[36]

The matter, however, did not end there. A New York law dating to 1817 allowed the captain of a ship who discovered a hidden fugitive to obtain from the mayor an order to return him. At the captain's request, Democratic mayor Andrew H. Mickle directed the police to arrest Kirk. "The whole police force of the city," complained the *Tribune*, "turned slave-catcher." That afternoon, cartmen were observed removing a crate labeled "American Bible Society" from the antislavery office. Police followed the cart, opened the box, and discovered Kirk. (Jay, who feared exactly such an outcome, had suggested that a black boy be placed in the box, allowing Kirk to slip away as the police were led astray.) Jay returned to Judge Edmonds for another writ of habeas corpus. This time, Edmonds declared the 1817 law unconstitutional, in accordance, he said, with the *Prigg* ruling that only the federal government possessed the authority to legislate concerning fugitives. Once again, Kirk was discharged from prison. He rode off in a carriage, seated alongside Elias Smith and Isaac T. Hopper's son Josiah. Gay and Jay arranged for him to be sent to Boston, "beyond the reach of any bloodhounds." Francis

Jackson of the Boston Vigilance Committee subsequently reported that Kirk was attending school and had learned shoemaking. Thirty years later, he was still practicing that craft in Boston.[37]

For two weeks, Gay worked feverishly on the Kirk case. "Wasn't it a glorious triumph," he exulted to Wendell Phillips, noting that his office had fewer than half-a-dozen people to carry out such endeavors. Gay could not refrain from using the case to reinforce Garrisonian doctrine and lambaste the Liberty party. "When the Union is dissolved," he wrote in the *Standard,* "a fugitive slave will be safe here . . . and *not before.*" He claimed that Horace Dresser, the Vigilance Committee attorney now associated with the Liberty party, had tried to take over the case before Jay's arrival in court and had muddied the legal waters by making improper motions. Nonetheless, New York's antislavery community, few of whom shared Gay's Garrisonian outlook, hailed the Kirk case as a great victory. The *Tribune* saluted the "legal knowledge and indefatigable exertions of Mr. Jay" and "the logical force . . . and remarkable power of expression of Mr. White." "Mr. Gay and Mr. Smith," declared a religious newspaper in Boston, "deserve the thanks of all lovers of freedom. . . . It is a marked sign of progress that a slave cannot be reclaimed, even in the great Babylon of American trade, without creating an excitement that shakes it throughout its borders." Southerners found the outcome outrageous. "We have long ago come to the conclusion," declared a Richmond newspaper, "that the courts in the non-slaveholding states will cease to enforce the laws in relation to fugitive slaves."[38]

Edmonds's handling of another case heightened southern annoyance and would be cited in Congress in 1850 as evidence of the need for a new fugitive slave law. In December 1848, John Lee, a slaveowner in Frederick County, Maryland, dispatched two men to New York to apprehend the alleged fugitive Joseph Belt. Presumably exercising the right of recaption, they seized Belt on a city street in broad daylight and spirited him to Brooklyn, where they held him captive for two days while awaiting a ship bound for Maryland. John Jay II rushed to Judge Edmonds to request a writ of habeas corpus, which the judge duly issued, not only directing two policemen to retrieve Belt, but also ordering the arrest of two other officers who had assisted the slave catchers. (Another judge subsequently cleared the latter two of carrying out an illegal arrest, even though Edmonds himself testified against them.) When Edmonds convened a hearing to determine Belt's status, "great numbers of . . . the colored population" gathered in his courtroom. Thomas Lee, the nephew of the Maryland claimant, arrived to testify that he recognized Belt as his uncle's slave. Edmonds demanded proof that the laws of Maryland in fact established slavery; when a statute book was produced, he responded that there was no evidence that it contained a correct version of the state's laws. New York, he continued, presumed the freedom of every person in the state and did not allow anyone to seize and hold another individual. He ordered Belt's release. Lee returned to Maryland, and Belt, according to the *Standard,* left the city via the underground railroad.[39]

The ramifications of Belt's case continued after his departure from New York. Despite the fact that the two police officers who rescued him were performing an official duty, the "friends of Belt" took up a collection to defray the expenses the men had incurred as well as to assist the "poor colored hack driver" who had conveyed the policemen to Brooklyn in the midst of a snowstorm and "whose feet were froze, so as to disable him from work for a month." In this instance, John Jay II had been engaged by the New York State Vigilance Committee, not Gay's group. But the committee's treasurer, William Harned, reported that demands for assistance the previous fall had "exhausted" its resources. A brief public spat ensued over who bore responsibility for providing the money, Gay's antislavery office or the Vigilance Committee. Eventually, in a display of unity, Elias Smith of Gay's office drew up an appeal for funds to assist Harned. It raised forty-seven dollars.[40]

Cases like these, as the American and Foreign reported at its annual meeting in New York City in 1849, helped to "erase from the minds of Northerners the notion that the Constitution forbids efforts" to aid fugitive slaves.[41] At the same time, the Mexican-American War of 1846–48, which resulted in the acquisition of vast new territories in the present-day Southwest, moved to center stage of American politics the question of whether slavery's westward expansion should be allowed to continue. The spread of free-soil sentiment increased the number of northerners sympathetic to runaways. By the same token, consternation among slaveholders, especially in the Upper South, grew stronger as the number of runaways, along with obstacles to their recovery, proliferated.

Particularly alarming to slaveholders was the attempted escape from the nation's capital, in April 1848, of seventy-six men, women, and children, all slaves, on the schooner *Pearl*. The organizer of this audacious enterprise was William L. Chaplin, formerly the corresponding secretary of the New York State Anti-Slavery Society and an active member of the Albany Vigilance Committee. Chaplin had come to Washington to report for an antislavery newspaper and to take the place of Charles T. Torrey, the underground railroad operative who died in a Maryland prison. Unfortunately, after the *Pearl* slipped away from Washington, the winds picked up and the ship had to anchor on the Potomac River near the mouth of Chesapeake Bay to await a change in the weather. A steamer dispatched by the authorities overtook it, and the two-man crew was arrested and fined. Unable to pay, they languished in prison until pardoned by President Millard Fillmore in 1852.

The *Pearl* slaves were remanded to their owners; most were quickly sold, including fifty to a single slave trader. Two, sixteen-year-old Mary Edmonson and her sister Emily, thirteen, gained their freedom after their formidable purchase price of $2,250 was raised by the New York State Vigilance Committee, people attending a mass meeting at the New York Tabernacle, and the congregations of James W. C. Pennington and Henry Ward Beecher. A recent recruit to the ranks of local abolitionists, Beecher had taken up the ministry of Brooklyn's Plymouth Church in 1847 and was on his way to becoming the nation's most celebrated prelate. (After the Civil War, the *Brooklyn Eagle* would call Beecher the "Hercules of American Protestantism," although he would also achieve notoriety in the era's most sensational scandal when it was revealed that he had practiced Christian love a bit too literally with his parishioner Elizabeth Tilton, the wife of the prominent reformer Theodore Tilton.) Beecher helped to raise funds for the New York State Vigilance Committee, and his church provided shelter to fugitives. From his pulpit, he held mock "auctions" of female slaves, to raise money from parishioners to purchase their freedom. Chaplin, who was not on board the *Pearl,* returned to the North and secured a position as "general agent" of the New York State Vigilance Committee.[42]

The entire attempted escape, although unsuccessful, exemplified some of the worst fears of slaveholders. While many escapes were wrongly attributed to "enticement" by northerners, here was a flesh-and-blood abolitionist who really did travel to the South to help slaves abscond. Moreover, numerous slaves, far beyond those on board the ship, knew of the plan, but not one had betrayed it.

The growing number of slaves attempting to escape to freedom heightened fears about the stability and future of slavery in the states bordering on free soil. As early as 1817, southern members of Congress had proposed measures to strengthen the Fugitive Slave Act of 1793. When John C. Calhoun composed his Address of the Southern Delegates in Congress at the beginning of 1849, the first grievance in his long recital of the North's aggressions was the "flagrant breach" of the Constitution's fugitive slave clause. Without mentioning the underground railroad by name, Calhoun blamed "secret combinations" in the free states for having "enticed" runaways from their owners, "to the great annoyance and heavy pecuniary loss of the bordering southern states." Not long afterward, a Richmond newspaper called for an armed "foray" into Pennsylvania and Ohio to teach northerners not to assist fugitives. Others demanded a stronger fugitive slave law, which abolitionists vowed to resist. A decade of sectional strife over fugitive slaves, in which New York City would play a crucial part, lay ahead.[43]

5

THE FUGITIVE SLAVE LAW AND THE CRISIS OF THE BLACK COMMUNITY

I

In January 1850, at the direction of Virginia's legislature, James M. Mason introduced in the U.S. Senate a measure outlining new procedures for the return of fugitive slaves. A version quickly became part of a plan of sectional reconciliation designed by Henry Clay, the senator from Kentucky nearing the end of an illustrious career in national politics. Antagonism between free and slave states had deepened in the previous few years, sparked by the enactment of northern personal liberty laws that impeded the rendition of runaways, demands for the abolition of slavery in Washington, D.C., and the growing controversy over whether southerners should be able to carry their human property into western territories. National politics had become so polarized that when Congress assembled in December 1849, threats of southern secession filled the air and it took sixty-three ballots to elect a Speaker of the House. The members finally decided on Howell Cobb, a Georgia Democrat and the owner of over 200 slaves, making him one of the nation's largest slaveowners.

Clay's proposal aimed to settle all outstanding points of conflict between North and South to the extent that they intersected with national politics. The Fugitive Slave Bill accompanied Clay's "omnibus" compromise measure, which among other things provided for the admission of California as a free state; the establishment, without reference to slavery, of territorial governments in the rest of the lands acquired in the Mexican-American War; and the abolition of the domestic slave trade, but not slavery itself, in the nation's capital.

Of all the South's grievances, Clay declared when he discussed his plan in the Senate in February, "the most irritating and inflammatory to those who live in the slave States" was the escape of fugitive slaves. Clay had recently given a good deal of thought to this question. Late in 1847, he felt compelled to respond to a public accusation by Lewis Hayden, who had escaped from Kentucky three years earlier and become an important antislavery activist in Boston, that Clay had once sold Hayden's wife and child to the Lower South. Clay offered a not very convincing denial. In 1849, Clay traveled to Newport, Rhode Island, with a slave, Levi, who promptly escaped, only to return after a short time. Clay then took Levi to Buffalo (in violation of New York's law prohibiting slave transit), where the slave disappeared again. Clay reacted philosophically. He would not pursue Levi, he wrote, "as it is probable that in a reversal of our positions I would have done the same thing." On the Senate floor, however, he insisted that responsibility for the return of runaways extended not only to the federal government but also to "the officers of every state" and, indeed, "to every man in the Union." But since northern states had erected "obstructions and impediments," it was up to Congress to enforce the Constitution. Clay also complained about the "unneighborly" actions of the northern states in rescinding the right of transit: "a man from a slave state cannot now . . . travel in a free state with his servant, although he has no purpose of stopping there any longer than a short time."[1]

There followed one of the most celebrated congressional debates in American history. On March 4, 1850, Mason read to the Senate the last speech of the dying John C. Calhoun, which rejected compromise. The North must yield on the issues in dispute, he declared, or the Union would dissolve. Three days later, Daniel Webster shocked many of his Massachusetts constituents by embracing Clay's proposals, including the Fugitive Slave Bill. On this question, he declared, the South's complaints had a "just foundation," although he would allow a trial by jury if the accused denied being a runaway. On March 11, William H. Seward, who had signed one of the first personal liberty laws as governor of New York, responded for the antislavery North. Conflict between freedom and slavery was inevitable, he insisted, and freedom must prevail: "you cannot roll back the tide of social progress." As to constitutional guarantees, Seward offered an arresting and, to the South, alarming, response: "there is a higher law than the Constitution." The rendition of fugitives, Seward declared, conflicted with "the laws of God."[2]

The debate over Clay's proposals occupied much of the spring and summer of 1850. At one point, Clay embraced the idea of a jury trial for accused fugitives, not in the North, however, but in the state from which they were alleged to have escaped, where they would be treated with "fairness and impartiality" (an assurance even Clay must have realized was absurd). At the end of July, the omnibus bill, buffeted by criticism from all sides, died in the Senate. Soon afterward, however, Senator Stephen A. Douglas of Illinois picked up the individual pieces and piloted each to passage, including the Fugitive Slave Bill. This was the Compromise of 1850.[3]

Partly because many Deep South congressmen felt the issue did not directly affect their constituents, and because many northerners wished to steer clear of the subject, the fugitive slave measure occupied less time in the ongoing debate than other aspects of the compromise. The House, in fact, passed the bill with no discussion at all, while many northern members "skulked in the corridors" to avoid casting a vote. In the Senate, a brief but heated exchange took place at the end of August. It revealed deep anxiety in the cotton kingdom about the depth of commitment in Maryland, Kentucky, and Virginia to the South's peculiar institution. The division within the slave states became apparent in discussion of a proposal by Senator Thomas Pratt of Maryland that the federal government compensate the owner when the return of a fugitive slave proved impossible. Deep South senators accused Pratt and his supporters of opening the door to a "mode of emancipation." Owners in the border region, they claimed, knowing that they would receive compensation, would allow slaves to run away and not pursue them. Senators from the cotton states also feared that allowing the federal government to interpose its "financial power" between master and slave would establish a dangerous precedent. John M. Berrien of Georgia warned that federal compensation for fugitives implied that the government "possesses the power of emancipation," since once the master has been paid, the slave would presumably be free.[4]

But representatives of the slave states of the Upper South rallied behind Pratt's idea. "Depredations to the amount of hundreds of thousands of dollars are committed upon the property of the people of the border slave states of this Union annually," proclaimed David Atchison of Missouri, and the federal government ought to reimburse them. With southern senators divided and northerners mostly opposed, the proposal failed. Of course, such a debate would never have taken place had it not been for the actions of slaves who ran away seeking freedom, the effectiveness of the underground railroad networks that came to their aid, and the growth of antislavery sentiment in the North. In earlier days, declared Pratt, hundreds of slaves who had escaped from Maryland were returned, but since the rise of the abolitionist movement, "I do not know a single case in which the fugitive has been surrendered to his master." Mason mentioned the Joseph Belt case in New York City to demonstrate the "tone of feeling among the people in the free states" that had made the rendition of fugitives impossible.[5]

Shortly before this debate unfolded, William L. Chaplin, the mastermind of the *Pearl* incident, returned to Washington to put an exclamation point on the fugitive slave issue. Early in August 1850, Chaplin hired a carriage and attempted to transport to Pennsylvania two slaves owned by Alexander H. Stephens and Robert Toombs, members of the House of Representatives from Georgia. The Washington Guard, a local militia unit, was waiting for him. They apprehended Chaplin and moved him to a jail in Maryland, where he was charged with larceny, assault, and other crimes. Bail was set at $25,000, an enormous sum, which abolitionists duly raised, with Gerrit Smith contributing $10,000 himself. Once released from prison, Chaplin headed north and remained there. He did not appear for his trial, and the bail money was forfeited. One of the slaves, Garland White, later escaped and went on to serve as chaplain for a regiment of black soldiers during the Civil War. He was part of the Union force that liberated Richmond, the Confederate capital, in April 1865.[6]

While Congress deliberated, slaves continued to escape (thirty-five fled from one county in Maryland on a single day in August 1850, according to the *National Anti-Slavery Standard*), and abolitionists prepared to resist the new law. That month, a black crowd rescued two fugitives who had been apprehended in Harrisburg, Pennsylvania. At the same time, Gerrit Smith, in the name of the New York State Vigilance Committee, called for opponents of the Fugitive Slave Bill to gather in Cazenovia, in the heart of upstate New York's "burned-over district," home to every kind of religious enthusiasm and social reform movement. Smith issued a special invitation to "fugitives from the prison house of southern despotism" to attend. The two-day convention opened on August 21, 1850, with 2,000 persons in attendance, including some fifty fugitives (among them Frederick Douglass) as well as many prominent abolitionists. The meeting endorsed a "Letter to the American Slave" composed by Smith, which described slaves as "prisoners of war" entitled to "plunder, burn, kill," if necessary, "to promote your escape." It assured fugitives they would be safe if they reached New York, while condemning as "grossly inconsistent" individuals—he had in mind northern leaders of the Democratic and Whig parties—who claimed to be critics of slavery but felt obligated to obey "pro-slavery" laws.[7]

Mainstream reaction to the Cazenovia meeting was unfriendly. A Buffalo newspaper called Smith a "madman." But the gathering reverberated in Washington. A large number of fugitive slaves, complained Senator David L. Yulee of Florida, had openly taken part in a "public convention," yet "no public officer nor citizen" made any attempt to arrest them. "What sort of good faith—what sort of justice," he asked, "call you this?" Some Garrisonians, committed to the philosophy of moral suasion, found the resolutions and speeches too belligerent.[8] But at the very least, the gathering suggested that the fugitive slave question was leading many abolitionists to abandon their long-standing belief in nonviolence.

On September 18, 1850, two days after its final approval by Congress, President Fillmore affixed his signature to the Fugitive Slave Bill. Compared with the brief measure of 1793, the statute was long, complicated, and draconian. It created a new category of federal official, that of U.S. commissioner, appointed by a federal judge and authorized to hear the case of an accused fugitive and to issue a certificate of removal, a document that could not be challenged in any court. The fugitive could neither claim a writ of habeas corpus nor testify at the hearing, whose sole purpose was to establish his or her identity. For this, a document from the owner's state with a physical description of the accused would constitute "conclusive" proof. The commissioner would receive a fee of five dollars if he decided against the owner and ten dollars if he issued a certificate of removal, on the grounds that the latter involved more paperwork. (This set the price of a northern conscience at five dollars, abolitionists complained.) Federal marshals could deputize individuals to execute a commissioner's orders and, if necessary, call on the assistance of local officials and even bystanders. The act included severe civil and criminal penalties for anyone who harbored fugitive slaves or interfered with their capture, as well as for marshals and deputies who failed to carry out a commissioner's order or from whom a fugitive escaped. No action by a state or local judge and no local law could interfere with the process; northern personal liberty laws were specifically mentioned in the act as examples of illegitimate "molestation" of the slaveowner. To forestall resistance, the federal government at its own expense could deliver the fugitive to his or her owner.[9]

The Fugitive Slave Law of 1850 embodied the most robust expansion of federal authority over the states, and over individual Americans, of the antebellum era. It could hardly have been designed to arouse greater opposition in the North. It overrode numerous state and local laws and legal procedures and "commanded" individual citizens to assist, when called upon, in rendition. It was retroactive, applying to all slaves who had run away in the past, including those who had been law-abiding residents of the free states for many years. It did nothing to protect free blacks from kidnapping.[10]

Southern political leaders insisted that compliance with the new law constituted the key test of the Compromise of 1850. On its "faithful execution," declared the Georgia Platform, a document issued by a convention of supporters of the compromise measures, depended the preservation of the Union. For this very reason, many citizens of the free states, especially in the Lower North, declared their support for the law. So did the national platforms of the Democratic and Whig parties in 1852. Yet Senator Mason, with whom it had originated, told the Senate that he had "little hope" that the measure would prove effective. "The disease," he remarked, "is seated too deeply to be reached by ordinary legislation," and the "spirit of the people" would render the law "inoperative."[11]

In May 1850, the American and Foreign Anti-Slavery Society predicted that the congressional bill then under consideration would awaken northerners to the plight of fugitive slaves and change how the underground railroad operated. "Heretofore," it declared, "the fugitive has been aided in secret." Now, "men will strive who can most openly do him service."[12]

II

The first arrest under the Fugitive Slave Act of 1850 took place in New York City. On September 26, 1850, eight days after President Fillmore signed the measure, two deputy U.S. marshals arrested James Hamlet at his job as a porter in a local store. Hamlet had left Baltimore two years earlier on a train to Philadelphia and then made his way to New York. He settled on South Third Street in Williamsburg, a Brooklyn village with a small black population, along with his wife and three children, all born in Maryland. In 1850, Hamlet's owner, Mary Brown, learned of his presence in New York and hired a "police firm" to retrieve him. The slave catchers advised waiting for the new law to go into effect. As soon as it did, a representative of the firm, together with Brown's son Gustavus and her son-in-law Thomas J. Clare, brought relevant documents to New York and presented them to Alexander Gardiner, the newly appointed U.S. commissioner. Gardiner ordered marshals to bring Hamlet to his office.[13]

The Hamlet case, the *New York Tribune* noted sardonically, exhibited "very little of the 'law's delay.'" Indeed, events proceeded so swiftly that abolitionists had little time to react. The hearing took place the day after Hamlet's arrest. Although "a large number of colored persons" gathered at the commissioner's office, he allowed only one to witness the proceedings. Brown's representatives identified Hamlet as her slave. Hamlet insisted before the hearing that he and his parents had been manumitted but that their free papers had been lost; however, in accordance with the provisions of the new law, Commissioner Gardiner did not allow him to testify. During the proceedings, an attorney hurriedly engaged by a friend of Hamlet's appeared, asked a few questions, and declared himself satisfied that the law was being complied with. Gardiner ordered Hamlet remanded to Mrs. Brown. When Clare stated that he had "reason to believe" that a rescue "by force" was being planned, the commissioner directed marshals to deliver Hamlet to Baltimore at the federal government's expense. Hamlet was handcuffed and hurried to a waiting steamboat. The day after his arrest he was back in Maryland, lodged in prison. His wife knew nothing of these events until after his departure.[14]

Hamlet's story, however, did not end there. At some point during his brief stay in New York City, Mary Brown's son-in-law stated that she would allow Hamlet to purchase his freedom for $800. Two thousand members of the city's black organizations, "with a slight and visible sprinkling of white abolitionists," gathered at the African Methodist Episcopal Zion Church on Church Street to collect contributions. In an indication of widespread consternation over how the new law had been implemented, the *Journal of Commerce*, the voice of the city's mercantile community and, in the words of the *National Anti-Slavery Standard*, "a paper which has distinguished itself more than any other in the northern states as an apologist of slavery," launched its own fund-raising campaign. As soon as the money was collected, John H. Woodgate, a "respectable merchant," carried it to Baltimore and negotiated the transaction. A week after his arrest, Hamlet was back in New York, a free man.[15]

The *Hamlet* case galvanized the city's black community. On October 5, a "great mass meeting of colored citizens" assembled at City Hall Park—the first black gathering ever to take place at that site—to celebrate Hamlet's arrival. The meeting attracted several thousand persons, including representatives of both of the city's outposts of the underground railroad. Louis Napoleon, the chief operative assisting fugitives out of the American Anti-Slavery Society office, was among the organizers, and the speakers included Charles B. Ray of the New York State Vigilance Committee and Jacob R. Gibbs, the underground railroad agent who had relocated a few years earlier from Baltimore to New York.

Another speaker was William P. Powell, the veteran black abolitionist who operated a boarding house for black sailors, which had moved several times but in 1850 was located at 330 Pearl Street, near the East River. Powell, who frequently hid escaped slaves in the building, had recently helped to create a new black organization, the Committee of Thirteen, pledged to assist fugitives seized in New York. After Hamlet's arrest, he led a group of black sailors in a march on City Hall to demand that Mayor Caleb S. Woodhull protect black New Yorkers. Woodhull himself addressed the celebration in the park and promised that the police would no longer participate in the apprehension of fugitive slaves. When Hamlet spoke, "the greatest excitement prevailed." He told the crowd that after his return to Maryland, slave buyers had been warned not to purchase him as "he had tasted liberty, and therefore could never be held again in chains." At the event's conclusion, Hamlet was "borne in triumph" to a ferry terminal, from which hundreds of black New Yorkers escorted him to his home in Williamsburg. "It was quite a day of rejoicing," the *Tribune* reported, "among the colored people of the village."[16]

The American and Foreign Anti-Slavery Society seized on the Hamlet affair to reinvigorate itself, although, as time would reveal, only temporarily. It quickly produced a pamphlet by Lewis Tappan on the new law and the *Hamlet* case. Thirteen thousand copies sold in the first three weeks, and the pamphlet quickly went through three editions. The society also distributed through the mail a pledge "not to obey the Fugitive Slave Bill." By January 1851, it had garnered over 1,600 signatures. Its annual meeting in 1851 was almost entirely devoted to fiery speeches denouncing the new law and pledging to resist it. The longest was delivered by Henry Ward Beecher.[17]

Some New York merchants shared the widespread indignation over the treatment of James Hamlet and contributed funds for his freedom. But even though the purchase had been perfectly legal, the business community quickly drew back from any hint of resistance to the new law. "The commercial, trading, manufacturing interests . . . that trade so much with the South," Lewis Tappan observed, "are favorable to acquiescence in the law." In the aftermath of the Hamlet affair, a large public meeting called by merchants and bankers from both the Whig and Democratic parties issued a public statement endorsing enforcement of the Fugitive Slave Act. The gathering established the Union Safety Committee (a kind of Vigilance Committee in reverse) to mobilize public opinion in favor of the Compromise of 1850 and to support the return of fugitives to slavery. Its membership reads like a list of New York's most prominent businessmen, including sugar trader and banker Moses Taylor; merchant and banker William H. Aspinwall; and William B. Astor, the son of the fur trader and real estate speculator John Jacob Astor and reportedly the richest man in America.

The Union Safety Committee raised $25,000 to finance its operations. The largest contribution came from Brown Brothers, the banking and merchant enterprise with close ties to the South. Only a handful of business leaders refused to join. Among them were the silk merchants Henry C. Bowen and Theodore McNamee, who placed a notice in the newspapers stating, "Our goods, and not our principles, are in the market." Years later, the black abolitionist Philip A. Bell would cite them as rare examples of prominent New Yorkers who braved the "political and social ostracism . . . which an avowal of abolition principles entailed."[18]

In some parts of the North, the Fugitive Slave Law quickly became unenforceable. Slave catchers tried without success to apprehend fugitives in New Bedford, Massachusetts. One abolitionist in the strongly antislavery Western Reserve of northern Ohio commented, "I doubt if a man could be found to act as a 'Commissioner' to hunt fugitive slaves." In New York City, however, led by the merchant community, public sentiment quickly turned in favor of enforcement. Even the pastor of St. Philip's Episcopal Church, one of the city's largest black congregations, declared it a "Christian duty" to obey "the law of the land." Abolitionists found New York even more inhospitable than in the past. In May 1850, while the new law was making its way through Congress, the annual public meeting of the New York State Vigilance Committee was "beset by rioters" who interrupted the speakers and at one point stormed the platform. In 1851 and 1852, because "no public hall could be procured," the AASS held its annual meetings not in New York, as had become customary, but in Rochester and Syracuse. The following year, Sydney Howard Gay wrote of his newspaper, the *National Anti-Slavery Standard,* "The opposition to it in the city of New York is most bitter and inveterate, while its friends [are] so few as hardly to be appreciable."[19]

Just two months after James Hamlet returned to New York, another alleged fugitive, twenty-five-year-old Henry Long, was arrested at the Pacific Hotel, where he worked as a waiter. Still wearing his white jacket and apron, Long appeared before U.S. Commissioner Charles M. Hall. Dr. William W. Parker, acting as representative of John T. Smith of Virginia, who claimed to be the owner, identified Long as a slave and testified that he had given him medical treatment at Smith's request. Parker related that Long had escaped by boat to New York in 1848. This time, abolitionists were not caught unawares, and their warring factions united to assist Long. The *National Anti-Slavery Standard* raised money for Long's defense, with contributions to be sent to Lewis Tappan, Sydney Howard Gay, or Horace Greeley. The leader of the New York State Vigilance Committee, Charles B. Ray, attended the hearing along with Tappan. When Tappan rose to urge a delay, the federal marshal, Benjamin H. Tallmadge, remarked that he had no standing to say anything. Tappan replied that he found it outrageous that Tallmadge, the son of an aide-de-camp of George Washington, should wish to "hurry a man claiming to be a freeman off to slavery."[20]

No fewer than three lawyers appeared for Long—John Jay II, Joseph L. White, and Charles Whitehead. The Union Safety Committee hired an attorney to represent Smith. Long's lawyers employed every legal device at their disposal. When the attorney for the owner sought to introduce evidence that Long had admitted privately to being a fugitive slave, Jay and White succeeded in having the "confession" excluded on the grounds that the law prohibited an alleged slave's testimony. They produced several black witnesses who testified to having known Long in New York City in 1847, before his supposed escape. Overall, the lawyers managed to delay the proceedings for three weeks, during which Long's case "created quite an excitement" in the city. A few of Long's supporters preferred direct action to legal maneuvering. James Williams, a fugitive slave from Maryland, resolved to "fight" for Long's freedom. With another man, he attacked Dr. Parker at night in a public square. Parker drew a revolver, and the two assailants fled.[21]

All these efforts were in vain. Early in January 1851, a judge ordered Long returned to Virginia. By now, Ambrose Kingsland, a wealthy sperm-oil dealer backed by the Union Safety Committee, had been elected mayor; he repudiated his predecessor's promise not to employ the police in fugitive matters. Two hundred policemen, accompanied by an armed gang headed by the Tammany Hall ward boss Isaiah Rynders, led Long to the ferry to transport him to New Jersey. There, with federal marshals, he boarded a train to Richmond. A "large concourse of blacks hovered about the procession" but could do nothing to prevent Long's return to slavery.[22]

Soon after he reached Virginia, the "black rascal," as the *Richmond Enquirer* described Long, was sold at public auction to a slave dealer from Georgia for $750. Not everyone in the latter state welcomed Long's arrival. Upper South owners, an Augusta newspaper complained, had been selling off large numbers of "vicious and unruly negroes," whose presence threatened to "corrupt the morals" of Georgia's slave population. Indeed, later in 1851, Long was arrested for "making abolition speeches to a party of slaves" near Atlanta.[23]

"The majesty of the Fugitive Slave Law has been vindicated," one member of the Virginia legislature exulted. But even though Long had been identified at the outset, a southern newspaper complained, the proceedings had dragged on for weeks and the cost of rendition exceeded Long's value as a slave. The whole affair, the paper warned, would discourage future claimants—"it will be the last attempt . . . to recover a fugitive in New York." Sadly, this did not turn out to be the case. In September 1851, a few months after Long's rendition, a U.S. commissioner returned to slavery John Bolding, claimed as a fugitive from South Carolina. Early in 1852, the same fate befell James Trasker, who had absconded from Maryland in 1844. Trasker was married and the father of three children.[24]

Fugitive slave renditions continued to take place in New York City until the eve of the Civil War. On occasion, as in the case of James Hamlet, money was raised to purchase the slave's freedom (a new kind of slave market now operated in the city, the *National*

Anti-Slavery Standard observed). One such instance involved Horace Preston, a fugitive from Baltimore who in April 1852 came before Commissioner George W. Morton. Like James Hamlet, the twenty-eight-year-old Preston was a married man who lived in Williamsburg. Even by the standards of fugitive slave proceedings, the one involving Preston was highly irregular. A police officer had notified the owner by telegram of Preston's presence in New York and then had him arrested on a pretended charge of petty theft so he could be held until the owner's son arrived from Baltimore. Preston's wife did not learn of her husband's plight until an acquaintance told her that he had been taken to the U.S. courthouse.[25]

The atmosphere at Preston's hearing proved volatile. As usual, John Jay II appeared to represent the accused fugitive. When Richard Busteed, the lawyer for the alleged owner, testified about Preston's identity, Jay pointed out that no bill of sale or other document had been produced demonstrating his status as a slave. Jay insisted that there was "reason to believe" that Preston's mother had been manumitted before his birth, making Preston a free man. When Busteed heatedly denied this, Jay called him a "rank perjurer," whereupon Busteed left the witness chair and "struck Jay a violent slap on the left side of the head."

Referring to a case "where a man having the accent of an Irishman was held to be an Irishman," Busteed insisted that in all "probability" Preston, being black, was a slave. This was an odd argument, considering that ever since the late eighteenth century, when Maryland planters began to shift from tobacco to less labor-intensive grain production, leading to widespread manumissions, the state's free black population had been growing. By 1850, nearly half of Maryland's black population was free. Commissioner Morton did not allow any testimony on Preston's behalf, but he did admit a statement by the alleged owner's son that at the police station Preston had admitted to being a fugitive. When the commissioner ordered Preston returned to slavery, a "great commotion" followed. "Legal gents," according to the *New York Times*, shouted out, "Pretty land of liberty this" and "Shame on a free country." Despite the protests of a "large number of colored people" at the courthouse, federal marshals transported Preston by train to Baltimore. Abolitionists, however, raised $1,200 to purchase Preston's freedom. Within a month he had returned to Brooklyn.[26]

The passage of the Fugitive Slave Law created a crisis in northern black communities. In the first three months after the law went into effect, hundreds of men, women, and children—the exact figure remains unknown—fled to Canada from the northern states. In 1850, a quarter of Boston's black adults had been born in the South, most of them escaped slaves. In the wake of the new law, sixty parishioners of the Twelfth Baptist Church, known as the "fugitive slave church," along with dozens of other individuals, abandoned the city for Canada. "It is horrible," wrote Wendell Phillips, "to see the distress of families torn apart." A notice in the *Liberator* pleaded for donations to assist the refugees "pressing northward . . . in increasing numbers." Even in upstate New York, where antislavery sentiment predominated, fugitive slaves and their families embarked for Canada. Their ranks included one-third of the 600 African Americans living in and around Syracuse and almost the entire congregation of Rochester's Abyssinian Baptist Church, including the minister.[27]

All told, over 300 fugitive slaves are known to have been returned to their owners during the 1850s, either by federal commissioners or without any legal process. An example of the latter occurred in 1853, when the mayor of Norfolk learned that seven slaves had escaped on a vessel headed for New York. He wired the shipping company's agent there, who arranged for the fugitives to be apprehended when the boat anchored in New York harbor. Twelve fugitives were remanded from New York City during the decade in accordance with the new law. This represented a tiny fraction of the hundreds of fugitives who lived in the city, but enough to reinforce New York's reputation as an unsafe environment for fugitive slaves and to strike fear among the city's black population.[28]

In her memoir published in 1861, Harriet Jacobs vividly recalled the panic that set in. Individuals became "impromptu vigilance committees," scanning the newspapers and streets for the arrival of southerners. "All that winter, I lived in a state of anxiety. When I took the children out to breathe the air, I closely observed the countenances of all I met. I dreaded the approach of summer, when snakes and slaveholders made their appearance." Jacobs went on to describe the havoc wrought on black families:

> While fashionables were listening to the thrilling voice of Jenny Lind in Metropolitan Hall, the thrilling voices of poor hunted colored people went up, in an agony of supplication, to the Lord. . . . Many families, who had lived in the city for twenty years, fled it now. . . . Many a wife discovered a secret she had never known before—that her husband was a fugitive, and must leave her to insure his own safety. Worse still, many a husband discovered that his wife had fled from slavery years ago, and . . . the children of his love were liable to be seized and carried into slavery.

Harriet Jacobs fled to Boston in 1852 after learning that her owner "was making preparations to have me caught." Only the following year, when her white employer purchased her freedom and that of her children, did Jacobs's family become secure. Her brother John, who had addressed the black meeting at Zion Church after James Hamlet's rendition, abandoned the city for California, from where he shipped out to Australia. Another fugitive slave, who had somehow managed to walk all the way from Louisiana to Brooklyn, sailed to the Pacific Ocean on a whaling vessel. "I thought I could not be safe," he wrote, "until I had got to the other side of the globe."[29]

Not all those who fled New York were fugitive slaves, since free blacks could easily find themselves caught up in the law's draconian net. One of the first renditions in the North illustrated this danger. Abraham Gibson was seized in Philadelphia, brought before a commissioner, identified as a fugitive slave, and quickly dispatched to Maryland, where his supposed owner declared him the wrong man. Not long after the return of James Hamlet, the abolitionist William P. Powell departed for England with his wife and seven children, although no member of the family had ever been a slave. Between 1850 and 1855, even as the city's overall population burgeoned thanks to continuing immigration from Europe, the number of blacks fell from 13,815 to 11,840, the lowest figure since the end of slavery in the state. The drop reflected not only the danger posed by the new law but also declining economic prospects as Irish and German newcomers pushed blacks out of positions as unskilled laborers and domestic servants, the only jobs available to the vast majority.[30]

Canada had long served as a refuge for black Americans, free as well as slave. During the 1840s, philanthropists established a number of black settlements in Canada West (present-day Ontario). The Canadian census of 1851 listed 4,669 blacks in that region, although unofficial estimates were considerably higher. By 1860, the black population had burgeoned to over 20,000, of whom an estimated 3,500 were fugitive slaves. Others were American-born free blacks seeking economic opportunities greater than those available in the United States. Black Americans, runaway slave and free, also settled in other parts of Canada. Canadian journals published by blacks from the United States—the *Voice of the Fugitive*, founded by the runaway slave Henry Bibb, and the *Provincial Freeman*, produced by the free-born Mary Ann Shadd Cary, the first black woman in North America to edit a newspaper—encouraged African Americans to emigrate. In 1856, the *Provincial Freeman* claimed that in the previous year over 1,000 fugitives had entered Canada from Detroit "on the U. G. R. R."[31]

Defenders of slavery depicted the refugees in Canada as destitute, helpless, and inclined toward criminality, thus demonstrating their lack of capacity for freedom. Abolitionists circulated reports of self-reliant black communities whose residents exhibited a healthy "spirit of enterprise." While hardly free from racism or, on occasion, incursions by slave catchers seeking to track down fugitives, Canada offered blacks greater safety and more civil and political rights—including serving on juries, testifying in court, and voting—than what existed in most of the United States. Despite entreaties from American officials, British authorities steadfastly refused to extradite fugitive slaves. Abolitionist gatherings in the United States pointedly contrasted Canada's "monarchial liberty" with their own country's "republican slavery," thus reversing the familiar self-image of the United States as an asylum for people seeking freedom in a world overrun with oppression.[32]

III

Soon after Henry Long's rendition in 1851, a correspondent of the *New York Tribune* outlined the obstacles his supporters had faced. Politicians and judges "manifested a bearing wholly in sympathy with the slaveholder." Police surrounded the courthouse, insulted Long's "black friends," and tried to prevent any black person from entering the courtroom; they even ejected the black physician James McCune Smith. The press, with a few exceptions, prejudged the case, referring to Long from the outset as a fugitive, not an "alleged slave." Except for John Jay, it proved "exceedingly difficult to retain the services of a respectable attorney to defend a poor alleged fugitive." On the other side, the Union Safety Committee not only engaged a lawyer for the claimant, but also contributed $800 to help defray the cost of Long's rendition. As a result, "some new friendships have been formed between our cotton merchants and cotton lawyers and southern customers and clients." To be sure, throughout the 1850s fugitive slaves kept arriving in the city. Nonetheless, as Jermain W. Loguen noted from Syracuse, runaway slaves were "in more danger" in "Eastern cities" like New York than in any other part of the country.[33]

Despite long odds against them, the Vigilance Committee's lawyers won occasional legal victories. One unusual case involved James Snowden, who escaped from Maryland in 1849 and secured work on a coastal vessel operating out of Providence, Rhode Island. On one voyage the following year, the captain anchored in New York harbor, and Snowden appropriated a small landing boat and paddled ashore. The captain followed Snowden and had him arrested for larceny. Before the trial, Snowden's owner arrived to claim him as a slave. But Jay convinced the court that the requirements of New York justice took precedence over the demands of the slaveowner. The judge sentenced Snowden to two years in prison for stealing the boat. In May 1852, as his incarceration was coming to an end, the Vigilance Committee secured a pardon from the governor, who was unaware of Snowden's status as a fugitive. The day before Snowden's scheduled release, according to the vivid imagination of a writer in the *Liberator,* the owner, in anticipation of retrieving his slave, was "drinking his champagne and smoking his cigars." But when he arrived at the jail the following day, Snowden was on his way to Canada.[34]

Another case involving strange twists and turns took place in 1853. Rose Cooper, "a large and showy woman" (according to an abolitionist account) from Mobile, Alabama, owned a slave, Emma, who married a free black man, Charles Trainer. Emma bore several children, among them Jane, born in 1844. Trainer attempted to purchase his daughter's freedom but was refused. In May 1853, Rose Cooper traveled to Cincinnati with Jane, followed by Trainer. Cooper then headed for New York, planning to embark by sea for San Francisco with the child. A friend in Cincinnati alerted Lewis Tappan, who had Jacob R. Gibbs locate the pair and asked Erastus D. Culver to obtain a writ of habeas corpus for Jane. (Culver, an antislavery lawyer who had served as a Whig member of Congress from upstate New York during the 1840s, moved to Brooklyn in 1851 and quickly became known for defending the rights of blacks in court.) Tappan and Louis Napoleon presented an affidavit to the police that led to Cooper's arrest for kidnapping. Jane's father, Charles Trainer, soon arrived from Cincinnati, and all appeared before a New York judge. The case devolved into a fight for custody of the child. Cooper's lawyers insisted that the marriage of a slave had no legal standing, and therefore Trainer had no parental rights.

Events then took a curious turn. Trainer failed to appear at a court session; he telegraphed Tappan that he had been abducted to Dunkirk, New York, not far from Buffalo. He refused to return unless the judge promised him protection. Tappan himself received threats that if he appeared at the courthouse, he would be assassinated. He came anyway, "putting my trust in God." The judge suddenly announced that he lacked jurisdiction ("after twenty days he finds this out," Tappan remarked). Culver located a Brooklyn jurist, Seward Barculo, willing to take over the case. On June 13, Barculo delivered the girl to her father, stating that regardless of the laws of Alabama, Trainer and his slave wife constituted a common-law marriage in New York. Rose Cooper, he continued, had no claim to Jane; once the child was brought into New York, she became free.[35]

The *Trainer* case underscored the legal area in which the Vigilance Committee experienced the greatest success: persuading New York jurists to enforce the freedom principle. This, it will be recalled, derived from the *Somerset* case in England. It defined slavery as a creature of local law, and held that any slave, with the exception of a fugitive, who entered a jurisdiction where the institution did not exist instantly became free. The freedom principle became part of New York statute law in 1841, when the legislature ended the right of southern owners to bring slaves into the state. (The Fugitive Slave Law did not alter this legal doctrine.)

In its 1853 annual report, the committee claimed to have secured the freedom of thirty-eight such slaves. By far the most prominent of these cases involved two women and six children aged one to ten owned by Jonathan Lemmon of Virginia and his wife Juliette. The Lemmons, their seven children, and the slaves arrived in New York on November 5, 1852, by sea from Norfolk, planning to board a steamboat for New Orleans and relocate from there to Texas. The vessel's black steward notified Louis Napoleon, Erastus D. Culver, and a black restaurateur of the slaves' presence. The next day, Napoleon brought to court a petition for a writ of habeas corpus, presumably written by someone else as the illiterate Napoleon signed it with his mark. Superior Court Judge Elijah Paine Jr. ordered the slaves brought before him. Culver and John Jay II, along with a young member of Culver's firm who had just been admitted to the bar and was trying his first case, future president Chester A. Arthur, represented the slaves. "The lobbies and passages" in the courthouse, the *Times* reported, "were crowded by colored persons."[36]

The question before the court, Culver argued, was simple: Did slavery exist in New York State? Within a week, Judge Paine declared the slaves free. The result, the *Times* exulted, constituted a clear vindication of the freedom principle. Any other decision would have made the city the center of "an extensive slave trade by sea," as it was far easier and cheaper to transport slaves from Maryland and Virginia to the southwest by ship via New York than over land. Accompanied by Louis Napoleon and "amid great cheering" from a crowd of black men and women, the eight liberated slaves rode off in a carriage. The Vigilance Committee held a public reception for them at a black church. They soon made their way to Canada, accompanied by Richard M. Johnson, a fugitive and the brother of one of the adult slaves. Johnson had settled in Cleveland, where he read about the case in a local newspaper, recognized the description of his sister, and immediately left for New York to join her (at considerable danger to himself).[37]

In the aftermath of the *Lemmon* decision, defenders and opponents of the Fugitive Slave Law launched rival fund-raising campaigns. An appeal by the *New York Tribune* collected over $1,000 for the liberated slaves "to begin their new life with." Fifty dollars went to reward the police officer who had custody of the slaves during the court proceedings and who had turned down an offer of $1,000 to deliver them surreptitiously to their owners. "Downtown merchants" collected $5,280 to reimburse the Lemmons for their lost property; Judge Paine himself contributed $100. The fund represented a shrewd investment, according to the *Tribune*. "Our jobbers . . . will probably get it all back in the increase of their southern business."[38]

While not widely remembered today, what one southern newspaper called "the robbery of Mr. Lemmon" caused consternation in the slave states and exacerbated the sectional conflict. Although the slaves had long since departed, the Virginia legislature in 1853 resolved to pursue an appeal of Judge Paine's decision, in order to establish owners' legal right to transport slaves through free states. The *Tribune* warned that were Virginia to win the appeal, "gangs of men, women, and children chained together" would be seen on the city's streets as they were marched from one ship to another. New York's attorney general took over the defense of the decision and hired Culver and Jay to assist him. After many delays, the appeal came before the New York Supreme Court in October 1857. During the proceedings, Charles O'Conor, a Democratic politician representing Virginia, asked if the Louis Napoleon who had launched the case was the former emperor of France. "A much better man," Jay replied.[39]

In December 1857, the state Supreme Court upheld Paine's ruling, a decision reaffirmed by the New York Court of Appeals, the state's highest court, in April 1860. The *Lemmon* case, wrote a Mississippi newspaper, involved principles "scarcely less important than those settled in the Dred Scott decision." But for reasons that are not entirely clear, Virginia decided not to appeal to the U.S. Supreme Court. Some Republicans feared, however, that they might in the future, and that the court would use the case to prohibit any state from keeping slaves out of its territory. Abraham Lincoln himself warned that the *Lemmon* case provided the opportunity for a "new Dred Scott decision" that would nationalize slavery by carrying it into the North. The issue became moot when Virginia seceded from the Union.[40]

Despite the fact that Pennsylvania and New York had long since eliminated the right of slave transit, and despite the *Lemmon* verdict, owners continued to travel to these states with their slaves. Some seized the opportunity to escape from bondage. In October 1855, Sydney Howard Gay provided aid to Rebecca Gill and Emeline Brown after they "left their mistress, Mrs. Hewitt, who brought them from Louisville" to New York City.[41]

The most celebrated case of these years involving the freedom principle centered on Jane Johnson and her sons Daniel and Isaiah, ages seven and eleven, the slaves of John Hill Wheeler, a prominent North Carolina politician whom President Franklin Pierce had appointed ambassador to Nicaragua. The situation bore a striking resemblance to the case of Jonathan Lemmon. On July 18, 1855, a day after dining with the president, Wheeler, with the slaves, trav-

THE PHILADELPHIA VIGILANCE COMMITTEE. Produced sometime in the 1850s, this collection of photographs includes seven underground railroad activists in Philadelphia, plus Thomas Garrett (middle row, left), who forwarded fugitive slaves to that city from Wilmington, Delaware. Among those depicted are James Miller McKim (top left); William Still (bottom right); Passmore Williamson (bottom center); and Robert Purvis (middle right). Many of the fugitives who reached New York in the 1850s had passed through Philadelphia. (Courtesy of Boston Public Library Print Department)

THE RESURRECTION OF HENRY BOX BROWN AT PHILADELPHIA. In one of the most celebrated escapes of the antebellum years, Henry Brown, a slave in Richmond, had himself concealed in a crate and shipped to the antislavery office in Philadelphia. This lithograph from 1851 shows James Miller McKim, with a hatchet, and William Still, holding the top of the crate, as Brown emerged. The man on the left may be the printer, Thomas Sinclair, and on the right, the abolitionist Charles D. Cleveland, who operated a school for girls.

(Library Company of Philadelphia)

GRACEANNA LEWIS, a member of one of the rural Quaker families that assisted fugitives who passed through southeastern Pennsylvania. (Chester County Historical Society)

WILLIAM WHIPPER, a prominent black businessman and abolitionist in Columbia, Pennsylvania, who dispatched many fugitives to Philadelphia and upstate New York. (I. Garland Penn, *The Afro-American Press and Its Editors*)

THE FOLLIES OF THE AGE, VIVE LA HUMBUG!! This popular print from 1855 depicts in the lower right corner the abolitionist Passmore Williamson urging Jane Johnson to escape from slavery. Johnson and her two children had been brought to Philadelphia by their owner, John Hill Wheeler, on their way to New York to board a ship for Nicaragua, where Wheeler was to take up a position as American ambassador. Williamson, along with William Still and several other black men, approached Johnson on a ferry as the party was about to depart. She and her children did become free. As the title suggests, the print is unsympathetic—other "follies" include a train wreck, a free lover, a carnival huckster, and a shop selling patent medicines. But it illustrates how widely known the Johnson case had become. (Library Company of Philadelphia)

MARIA WESTON CHAPMAN, the fashionable organizer of the annual Boston Anti-Slavery Bazaar that raised money for the American Anti-Slavery Society. (Portraits of American Abolitionists, Massachusetts Historical Society)

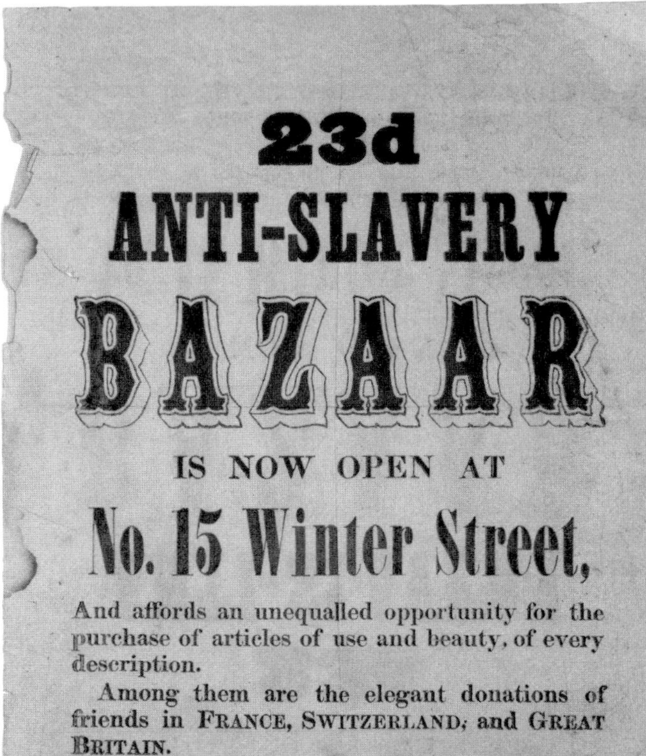
23d
ANTI-SLAVERY
BAZAAR
IS NOW OPEN AT
No. 15 Winter Street,

And affords an unequalled opportunity for the purchase of articles of use and beauty, of every description.

Among them are the elegant donations of friends in FRANCE, SWITZERLAND, and GREAT BRITAIN.

A broadside advertising the annual bazaar for 1856, emphasizing the "elegant" imported goods on sale. (Library of Congress)

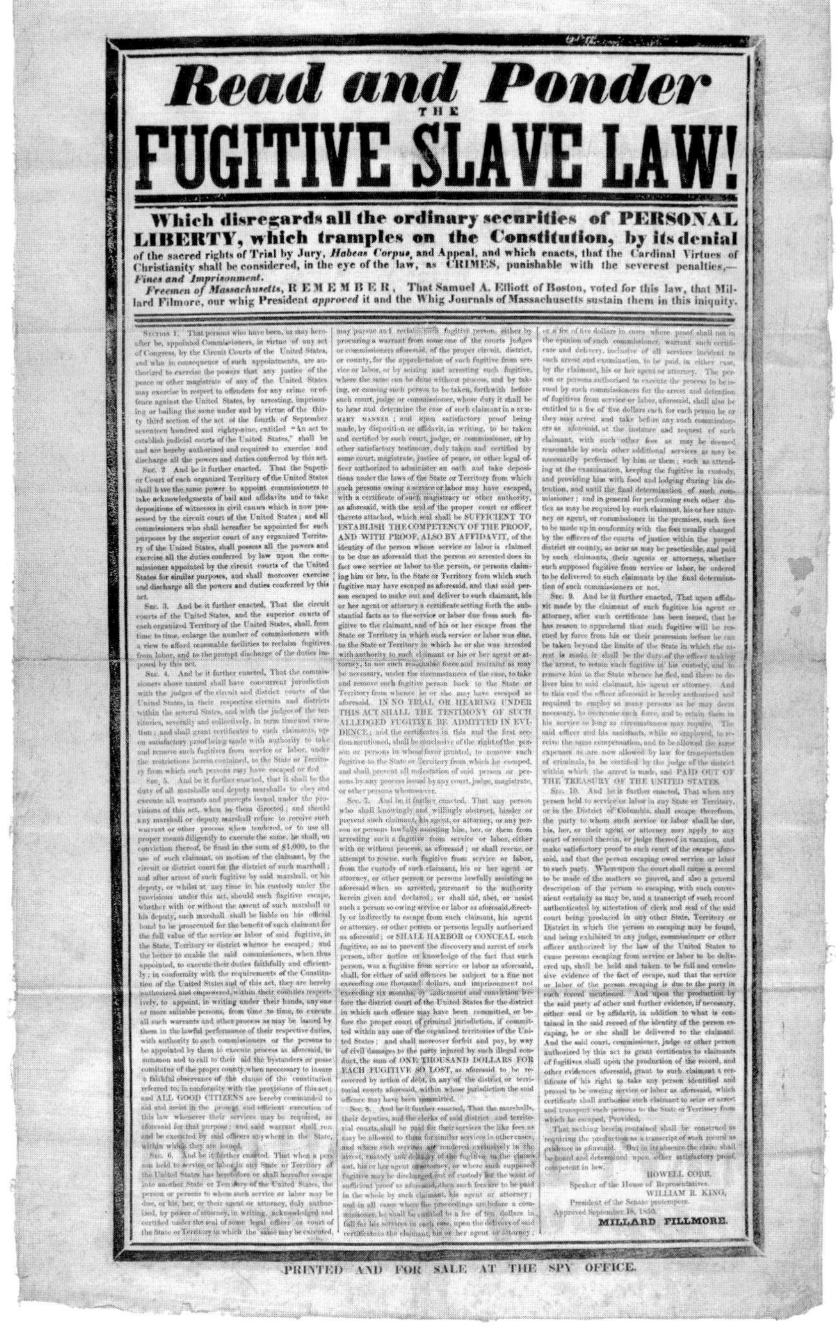

Read and Ponder
THE
FUGITIVE SLAVE LAW!

Which disregards all the ordinary securities of PERSONAL LIBERTY, which tramples on the Constitution, by its denial of the sacred rights of Trial by Jury, *Habeas Corpus*, and Appeal, and which enacts, that the Cardinal Virtues of Christianity shall be considered, in the eye of the law, as CRIMES, punishable with the severest penalties,—*Fines and Imprisonment.*

***Freemen of Massachusetts*, R E M E M B E R, That Samuel A. Elliott of Boston, voted for this law, that Millard Filmore, our whig President *approved* it and the Whig Journals of Massachusetts sustain them in this iniquity.**

SECTION 1. That persons who have been, or may hereafter be, appointed Commissioners, in virtue of any act of Congress, by the Circuit Courts of the United States, and who in consequence of such appointments, are authorized to exercise the powers that any justice of the peace or other magistrate of any of the United States may exercise in respect to offenders for any crime or offence against the United States, by arresting, imprisoning or bailing the same under and by virtue of the thirty third section of the act of the fourth of September seventeen hundred and eighty-nine, entitled "An act to establish judicial courts of the United States," shall be and are hereby authorized and required to exercise and discharge all the powers and duties conferred by this act.

SEC. 2 And be it further enacted. That the Superior Court of each organized Territory of the United States shall have the same power to appoint commissioners to take acknowledgments of bail and affidavits and to take depositions of witnesses in civil causes which is now possessed by the circuit court of the United States; and all commissioners who shall hereafter be appointed for such purposes by the superior court of any organized Territory of the United States, shall possess all the powers and exercise all the duties conferred by law upon the commissioner appointed by the circuit courts of the United States for similar purposes, and shall moreover exercise and discharge all the powers and duties conferred by this act.

SEC. 3. And be it further enacted, That the circuit courts of the United States, and the superior courts of each organized Territory of the United States, shall, from time to time, enlarge the number of commissioners with a view to afford reasonable facilities to reclaim fugitives from labor, and to the prompt discharge of the duties imposed by this act.

SEC. 4. And be it further enacted, That the commissioners above named shall have concurrent jurisdiction with the judges of the circuit and district courts of the United States, in their respective circuits and districts within the several States, and with the judges of the territories, severally and collectively, in term time and vacation; and shall grant certificates to such claimants, upon satisfactory proof being made with authority to take and remove such fugitives from service or labor, under the restrictions herein contained, to the State or Territory from which such persons may have escaped or fled

SEC. 5. And be it further enacted, that it shall be the duty of all marshalls and deputy marshalls to obey and execute all warrants and precepts issued under the provisions of this act, when to them directed; and should any marshall or deputy marshall refuse to receive such warrant or other process when tendered, or to use all proper means diligently to execute the same, he shall, on conviction thereof, be fined in the sum of $1,000, to the use of such claimant, on motion of the claimant, by the circuit or district court for the district of such marshall; and after arrest of such fugitive by said marshall, or his deputy, or whilst at any time in his custody under the provisions under this act, should such fugitive escape, whether with or without the assent of such marshall or his deputy, such marshall shall be liable on his official bond to be prosecuted for the benefit of such claimant for the full value of the service or labor of said fugitive, in the State, Territory or district whence he escaped; and the better to enable the said commissioners, when thus appointed, to execute their duties faithfully and efficiently; in conformity with the requirements of the Constitution of the United States and of this act, they are hereby authorized and empowered, within their counties respectively, to appoint, in writing under their hands, any one or more suitable persons, from time to time, to execute all such warrants and other process as may be issued by them in the lawful performance of their respective duties, with authority to such commissioners or the persons to be appointed by them to execute process as aforesaid, to summon and to call to their aid the bystanders or posse comitatus of the proper county, when necessary to insure a faithful observance of the clause of the constitution referred to, in conformity with the provisions of this act; and ALL GOOD CITIZENS are hereby commanded to aid and assist in the prompt and efficient execution of this law whenever their services may be required, as aforesaid for that purpose; and said warrant shall run and be executed by said officers anywhere in the State, within which they are issued.

SEC. 6. And be it further enacted. That when a person held to service or labor in any State or Territory of the United States has heretofore or shall hereafter escape into another State or Territory of the United States, the person or persons to whom such service or labor may be due, or his, her, or their agent or attorney, duly authorized, by power of attorney, in writing, acknowledged and certified under the seal of some legal officer or court of the State or Territory in which the same may be executed, may pursue and reclaim such fugitive person, either by procuring a warrant from some one of the courts judges or commissioners aforesaid, of the proper circuit, district, or county, for the apprehension of such fugitive from service or labor, or by seizing and arresting such fugitive, where the same can be done without process, and by taking, or causing such person to be taken, forthwith before such court, judge or commissioner, whose duty it shall be to hear and determine the case of such claimant in a SUMMARY MANNER; and upon satisfactory proof being made, by disposition or affidavit, in writing, to be taken and certified by such court, judge, or commissioner, or by other satisfactory testimony, duly taken and certified by some court, magistrate, justice of peace, or other legal officer authorized to administer an oath and take depositions under the laws of the State or Territory from which such persons owing a service or labor may have escaped, with a certificate of such magistracy or other authority, as aforesaid, with the seal of the proper court or officer thereto attached, which seal shall be SUFFICIENT TO ESTABLISH THE COMPETENCY OF THE PROOF, AND WITH PROOF, ALSO BY AFFIDAVIT, of the identity of the person whose service or labor is claimed to be due as aforesaid that the person so arrested does in fact owe service or labor to the person, or persons claiming him or her, in the State or Territory from which such fugitive may have escaped as aforesaid, and that said person escaped to make out and deliver to such claimant, his or her agent or attorney a certificate setting forth the substantial facts as to the service or labor due from such fugitive to the claimant, and of his or her escape from the State or Territory in which such service or labor was due, to the State or Territory in which he or she was arrested with authority to such claimant or his or her agent or attorney, to use such reasonable force and restraint as may be necessary, under the circumstances of the case, to take and remove such fugitive person back to the State or Territory from whence he or she may have escaped as aforesaid. IN NO TRIAL OR HEARING UNDER THIS ACT SHALL THE TESTIMONY OF SUCH ALLEDGED FUGITIVE BE ADMITTED IN EVIDENCE; and the certificates in this and the first section mentioned, shall be conclusive of the right of the person or persons in whose favor granted, to remove such fugitive to the State or Territory from which he escaped, and shall prevent all molestation of said person or persons by any process issued by any court, judge, magistrate, or other persons whomsoever.

SEC. 7. And be it further enacted, That any person who shall knowingly and willingly obstruct, hinder or prevent such claimant, his agent, or attorney, or any person or persons lawfully assisting him, her, or them from arresting such a fugitive from service or labor, either with or without process, as aforesaid; or shall rescue, or attempt to rescue, such fugitive from service or labor, from the custody of such claimant, his or her agent or attorney, or other person or persons lawfully assisting as aforesaid when so arrested, pursuant to the authority herein given and declared; or shall aid, abet, or assist such a person so owing service or labor as aforesaid, directly or indirectly to escape from such claimant, his agent or attorney, or other person or persons legally authorized as aforesaid; or SHALL HARBOR or CONCEAL such fugitive, so as to prevent the discovery and arrest of such person, after notice or knowledge of the fact that such person, was a fugitive from service or labor as aforesaid, shall, for either of said offences be subject to a fine not exceeding one thousand dollars, and imprisonment not exceeding six months, by indictment and conviction before the district court of the United States for the district in which such offence may have been committed, or before the proper court of criminal jurisdiction, if committed within any one of the organized territories of the United States; and shall moreover forfeit and pay, by way of civil damages to the party injured by such illegal conduct, the sum of ONE THOUSAND DOLLARS FOR EACH FUGITIVE SO LOST, as aforesaid to be recovered by action of debt, in any of the district or territorial courts aforesaid, within whose jurisdiction the said offence may have been committed.

SEC. 8. And be it further enacted, That the marshalls, their deputies, and the clerks of said district and territorial courts, shall be paid for their services the like fees as may be allowed to them for similar services in other cases, and where such services are rendered exclusively in the arrest, custody and delivery of the fugitive to the claimant, his or her agent or attorney, or where such supposed fugitive may be discharged out of custody for the want of sufficient proof as aforesaid, then such fees are to be paid in the whole by such claimant, his agent or attorney; and in all cases where the proceedings are before a commissioner, he shall be entitled to a fee of ten dollars in full for his services in each case, upon the delivery of said certificate to the claimant, his or her agent or attorney; or a fee of five dollars in cases where proof shall not in the opinion of such commissioner, warrant such certificate and delivery, inclusive of all services incident to such arrest and examination, to be paid, in either case, by the claimant, his or her agent or attorney. The person or persons authorized to execute the process to be issued by such commissioners for the arrest and detention of fugitives from service or labor, aforesaid, shall also be entitled to a fee of five dollars each for each person he or they may arrest and take before any such commissioners as aforesaid, at the instance and request of such claimant, with such other fees as may be deemed reasonable by such other additional services as may be necessarily performed by him or them; such as attending at the examination, keeping the fugitive in custody, and providing him with food and lodging during his detention, and until the final determination of such commissioner; and in general for performing such other duties as may be required by such claimant, his or her attorney or agent, or commissioner in the premises, such fees to be made up in conformity with the fees usually charged by the officers of the courts of justice within the proper district or county, as near as may be practicable, and paid by such claimants, their agents or attorneys, whether such supposed fugitive from service or labor, be ordered to be delivered to such claimants by the final determination of such commissioners or not.

SEC. 9. And be it further enacted, That upon affidavit made by the claimant of such fugitive his agent or attorney, after such certificate has been issued, that he has reason to apprehend that such fugitive will be rescued by force from his or their possession before he can be taken beyond the limits of the State in which the arrest is made, it shall be the duty of the officer making the arrest, to retain such fugitive in his custody, and to remove him to the State whence he fled, and there to deliver him to said claimant, his agent or attorney. And to this end the officer aforesaid is hereby authorized and required to employ so many persons as he may deem necessary, to overcome such force, and to retain them in his service so long as circumstances may require. The said officer and his assistants, while so employed, to receive the same compensation, and to be allowed the same expenses as are now allowed by law for transportation of criminals, to be certified by the judge of the district within which the arrest is made, and PAID OUT OF THE TREASURY OF THE UNITED STATES.

SEC. 10. And be it further enacted, That when any person held to service or labor in any State or Territory, or in the District of Columbia, shall escape therefrom, the party to whom such service or labor shall be due, his, her, or their agent or attorney may apply to any court of record therein, or judge thereof in vacation, and make satisfactory proof to such court of the escape aforesaid, and that the person escaping owed service or labor to such party. Whereupon the court shall cause a record to be made of the matters so proved, and also a general description of the person so escaping, with such convenient certainty as may be, and a transcript of such record authenticated by attestation of clerk and seal of the said court being produced in any other State, Territory or District in which the person so escaping may be found, and being exhibited to any judge, commissioner or other officer authorized by the law of the United States to cause persons escaping from service or labor to be delivered up, shall be held and taken to be full and conclusive evidence of the fact of escape, and that the service or labor of the person escaping is due to the party in such record mentioned. And upon the production by the said party of other and further evidence, if necessary, either oral or by affidavit, in addition to what is contained in the said record of the identity of the person escaping, he or she shall be delivered to the claimant. And the said court, commissioner, judge or other person authorized by this act to grant certificates to claimants of fugitives shall upon the production of the record, and other evidences aforesaid, grant to such claimant a certificate of his right to take any person identified and proved to be owing service or labor as aforesaid, which certificate shall authorise such claimant to seize or arrest and transport such persons to the State or Territory from which he escaped, Provided,

That nothing herein contained shall be construed as requiring the production as a transcript of such record as evidence as aforesaid. But in its absence the claim shall be heard and determined upon other satisfactory proofs, competent in law.

HOWELL COBB,
Speaker of the House of Representatives.
WILLIAM R. KING,
President of the Senate protempore.
Approved September 18, 1850.
MILLARD FILLMORE.

PRINTED AND FOR SALE AT THE SPY OFFICE.

A broadside published by Boston abolitionists condemning a Whig member of Congress who voted for the Fugitive Slave Act of 1850, as well as President Millard Fillmore, who signed the measure, and the local Whig press, which supported it. It includes excerpts from the law and some of the reasons that it outraged many northerners. (Gilder-Lehrman Collection)

THE FUGITIVE SLAVE LAW.....HAMLET IN CHAINS.

THE FUGITIVE SLAVE LAW . . . HAMLET IN CHAINS. An engraving from the *National Anti-Slavery Standard*, October 17, 1850, depicts James Hamlet, the first person returned to slavery under the Fugitive Slave Act of 1850, in front of city hall in New York. Flags fly from the building, emblazoned with popular American maxims violated by Hamlet's rendition. By the time this appeared in print, New Yorkers had raised the money to purchase Hamlet's freedom and he was back in the city. (Rare Books and Manuscripts Library, Columbia University)

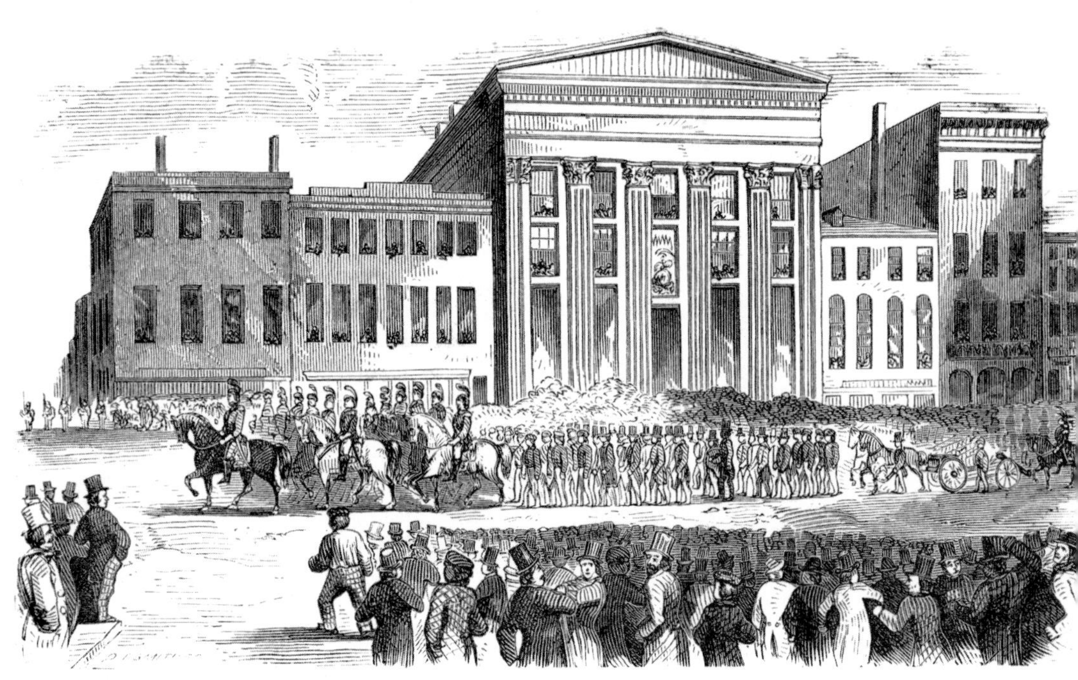

MARSHAL'S POSSE WITH BURNS MOVING DOWN STATE STREET. This engraving shows some of the 1,600 marshals, soldiers, and militiamen who marched the fugitive slave Anthony Burns to a Boston dock in 1854, for his return to Virginia. (Schomburg Center for Research in Black Culture, New York Public Library)

eled by train from Washington to Philadelphia en route to New York, where he intended to board a ship bound for Central America. While Wheeler was having dinner at a Philadelphia hotel adjacent to the dock, Johnson told a black waiter that she was a slave who did not wish to leave with her owner. He quickly notified William Still of the Philadelphia Vigilance Committee that three slaves were in the city and "they want liberty." With Passmore Williamson, a Quaker abolitionist, Still and five black dockworkers boarded the ferry on which the party was departing. Williamson informed Johnson that she and the children were entitled to their freedom and could leave the ship. Johnson responded, "I am not free, but I want my freedom." After a brief scuffle, Johnson and her sons disembarked with Still and Williamson. They were soon dispatched to New York, where Gay arranged for their passage to Boston. On behalf of the Boston Vigilance Committee, the black abolitionist William C. Nell met them at the train station.

Meanwhile, Wheeler obtained a writ of habeas corpus directing Williamson to produce the slaves, and filed charges against him, Still, and several other black men for riot and assault. In what the *New York Tribune* called "a bold and perilous move," Jane Johnson returned to Philadelphia from Boston to testify at the ensuing trial. She denied Wheeler's claim that she had been abducted: "I went away of my own free will; I always wished to be free." Wheeler found this impossible to believe. "Jane (servant)," he wrote in his diary, had been "induced" to perjure herself. Federal marshals planned to seize Johnson when her testimony concluded, but local officials sent a squad of police to protect her, and a wild carriage chase ensued. Johnson remained in the city until early September, staying at the home of the abolitionists James and Lucretia Mott, and even spoke at an antislavery convention. She then left Philadelphia for Boston; on the way, Gay again paid for her lodging and travel.

The case ended up as a triumph for the Vigilance Committee. The judge declared that Johnson and the children had become free the moment they set foot in Pennsylvania, and the assault cases mostly resulted in verdicts of acquittal. Williamson, however, served more than three months in prison for contempt of court, since he had failed to produce Johnson and the boys. The jailers treated him with uncommon solicitude. A steady stream of supporters, including Harriet Tubman and Frederick Douglass, visited him in his cell, and when Williamson's wife gave birth, a prison official escorted him to see her.[42]

Jane Johnson married in Boston and received financial assistance from the Boston Vigilance Committee as well as the poet Henry Wadsworth Longfellow, who privately donated money to black newspapers, churches, and fugitive slaves. Without his slaves, Wheeler sailed from New York for Nicaragua, where his bad luck continued. In 1856, the State Department recalled him for extending recognition, without authorization from Washington, to the regime set up in Nicaragua by the filibusterer William Walker, who restored slavery in that country and reopened the African slave trade. (Wheeler had concluded that "the race of Central Americans" was "incapable of self-government.") The following year, another of Wheeler's slaves, Hannah Bond, escaped from North Carolina. Sometime in the late 1850s, under the name Hannah Crafts, she produced *The Bondwoman's Narrative*, the first novel written by a black American woman. Among the slaves mentioned in the book is one Jane, who had recently escaped from slavery.[43]

IV

Despite abolitionists' success in winning the liberty of the Lemmon slaves, Jane Johnson and her children, and other slaves brought to the North by their owners, the freedom principle had no bearing on fugitive slaves. For them, especially after 1850, the only sure avenue to freedom involved seeking refuge in Canada. And at the same time that it inspired heightened efforts to aid fugitives in the courts, the passage of the Fugitive Slave Law reinvigorated and radicalized the underground railroad. New local vigilance committees sprang up, and increasing numbers of abolitionists abandoned moral suasion to embrace the use of force.

At public meetings throughout the North, speakers, black and white, invoked the heritage of the American Revolution to justify violent resistance to an unjust law. At the 1852 national convention of the Free Soil party, an organization devoted to stopping the westward expansion of slavery, Frederick Douglass proclaimed, "The only way to make the Fugitive Slave Law a dead letter [is] to make half a dozen or more dead kidnappers." A New Bedford abolitionist urged fugitives to "practice the art of using firearms" so that they could shoot slave catchers. New York City was no exception. Speakers at the public meeting that raised money to free James Hamlet called for resistance. "Liberty is worth fighting for," declared one member of the audience, and the gathering advised fugitives to "arm themselves with the surest and most deadly weapons, to resist unto the death." White abolitionists, the *Brooklyn Eagle* complained, "were foolish enough to endorse the frenzied ravings of the negroes."[44]

Rhetoric advocating armed resistance to the new law often amounted to little more than bravado. In parts of the North, however, efforts to assist fugitives took a violent turn. Dramatic attempts to rescue runaway slaves punctuated the 1850s—one study counts over eighty such confrontations. Before 1850, altercations of this kind had mostly been confined to the borderlands between slavery and freedom; now they occurred in many parts of the North. In October 1850, hundreds of armed blacks gathered at a jail in Detroit where a fugitive was being held. The frightened owner quickly agreed to allow his freedom to be purchased. In September

1851, a predominantly black crowd in Christiana, Pennsylvania, routed a group of slave catchers that included a federal marshal and a Maryland owner, who were attempting to apprehend four fugitives. The crowd, which numbered over 100 men and women, many of them armed, was led by William Parker, a runaway slave at whose home two of the fugitives were hiding. The slaveowner died in the affray, Parker and the fugitives fled to Canada, and the Fillmore administration obtained indictments for treason—a capital crime—against forty-one men, the largest such mass indictment in American history. But pursuing the case proved almost impossible in an area with strong sympathy for fugitives. Only one person, a white miller who claimed to have been an innocent bystander, was brought to trial. After deliberating for only fifteen minutes, the jury returned a verdict of not guilty.[45]

The following month, similar events unfolded in Syracuse, a city in the heart of upstate New York's burned-over district. A vigilance committee formed after the passage of the Fugitive Slave Act openly vowed to resist enforcement. On October 1, 1851, a federal marshal arrested Jerry McHenry, who had escaped from North Carolina eight years earlier and settled in Syracuse. A Liberty party convention happened to be meeting in the city; it adjourned to besiege the commissioner's office. A group that included the abolitionists Gerrit Smith and Samuel J. May and the fugitive slave Jermain W. Loguen met to plan a rescue. May, a Garrisonian and advocate of moral suasion, nonetheless felt he "could not preach non-violence to the crowd clamoring for his release." That night, about fifty men, a cross section of the city's population—blacks and whites, clergymen, physicians, lawyers, and laborers—stormed the police station and rescued McHenry. Five days later, he crossed the border into Canada. Indictments soon followed. Loguen fled to Canada, where he remained for a year, and four men were brought to trial, but the government obtained only one conviction, for the relatively minor crime of interfering with a legal process. A year after the rescue, May organized an anniversary celebration attended by 5,000 persons. The "rescue of Jerry," he wrote, had the same "significance" as "the destruction of the tea in Boston Harbor."[46]

Boston itself witnessed several confrontations over the rendition of fugitives. The Vigilance Committee of the 1840s had fallen into abeyance, but a new one emerged in the wake of the Fugitive Slave Act. It consisted of over 200 Bostonians (all men), ranging from abolitionists and business and religious leaders to persons of "the humblest pursuits and callings." Among the members was Francis G. Shaw, a wealthy businessman whose son, Robert Gould Shaw, would die commanding the celebrated black Fifty-Fourth Massachusetts Infantry during the Civil War. Austin Bearse, the captain of a schooner, the *Moby Dick* (Herman Melville's novel appeared in 1851), served as the committee's "doorkeeper." On one occasion, Bearse and an interracial party of men sailed out to a North Carolina vessel anchored offshore, seized a fugitive whom they had learned was on board, and spirited him off to the city, from which he was sent to Canada. Nearly all the members of the committee were white, but a group of black abolitionists, including Lewis Hayden and William C. Nell, did most of the day-to-day work of arranging shelter (generally in the homes and churches of black Bostonians) and transportation for fugitives who arrived in the city. A list compiled by the revitalized committee indicates that between 1850 and 1858 it aided over 400 fugitive slaves.[47]

In December 1850, members of the Boston Vigilance Committee learned that slave hunters had arrived seeking to apprehend William and Ellen Craft. Two years earlier, the couple had escaped from Georgia by train, with the light-skinned Ellen Craft disguised as a sickly planter accompanied by his personal slave. The committee distributed broadsides identifying the slave catchers, harassed them on the streets, and had them arrested for defamation for calling the Crafts slaves. The pursuers left the city, and the committee paid for the Crafts to flee to Canada and then England, where they became popular speakers on the antislavery lecture circuit. They did not return to the United States until 1869. In February 1851, a slaveowner arrived in Boston seeking to retrieve Shadrach Minkins, who had escaped from Virginia in 1850 and found a job in a Boston coffeehouse. Two deputy U.S. marshals arrested Minkins, the first fugitive seized in New England under the new law. But as the hearing before a U.S. commissioner progressed, a crowd of men led by Lewis Hayden entered the courtroom "like a black squall" and carried Minkins off. Eight, including Hayden, were put on trial for taking part in the rescue, but none was convicted. Minkins ended up in Montreal.[48]

Only twice did Boston's activists fail. In April 1851, authorities arrested Thomas Sims, a seventeen-year-old fugitive from Georgia, a month after he reached the city by stowing away on a coastal vessel. In the wake of the Minkins rescue, the police placed him under heavy guard, and although the Vigilance Committee concocted various rescue plans, none came to fruition. As he boarded the ship that would return him to bondage, a man cried out, "Sims! Preach liberty to the slaves!" When Sims arrived in Georgia, he was punished by a whipping in a public square and then sold to an owner in Mississippi. He remained a slave until escaping to Union lines in 1863. Fourteen years later, Sims obtained a job as a messenger for the Department of Justice in Washington, D.C., through the efforts of Charles Devens, who as a federal marshal had arrested him in 1851 and now served as Rutherford B. Hayes's attorney general.[49]

Like New York, Boston was home to merchants and cotton manufacturers who prospered from trade with the South, and many newspapers applauded the rendition of Sims as a vindication of the rule of law. But the strength of the abolitionist movement and the militancy of a free black community willing to resort to violence to defend runaway slaves made it extremely difficult and expensive to enforce the Fugitive Slave Act. Only one additional runaway was returned from the city. Anthony Burns, a twenty-one-year-old slave in Richmond, escaped by boat to Boston early in 1854 with the aid of a sympathetic sailor. His whereabouts became known when a letter Burns wrote to his brother was intercepted by the brother's owner. Burns's owner traveled to Boston and appeared before Edward G. Loring, a prominent jurist acting as U.S. commissioner. Hundreds of persons gathered at the courthouse, but guards repulsed a rescue attempt. Following the letter of the law, Loring ordered Burns returned to slavery. It took some 1,600 men—police, militia units, and three companies of infantry and marines—to march Burns to a waiting ship. Crowds gathered along the way, hissing at the procession. Within a year, abolitionists had raised the money for his purchase, and Burns returned to Boston. He soon departed for Oberlin, Ohio, where he attended college and studied for the ministry. He moved to Canada in 1860 and died there two years later.[50]

The *Burns* case polarized Massachusetts politics. In the *Liberator*, Garrison lamented that neither the governor nor the mayor had spoken out against the rendition. But coming at the height of the northern uproar over the Kansas-Nebraska Act, which repealed the Missouri Compromise of 1820 and opened parts of the old Louisiana Purchase to slavery, the case reinforced antislavery sentiment. Ten abolitionists were indicted for rioting; all won acquittal. A new personal liberty law, enacted in 1855 over the governor's veto, barred state and local officials from assisting in renditions, granted accused fugitives a jury trial, and required any state judge who accepted appointment as a federal commissioner to resign from the bench. Loring himself was dismissed from a position at Harvard Law School and four years later removed from his judgeship, although President James Buchanan appointed him to the federal judiciary, where he served until his death in 1877. Anthony Burns proved to be the last person remanded to slavery from anywhere in New England.[51]

Nothing remotely like these confrontations occurred in New York City. No apprehended fugitive was rescued by force in the city during the 1850s. Nonetheless, the outposts of the underground railroad intensified their operations, aided by the completion of the rail network in the state, which facilitated sending fugitives to Albany and on to Canada. In the decade before the Civil War, New York City consolidated its position as a crucial hub in a complex set of networks that stretched along the metropolitan corridor of the East Coast, assisting fugitives from Delaware, Maryland, Virginia, and the District of Columbia. Despite the new federal law, over 1,000 fugitive slaves passed through New York City in the 1850s, aided by the underground railroad on their journey to freedom.[52]

6

THE METROPOLITAN CORRIDOR: THE UNDERGROUND RAILROAD IN THE 1850S

I

In 1858, a correspondent for the *New York Tribune* identified Philadelphia and New York as "the great central stations of that glorious humanitarian institution of modern times, the Underground Railroad."[1] And the effectiveness of the underground railroad in New York City during its heyday in the 1850s stemmed in considerable measure from the revitalization of the Philadelphia Vigilance Committee under the leadership of William Still.

The youngest of eighteen sons and daughters of a Maryland slave father who had purchased his freedom and a fugitive slave mother, Still was born in Medford, New Jersey, in 1821. He moved to Philadelphia in 1844, where he worked as a handyman until the Pennsylvania Anti-Slavery Society hired him as a "clerk" and janitor at its office in 1847. These titles belied his wide-ranging responsibilities. Still ran the society's headquarters and was Philadelphia's key operative in assisting fugitives, sometimes hiding them in his own home. He kept detailed records of their stories and destinations and how he aided them, which became the basis for his 1872 book, *The Underground Railroad*. Although it recorded illegal actions, Still's journal was known in antislavery circles and beyond. Indeed, the Philadelphia Vigilance Committee publicly announced that its books were open for inspection, including "accurate accounts of the number of escapees, the amount of expenditures, receipts, etc." The most detailed record now extant of how the underground railroad operated, Still's journal lists well over 400 fugitives he received and sent on their way between 1853 and early 1857.[2]

Still's work depended on a network of white and black agents that by the early 1850s reached deep into the slave states of the Upper South. A number of sea captains "did good service" for Still on the maritime underground railroad. Thousands of vessels, of every size, shape, and description, sailed regularly between ports up and down the Atlantic coast. Numerous blacks, free and slave, worked on the region's docks and ships. Still used black sailors to carry letters between fugitive slaves in Canada and their families who remained in bondage and to local white persons the runaways had indicated could be trusted.[3]

Norfolk, Virginia, had a particularly active network. The owners of some ships, a Norfolk newspaper complained in 1850, "actually [made] the abduction of slaves a matter of trade and a source of profit." A clandestine "society among the slaves" helped fugitives find hiding places, directed them to ships, and provided forged passes. Black stevedores and crew members secreted them on board. In April 1855, a slave mother and child arrived in New York on a ship from Norfolk, having been hidden by the black cook. When the boat docked, the cook went ashore and hired a carriage to remove them. Still identified Henry Lewey, a slave known as Blue Beard, as the "dextrous" manager of the underground railroad in Norfolk. Lewey's wife Rebecca escaped on one voyage to Philadelphia and passed through New York in March 1856. Blue Beard himself later joined her in Canada. Norfolk's city fathers found it impossible to discover the names of those who assisted fugitives. When a ship en route from Norfolk to Philadelphia was driven ashore during a storm in 1855, leading to the discovery of five fugitives on board, a local newspaper hoped that when a case against the captain came to trial, "some clue may be obtained which will lead to the discovery of the president, directors and agents of the underground railroad from Norfolk."[4]

Strict state and local laws, of course, prohibited aiding slaves to escape by sea. Ships were sometimes searched, and captains and crew members jailed. In 1856, a "New York negro" who worked on a schooner about to sail from Richmond was arrested after the discovery of two absconding slaves on board. Two years later, a Virginia court sentenced William D. Bayliss, who carried fugitives, for a fee, in a false bottom on his schooner *Keziah,* to forty years in prison. He remained incarcerated in Richmond until Union forces liberated the city in 1865. Virginia passed a stringent new law for ship inspection in 1856; a local newspaper warned "the negro-loving captains of Yankee vessels" to take note. But far too many ships sailed to inspect them all.[5]

No one transported more fugitives to the North by sea than the intrepid Albert Fountain of Virginia. Little information exists about him other than his underground railroad activities. Fountain's schooner, the *City of Richmond,* which could carry forty cabin and fifty steerage passengers, established a regular packet service from Richmond and Norfolk to New York City in the early 1850s. He often stopped at Wilmington to drop off or pick up fugitives there. In Philadelphia, Fountain landed fugitives at night near League Island at the foot of Broad Street, where William Still arranged for them to be met. Thirty of the fugitive slaves who reached New York in 1855 and 1856 had escaped on Fountain's ship. A black ship carpenter worked with Fountain, informing potential runaways when his vessel was sailing. Fugitive slaves certainly appreciated Fountain's efforts. Thomas Page, who escaped from Norfolk on the *City of Richmond* in 1856, asked Still two years later to "give my love" to Fountain and to urge him to visit Boston, "as there are a number of his friends that would like to see him."

Like other captains, Fountain was not "averse to receiving compensation for his services," up to $100 per slave. He even offered to rescue the families of fugitives for a hefty fee. (Slave traders were not the only ones profiting from financial transactions involving slaves.) "Captain F.," Still wrote, "was certainly no ordinary man." On one occasion, when Fountain was about to sail from Norfolk with twenty-one slaves on board, the mayor and other officials arrived to inspect the ship. Fountain took an axe and began splintering boards on the deck, convincing them that no one had been hidden below.[6]

Most of the slaves who reached Philadelphia and New York had come by land. Many arrived from Washington, where after the death of Charles T. Torrey in 1846 and the departure of William L. Chaplin in 1850, Jacob Bigelow emerged as the key figure in a secret group of underground railroad operatives. A retired lawyer who had arrived in the nation's capital from Massachusetts in 1843 and helped to found the city's first gas company, Bigelow later wrote that he devoted "one-half of my time . . . to aid the oppressed." He raised money to purchase the freedom of slaves threatened with sale and arranged for fugitives to be sent to Wilmington and Philadelphia. In 1854, he asked Still to send a reliable man, "a white man would be best," willing to lead small groups of slaves out of the nation's capital "once or twice a week." The man would be paid and, Bigelow added, "might make a good living at it."

Unlike Torrey and Chaplin, Bigelow kept a low profile. In a city with strict laws against aiding fugitives and a police force on the lookout for runaways, he lived in constant fear of arrest. In 1855, he outlined to Still the difficulties of hiding slaves in the nation's capital. The home of "any colored citizen" could be "ransacked by constables . . . at any hour of day or night," and police offered "sharp colored men" rewards of up to $200 to betray fugitives. Bigelow signed his letters "William Penn," and urged Still to keep them in a safe place. In the letters, which alerted Still to the arrival of what Bigelow variously called freight, merchandise, or people "most anxious to travel," he inserted in brackets strong statements avowing his opposition to any actions that violated the law. When he began this practice, he told Still not to take the bracketed words seriously—they were "intended to have no significance whatever to you, only to blind the eyes of the uninitiated."[7]

Another key underground railroad operative south of the Mason-Dixon Line was Thomas Garrett, who operated an iron, coal, and hardware business in Wilmington, Delaware. A Quaker and follower of William Lloyd Garrison, Garrett kept meticulous count of the fugitives he aided over the course of three decades. By the outbreak of the Civil War he claimed that his "slave list" had surpassed 2,200. On one occasion, twenty-one slaves who had escaped together departed from Garrett's house through the rear entrance just as "the masters in pursuit arrived at his front door." Garrett seems to have served as the inspiration for the character of Simeon Halliday, a Quaker who helps slaves on their way to Canada, in *Uncle Tom's Cabin*. Some abolitionists referred to him as "President of the U. G. R. R."[8]

With large free black and Quaker communities, Wilmington, situated only five miles from the Pennsylvania state line, was a unique island of antislavery sentiment within a slave state, as much, Garrett wrote, "as in Boston, and quite as freely expressed." "The abolitionists are extremely active," wrote a local newspaper in 1849, "and we have reason to believe that the underground railroad extends a considerable distance down the state, and that branches have even entered Maryland." Free blacks in Wilmington were known to tear down handbills posted by slave catchers offering rewards for fugitives.

Garrett worked with a small group of black and white associates, including John Hunn, a Quaker who later described himself as "supt. of the underground railroad from Wilmington down the peninsula." They transported fugitives across the nearby state line in wagons, on boats, on foot, and by rail, and then put them on the "cars" (the Philadelphia, Wilmington and Baltimore Railroad) to Philadelphia. Garrett alerted Still by letter when to expect them, and Still sent men to meet them at the railroad station, the docks if they were coming by boat, or the border if they traveled on foot.[9]

Slavery had a small presence in Delaware—the census of 1860 recorded only 1,800 slaves in the state. Most of those Garrett assisted came from farther south, especially Maryland, Virginia, and Washington, D.C. Despite the waning of slavery in Delaware, however, aiding fugitives remained dangerous. A free black man, Samuel Burris, was sentenced in 1847 to be sold into slavery for fourteen years for this offense. (A white Quaker purchased Burris at auction and spirited him off to Philadelphia.) In 1848, with Supreme Court Chief Justice Roger B. Taney presiding, the U.S. Circuit Court fined Garrett $5,400 (later lowered to $1,500) and John Hunn $2,500 after two owners sued them for helping a black family of eight to escape. Garrett told the court that he thought the blacks were free, but "had I believed every one of them to be slaves, I should have done the same thing." Turning to the spectators, he declared, "If any of you know of any slave who needs assistance, send him to me."[10]

As time went on, the underground railroad in Delaware became less and less secretive. By 1855, Garrett could write that he dispatched fugitives "in open day on their way North," with little fear of the consequences. Two years later a newspaper reported a "general stampede" (as the press called group escapes) from Dover, the state capital, "by the underground railroad." In 1855 and 1856, Syd-

Gateway to Freedom

MAJOR SITES OF THE UNDERGROUND RAILROAD IN THE METROPOLITAN CORRIDOR

ney Howard Gay recorded the arrival in New York of nearly fifty fugitives who had been assisted by Garrett.[11]

Overall, however, it was common south of the Mason-Dixon Line for assistance to come from individuals unconnected with any network. Not surprisingly, fugitives tended to approach black persons for help in initiating or conducting their escapes. "Some colored people" offered Albert and Anthony Brown provisions on their way from Maryland to Wilmington, and "friendly colored people whom they happened to fall in with" gave shelter to a couple escaping from Alexandria when the wife became ill. Henry Chambers, a Maryland slave who accompanied his owner on a visit to Wilmington, was told by a local black man "how he could get clear" of slavery. The cook on a vessel sailing from Richmond asked Henry Johnson "if he would not like his freedom," and then concealed him on board for the journey to New York. Another ship's cook, with the approval of the captain so long as "his name not be used," hid William Thompson on board for a fee of five dollars. A group of sailors in Petersburg offered a slave named Charles passage to New York in exchange for helping them load the vessel.[12]

Some white southerners were also willing to assist fugitive slaves. White friends in Washington gave James Anderson the money that enabled him to hire Joseph Becket, a free black man who, for a fee, guided fugitives to the Pennsylvania border. Andrew Jackson, a slave from Cecil County, Maryland, told Gay that "a white man . . . piloted him some 4 or 5 miles on the road, only charging him 25 c. for his trouble." A white woman provided extraordinary assistance to David Lewis of Leesburg, Virginia. Lewis had permission to take his owner's horse to visit his mother. His female companion hired a carriage and, along with her daughter, accompanied him on a journey to Harrisburg, posing as a woman traveling with her coachman. Thus, they were able to traverse the fifty miles to the Pennsylvania border "unmolested by day light," and to stay overnight in a hotel in Chambersburg, where the proprietor told them "they would find friends in Harrisburg."[13]

Not all slaves who passed through Delaware and eastern Maryland went directly to Philadelphia. Their first stop was often Chester County in southeastern Pennsylvania, "the most enlightened county in the state" according to one abolitionist, but also a place that witnessed frequent incursions from slave catchers and kidnappers from Maryland, and whose local press castigated free blacks as a burden to society. Nonetheless, Chester was home to a sizable free black community whose churches sheltered fugitives, and to numerous farm families, mostly Quakers, who forwarded them to Still or directly to underground railroad operatives in upstate New York. Black and Quaker underground railroad networks in the county overlapped. Some of the blacks involved in the Christiana riot of 1851 worked as tenants on Quaker-owned farms. Samuel Ringgold Ward, who escaped from Maryland in the 1820s with his parents and became a prominent abolitionist, later wrote that when slave catchers arrived, "Quakers threw all manner of *peaceful* obstacles in their way, while the Negroes made it a little too *hot* for their comfort." Family connections linked the Quakers involved in these activities. Thomas Garrett's wife Rachel was the sister of Isaac Mendenhall, an underground railroad activist in Kennett Square, Pennsylvania. A group of Quaker abolitionists in and around that village a dozen miles from Wilmington organized themselves as the Progressive Friends. Garrett regularly attended meetings there in the 1850s. So did Oliver Johnson, who worked with Sydney Howard Gay on the *National Anti-Slavery Standard*.[14]

The Lewis family was typical of the Quaker clans in Chester County connected to the underground railroad. Graceanna Lewis, a niece of a founder of the American Anti-Slavery Society and later the country's leading female botanist and ornithologist, grew up in an abolitionist Quaker household. "There was never a time," she later wrote, "when our house was not a shelter for those escaping slavery." A member of the Progressive Friends, she published an accusatory missive to other Quakers bearing the formidable title *An Appeal to Those Members of the Society of Friends Who, Knowing the Principles of the Abolitionists, Stand Aloof from the Anti-Slavery Enterprise.* Among other fugitives, Lewis hid four men, including William Parker, on their way to Canada after the Christiana riot.

Lewis and her friends formed a "sewing society" to ensure that they had large quantities of "clean and nicely mended clothing on hand" so that fugitives could travel by rail without looking like slaves. She often forwarded them by wagon to nearby Phoenixville, where the Quaker farmer Elijah F. Pennypacker, according to Still, assisted "the majority of fugitives" proceeding through southeastern Pennsylvania. Farther west, the Quaker couple William and Phoebe Wright of York Springs (who had sheltered James W. C. Pennington in the late 1820s) received runaways from Delaware, Maryland, and Washington on their farm a dozen miles from the Maryland border. So did the black abolitionist William Whipper, who ran a successful lumber and shipping business in nearby Columbia and owned a small railroad. Whipper sent many fugitives by rail to the Wrights, directly to Still in Philadelphia, or north to New York State and Canada. By the 1850s, what had been a "rough network" of safe houses in southern Pennsylvania had evolved into a well-organized system for assisting fugitives.[15]

Once they crossed the Mason-Dixon Line into southern Pennsylvania, fugitives encountered many persons prepared to help them on their way, including militant free blacks willing, as evidenced at Christiana, to employ violence to do so. The Record of Fugitives compiled by Sydney Howard Gay in 1855 and 1856 reflects the wide range of individuals in that region who assisted fugitives on their way to Philadelphia and New York. Among them were the baggage master at the Harrisburg railroad station, who "befriended" runaways and sent them to Philadelphia, and a white person in Little York who took a fugitive man and wife to a black church. Names of many of the underground railroad operatives in southeastern Pennsylvania appear in Gay's Record, including William Whipper in Columbia and the Quakers William Wright, Mahlon B. Linton, Rowland Johnson, and Elijah Pennypacker. The role of the Friends in assisting fugitives was known to absconding slaves. In December 1855, Henry Cooper escaped on foot from Middletown, Maryland, to Pennsylvania. When he reached North Chester, he "stopped at a house and inquired for Quakers."[16]

The experience of one large, extended family of fugitives illustrates how the underground railroad operated in southeastern Pennsylvania in the years before the Civil War. On the night of October 16, 1855, Harriet Shepherd and her five children, ranging in age from three to seventeen, along with her brother John Bright and his wife and three teenage sons and a stepson, "borrowed" two horse-drawn carriages and departed from Chestertown, Maryland, "for a free country." The next morning they arrived in Wilmington, a little over fifty miles to the north, where they "bought some cakes" at a local store and asked a "colored man . . . to direct them to a Quaker." He brought them to Thomas Garrett, who sent them "hastily onward for fear of pursuit." That evening the group reached the Longwood Meeting House in Kennett Square, Pennsylvania, where a meeting of the Progressive Friends was in progress. One of the members put them up for the night, and on October 28 the two families arrived at Graceanna Lewis's home in Kimberton. "The case seems to us one of unusual danger," Lewis wrote to William Still, and she decided to separate the two families. Lewis sent Shepherd and her children "off of the usual route, and to a place where I do not think they can remain many days." Soon, they proceeded to Philadelphia, where they arrived on November 8. The Brights were sent to the home of Elijah Pennypacker in Phoenixville, from where their sons and stepson continued on to stay with Mahlon B. Linton in Newtown, north of Philadelphia. This family did not reach William Still's office until early December. All were eventually forwarded to Gay's office in New York and sent on their way northward.[17]

Until the passage of the Fugitive Slave Law, many runaway slaves remained in southern Pennsylvania, "scattered among the rural population" as farm laborers. Graceanna Lewis recalled numerous fugitives who worked in her family's home and on their farm. But many runaways who had established homes in the region departed in the 1850s. It was "far better" for them to head for Canada, William Still wrote, than to remain in Pennsylvania, given the "dread and danger hanging over the head of the fugitive."[18]

Those fugitives who reached Philadelphia were aided by the city's revitalized Vigilance Committee. The original Philadelphia Vigilant Committee, founded in 1837, had ceased to function effectively in the mid-1840s. After a series of renditions from the city, participants at a meeting in December 1852 organized the new committee "for the protection and assistance of fugitive slaves." The abolitionist James Miller McKim opened the gathering by noting that for some years "the friends of the fugitive" had been "embarrassed, for the want of a properly constructed, active" organization. With the old committee "disorganized and scattered," aid had been extended "by individuals, . . . in a very irregular manner." The new organization had nineteen members, although as generally was the case, a small acting committee did most of the day-to-day work. This consisted of four persons: the white abolitionist Passmore Williamson; the prominent black businessman Jacob C. White; the black antislavery veteran Nathaniel Depree; and William Still, the group's secretary. Mindful of earlier allegations of misuse of funds by Dr. James G. Bias, the meeting instructed Still to keep careful records, "especially of the money received and expended on behalf of every case claiming interposition." Still recorded every expense, down to six cents' postage on a letter to New Bedford.[19]

The Philadelphia Vigilance Committee advertised its meetings in local newspapers and held public events, including a gathering in 1854 to welcome Henry "Box" Brown on a visit to the city where he had first arrived in a crate five years earlier. Its fund-raising meetings and public appeals for money forthrightly announced what it did. "Fugitives from southern injustice are coming thick and fast," read one such notice in 1854. "The underground railroad never before did so large a business as it is doing now." Still also helped raise money for the purchase of slaves whose owners agreed to free them. In one poignant instance, a man walked into the antislavery office, explaining that he had purchased his own freedom in 1849 and now sought assistance in retrieving his wife and children. He turned out to be Peter Still, William's older brother. One of two children who had been left behind when his mother escaped from slavery, he had been sold at the age of six more than forty years earlier, before William's birth. Peter Still departed with letters of introduction to abolitionists in the North and Canada and managed to secure the daunting sum of $5,000 to liberate his family.[20]

In addition to his other activities, William Still was a prolific writer who published articles in black Canadian periodicals. He wrote about fugitives he assisted, although "for prudential reasons" he kept "dark" their names and the details of their escapes. Still's pieces also included commentaries on national affairs. In 1857, to enlighten those who had "fled for refuge," he published a long explanation in the *Provincial Freeman* of the *Dred Scott* decision. In an essay in June 1854, Still wrote, "A civil war or a dissolution of the Union may be upon us ere we realize it."[21]

Fugitive slaves were hardly safe when they reached Philadelphia. On one occasion in 1856, a sympathetic Philadelphia policeman came to Still's office to warn the Vigilance Committee to "be on the lookout" for a group of fugitives from Baltimore, for whom a sizable reward had been posted. But, during the 1850s, ten were remanded from the city in accordance with the Fugitive Slave Act, and others were removed without any legal proceedings. Early in 1857, Dr. James G. Bias and three other men posted a notice in a Philadelphia newspaper warning "all self-emancipated persons in this community" that "slave-hunters" were "lurking about the city." Thus, Still generally sent fugitives northward as quickly as he could, sometimes to New England or directly to upstate New York, but in about half the cases to New York City.[22]

Although fugitives reached New York by many routes, a considerable majority of the more than 200 persons listed in Sydney Howard Gay's Record of Fugitives had been forwarded from Philadelphia. Generally, Still put them on a train, telegraphed ahead announcing their impending arrival, and provided instructions on how to reach Gay's office. An abolitionist from Vermont recalled how, in 1856, while visiting Gay, a dispatch arrived from Still giving notice of " 'six parcels' coming by the train. And before I left the office, the 'parcels' came in, each on two legs." Frequently, someone from Gay's office met fugitives at the ferry terminal in New Jersey or Manhattan. Usually, this was Louis Napoleon, who lived in lower Manhattan until the late 1850s. Gay knew families willing to harbor fugitive slaves, and for a time, Napoleon rented "a room down town" to accommodate them.[23]

It is impossible to know precisely how many fugitive slaves Still dispatched to New York City, since normally he simply entered "forwarded" in his journal, without a destination. On some occasions, he did specifically mention New York. In April 1853, a group of slaves—six men and women from three different owners—arrived in Philadelphia from Baltimore. Still "forwarded them to the Committee in New York" at a cost of $14.50 for "bread, carriage hire and fare." Charlotte Harris arrived in Philadelphia from Wilmington with her nine-year-old son in July 1853. "They were satisfactorily examined," Still recorded, "and forwarded to N. Y. Expenses 5.25." Another fugitive dispatched by Still to New York was John Henry Hill, a literate twenty-five-year-old carpenter from Virginia who somehow managed to escape while being transported to be sold at a slave auction in Richmond. Hill hid out in that city for nine months; eventually he managed to get to Norfolk (with a pass he himself had written) and secured a place on the *City of Richmond*, Albert Fountain's vessel. Hill disembarked in Philadelphia and was soon sent to New York and on to Toronto. His wife and two children, all free, joined him in Canada.[24]

Isaac D. Williams escaped from Virginia in 1854, and after many harrowing experiences, he found his way with another fugitive to Still's office. He later related how Still and his contacts in New York operated. "After a very pleasant sojourn of several days, during which we recruited [sic] ourselves from the hardships we had endured," Williams wrote, "Mr. Still took us himself to the train and saw us off for New York City, where a man named [Jacob R.] Gibbs was to meet us. He came right into our car at the depot and reshipped us on to Syracuse, where we were to be met by a Mr. [Jermain] Loguen." Not long afterward they arrived in Canada.[25]

II

As the networks assisting fugitives consolidated to the city's south, the underground railroad in New York, in the words of the *Tribune*, did "a safe and increasing business." What Lewis Tappan called the "friendly rivalry" between the New York State Vigilance Committee and the group operating out of Sydney Howard Gay's office heightened activity in the city. Both national abolitionist organizations, the *Times* noted, "own stock in the underground railroad, and make no bones of drumming up passengers for it." On a single day in 1852, the *Tribune* reported, there passed through the city "no fewer than forty-one human chattels . . . all safely landed in Canada."[26]

A third organization assisting fugitive slaves, the Committee of Thirteen, also operated in New York in the early 1850s. It had been established in the wake of the passage of the Fugitive Slave Law. This group of black abolitionists from New York City and Brooklyn included Dr. James McCune Smith, the publisher Philip A. Bell, and, before his departure from the city, William P. Powell, owner of the Colored Seamen's Boarding House. (After Powell sailed for England, Albro Lyons and his wife Mary operated the establishment and continued to provide a hiding place for fugitive slaves.) Two "offshoots" quickly followed, committees of nine in Brooklyn, and five in the village of Williamsburg. All these groups offered legal assistance to fugitives and protection against slave catchers. Junius C. Morel, a member of the Committee of Thirteen, was a resident of the Brooklyn village of Weeksville (located in present-day Crown Heights), whose population of 366 in 1850 made it one of the country's largest free African American settlements. Weeksville offered a modicum of safety from kidnappers and slave catchers, and the committee used it as a place to hide fugitives.[27]

The Committee of Thirteen seems to have survived for only a few years. While it lasted, like other groups involved with the underground railroad, it operated both openly and in secret. In December 1851, it presented a memorial to the Hungarian patriot Lajos Kossuth, who had arrived in New York after the failed revolution of 1848. The committee identified the Hungarian uprising with "the struggles now going on in our own country" against slavery. When Governor Washington Hunt called on the New York legislature to appropriate funds for black colonization, the Committee of Thirteen organized rallies to expose the "ignorance and weakness" of Hunt's message. In April 1852, the committee held a public gathering at which it urged runaway slaves to leave the city, unless they were prepared to "send to perdition" owners intent on their recapture. Charles B. Ray, who had succeeded Gerrit Smith as head of the New York State Vigilance Committee, spoke at a number of these meetings. But the Committee of Thirteen established a greater reputation for discretion than Ray's own organization. Early in 1852, the Philadelphia Vigilance Committee forwarded to New York "for safe-keeping and disposal" one of the "Christiana patriots" (evidently a man who had escaped from jail after being arrested for participation in that affray). He carried with him a letter that explained, "We would have sent him to the New York Vigilance Committee; but as his case requires great secrecy, we prefer sending him to the Committee of Thirteen, as we have mutually acted together in these cases."[28]

Nonetheless, in the early 1850s most of the work of aiding fugitives continued to be done by the New York State Vigilance Committee. Beginning in late 1850, it had to deal not only with fugitives from the South, but also with blacks long resident in Pennsylvania and New Jersey who arrived in New York "on their way North or East, to escape from real or supposed danger of being recaptured and returned to slavery." In 1853, the committee claimed to have aided nearly 700 persons in the preceding two years. Along with forwarding fugitives to Boston, New Bedford, and Albany, it posted placards around the city warning when slave catchers had arrived, and raised funds for the purchase of slave relatives of black New Yorkers. "I have had so many of these cases recently," Ray wrote to Gerrit Smith at his upstate home, asking for financial aid, that he could not go back to the same donors in the city. Lewis Tappan remained a key "resident director," as the *New York Herald* called him. He attended most of the Vigilance Committee's meetings, generally held in private.[29]

The Vigilance Committee played a major role in one of the more dramatic escapes of this period, the flight of Anna Maria Weems, the teenage daughter of a free black man from Maryland and his slave wife. One daughter had managed to escape to the North and was adopted by Henry Highland Garnet, the fugitive slave who became a Presbyterian minister. In 1852, Anna Maria's father learned that the owner was planning to sell his wife and their other children. He embarked on a campaign to raise money to purchase their freedom. Charles B. Ray and Lewis Tappan coordinated efforts to gather funds, much of it collected in England as the Weems Ransom Fund, and managed to buy the freedom of the mother and an older sister. Two sons, however, were sold to an owner in Alabama.

Efforts to purchase Anna Maria proved fruitless, and Jacob Bigelow and Ray decided she should be "run off"—a difficult project since she slept in the bedroom of her owners. Eventually, in 1855, Bigelow managed to get her to Washington, where she remained for eight weeks. Then, dressed in boy's clothing, she was taken by carriage to William Still's office in Philadelphia. From there Anna Maria proceeded to New York, where Ray and Tappan received her. She spent Thanksgiving at Tappan's home in Brooklyn Heights. A few days later, accompanied by the black minister Amos N. Freeman, she embarked by train for Canada. On December 1, 1855, they crossed the Niagara Falls Suspension Bridge, a recently opened rail link between the two countries, and Anna Maria was delivered to an aunt and uncle who lived in a black settlement. By 1858, the rest of the family, including all her brothers, had been purchased.[30]

Despite Tappan's largesse, the committee, as always, found itself short of funds. It subsisted on local contributions, donations from Great Britain, and money raised by sympathetic groups in upstate New York, such as a "Ladies" society in Rochester, which gathered funds for the "Gentlemen's Vigilance Committee of New York." "Fugitives," Henry Ward Beecher declared in 1852, "make their appearance continually, pleading with a pathos deeper than words, for shelter and aid in their flight," and while the Vigilance Committee had spent $2,000 in the past year, "much more is needed." By 1855, the committee had run out of money, and the treasurer had to advance $100 from his own pocket to keep the organization afloat.[31]

In one notable instance, the Vigilance Committee's system of protecting fugitive slaves disastrously broke down. Stephen Pembroke and his teenage sons Robert and Jacob, the enslaved brother and nephews of James W. C. Pennington, absconded on foot from Sharpsburg, Maryland, on May 21, 1854. Upon reaching Chambersburg, Pennsylvania, thirty-three miles away, they boarded a train for Philadelphia, where they arrived the following day. William Still immediately communicated with Pennington and on May 24 dispatched his relatives, along with several other fugitives, by train to the New York State Vigilance Committee. Professional slave hunters, reportedly alerted via carrier pigeon by the Pembrokes' owners, managed to board the same train. The three fugitives alighted unobserved in Newark and made their way to New York City, where they were put up in a home the Vigilance Committee considered safe. But before daybreak, the slave catchers and a deputy marshal broke in and hurried the three before Commissioner George W. Morton. After a brief hearing that began at nine o'clock in the morning, Morton ordered them returned to the South. That evening, the Pembrokes were taken by ferry to New Jersey "under a strong guard of policemen" and put on a train for Baltimore. It all happened so quickly that no attorney was present to represent the slaves. When Erastus D. Culver turned up at the commissioner's office, the hearing had already ended.[32]

The Vigilance Committee and its supporters were stunned by the turn of events. A letter to the *New York Tribune,* signed "many sympathizers," complained that "a more barbarous star chamber proceeding was never witnessed in New York." Abolitionists managed to raise $1,000 to purchase Stephen Pembroke's freedom. Early in July 1854, a meeting at Pennington's church celebrated his brother's return to the city. But his sons remained in slavery; they had been "sold twice before my face," Pembroke told the gathering.

The debacle underscored once again the dangers facing fugitives in New York City. A " 'stool-pigeon' or traitor," William Still suspected, had revealed the hiding place. Still concluded that the capture of the Pembrokes revealed serious weaknesses in the New York committee's methods. He had "spared no pains to render their success sure," he complained, and the Pembrokes had arrived in New York with "sufficient time, it would seem, for their friends to have placed them beyond the reach of their infernal pursuers." He chastised Pennington for ignoring "how imminent their danger was." For "a length of time afterwards," Still later wrote, the Philadelphia Committee "felt disposed, when sending, to avoid New York as much as possible."[33]

Part of the problem may well have been the collapse of the American and Foreign Anti-Slavery Society, with which the Vigilance Committee was closely connected. Its last annual report was published in 1853. Soon afterward, Tappan noted that the society was "doing very little." In 1854, it dissolved. Many of the members transferred their energies to the American Missionary Association or to a new organization, the American Abolition Society, which adopted the position that the Constitution had actually outlawed slavery. Lewis Tappan became its president. At the same time, Tappan and Charles B. Ray, the head of the Vigilance Committee, had a falling-out over allegations that Ray had misused funds raised for the "ransom" of the Weems family. Tappan discovered that Ray had "invested" some of the money in real estate "for his own benefit." Ray explained that he felt he deserved monetary compensation for all the time he had spent on the case.[34]

Whatever the merits of the dispute, it did not bode well for the vitality of the New York State Vigilance Committee. The organization continued to maintain a presence in New York City until the eve of the Civil War. But in 1857, the Glasgow association that had been sending funds to the committee announced that assistance was "less needed" than in the past, since "a smaller number of fugitives are now passing through [its] hands." It added, "Some of them, as we are informed, are receiving aid from another Society"—undoubtedly Sydney Howard Gay's operation.[35]

Gay and the men Wendell Phillips called his "runners" had continued to assist fugitives in the early 1850s, but so secretly that information about their activities in these years is virtually nonexistent. Gay's newspaper, the *National Anti-Slavery Standard,* published information about fugitive slave cases in New York courts and reports of escapes and rescues in other parts of the North, but it said virtually nothing about the underground railroad in New York City. One editorial did praise the work of assisting fugitives as "an important branch" of the struggle against slavery, and noted that activities "that would excite the astonishment and admiration" of readers had of necessity been kept secret—one of Gay's few public intimations of his own involvement.[36]

Gay happened to be in Boston in June 1854 at the time of the rendition of Anthony Burns, mentioned in the previous chapter. He was galvanized by the spectacle of troops marching Burns to the dock amid the "groans and hisses" of crowds lining the streets. "I have seen a sight to remember and . . . to tell of," he wrote to his wife. He hoped it would be "the opening scene of a new history of Massachusetts." The event reinforced Gay's commitment to assisting fugitive slaves. A few months later, William Still resumed sending fugitives to New York. With the New York State Vigilance Committee in disarray, leadership of the underground railroad in the city passed to the group operating out of the American Anti-Slavery Society's office and headed by Sydney Howard Gay.[37]

III

Shortly after the Civil War, in his history of the sectional conflict, the antislavery politician Henry Wilson identified Gay as the leader of a "devoted band" of underground railroad agents in New York, a city with "southern connections, interests, and prejudices against the African race and its friends." Many recent historical works on the underground railroad, however, completely ignore Gay's activities. Nonetheless, by the mid-1850s Gay's office had become the major depot in New York City. It stood at the nexus of two key sets of underground railroad networks: those in southeastern Pennsylvania centered on rural free black and abolitionist Quaker families and William Still's office in Philadelphia, and the vigilance committees in New England and upstate New York. By this time, when Still referred to the "Vigilance Committee in New York," he meant Gay's office, and virtually every slave Still mentioned sending to the city in 1855 and 1856 turned up in Gay's Record of Fugitives. Compared to the complex networks of southeastern Pennsylvania, however, Gay oversaw a skeletal operation. He relied mainly on the two black men who worked in his office—Louis Napoleon and a printer, William H. Leonard—to both of whom he made numerous small payments for assisting fugitives. Napoleon was Gay's key associate, meeting fugitives when they arrived, finding lodging for them, and escorting them to the docks or train station for their onward journeys.[38]

James S. Gibbons and his wife, Abigail, also offered assistance. On one occasion, Gibbons alerted Gay that Sarah Moore, a fugitive slave who had escaped from North Carolina in the 1840s and was now living in New Haven, was in danger of recapture. Evidently her husband, who had "abandoned her" and taken their three small children with him, had betrayed her to authorities. Gay immediately dispatched Napoleon to find Moore and take her to Albany.

But at the railroad depot in New Haven, Napoleon noticed a man who matched Moore's description of her owner, accompanied by the same federal marshal who a year earlier had arrested Stephen Pembroke and his sons and returned them to slavery. Napoleon decided that he and Moore should get off the train in Springfield and travel to Albany the following day. From there, Moore proceeded alone to Syracuse while Napoleon returned to New Haven. Somehow, Napoleon located the children and arranged with a black woman to "walk off" with them. He then brought the children to Syracuse; he "never saw such a time," Gay recorded, as when the family was reunited. Gay carefully noted the money he had laid out—$64.74 for lodging and train fares.[39]

The number of underground railroad agents operating in New York was tiny, but many other individuals proved ready to assist fugitives and knew how to do so. William Thompson, who escaped by boat and train from Virginia, asked to be directed to a black church when he reached New York. "The persons in charge took him in" and sent for someone from Gay's office. The fugitive John Richardson arrived from Philadelphia thanks to a "colored man by the name of Jackson employed on one of the steamers to N.Y.," who "gave him a passage here, and put him in Napoleon's hands." Charles, mentioned earlier, a fugitive from Petersburg, was discovered by the captain hiding on a vessel and resigned himself to being sent back to his owner. But he "fell in with a coloured man" when the ship reached New York, "who, on learning his story," helped him escape from the vessel. Blacks working on the docks frequently directed to the antislavery office runaways who arrived on ships or by ferry from the rail depot in New Jersey. Although in the mid-1850s Fernando Wood, a notoriously pro-southern Democrat, was serving as New York's mayor, some policemen sympathized with fugitives. In an undated note, Gay recorded that "officer Brady" had brought the fugitive Elizabeth Anderson to his office.[40]

As late as 1855, James McCune Smith called New York a "poor neglected city" when it came to abolitionism. Secrecy was at a premium. Nonetheless, Gay kept detailed records of how much he expended helping fugitives with accommodations, clothing, and train and boat tickets, and where the money came from. "Sydney has the fugitive matter entirely in his own hands," his wife wrote in a letter to an abolitionist in Boston, "and takes care that no unnecessary expenditure of money is made." In 1855, Gay recorded donations of $48.66 from the "Ladies' Society" of Dundee, Scotland, and $94.50 from a "Ladies' Fair" in New York City. But expenses often exceeded income. When money ran short, Gay had to dig into his own pocket or into the funds the American Anti-Slavery Society provided for publication of the *Standard*. In 1856, "cash received" totaled $277, but expenses, including Napoleon's pay, amounted to $457, leaving a balance due to Gay of $180.[41]

When Gay was absent, Napoleon sometimes had to borrow money hurriedly from other abolitionists. Frequently, he turned to Rowland Johnson, a wealthy Quaker merchant dealing in Chinese goods who lived in Orange, New Jersey, not far from Manhattan. In April 1856, Abigail Hopper Gibbons persuaded Johnson to advance twelve dollars to Napoleon, and she promised it would be "refunded." The following month, with Gay home because of illness, Napoleon had to ask Johnson for another loan "to defray the expenses of 4 fugitives now here on their way to New Bedford." Gay was alert to the possibility that some who claimed to be fugitives were impostors. In 1857, a man appeared who claimed to have escaped from Virginia, but "discrepancies in his story made it doubtful." Nonetheless, Gay found a job for him on a ship and paid someone thirty-seven cents to "get his trunk for him."[42]

Despite simultaneously editing the *National Anti-Slavery Standard* and serving on the executive committee of the AASS and as president of the New York Anti-Slavery Society (an auxiliary of the AASS founded in 1853), Gay devoted much of his time in the 1850s to his underground railroad activities. In a letter of 1853, written after attending an executive committee meeting where he listened to an "attack on the Standard" and a proposal (not approved) to abandon the newspaper or appoint a new editor, Gay thought of resigning as editor and questioned the significance of abolitionist agitation. "We are doing so little, and much of that little wrong," he mused. But his work with fugitive slaves was certainly significant.[43]

To be sure, things did not always go smoothly. In August 1855, after Still resumed dispatching fugitives to New York City, Gay wrote a letter asking him to send them with "careful directions to this office," adding:

> There is now no other sure place, but the office, or Gibbs', that I could advise you to send such persons. Those to me, therefore, must come in office hours. In a few days, however, Napoleon will have a room down town, and at odd times they can be sent there. . . . When it is possible I wish you would advise me two days before a shipment of your intention, as Napoleon is not always on hand to look out for them on short notice. In special cases you might advise me by Telegraph thus: "One M. (or one F.) this morning."

A little over a year later, William H. Leonard, the black printer who worked on the *Standard*, complained to Still about the timing and accuracy of his messages. "Your favor of Thursday last was rather inopportune," he wrote. "It was only by chance that I was in the office. They had no person to pilot them to the office. Napoleon not being on hand. Ray not at home. On all such days we are closed." Leonard also noted that Napoleon had stopped going to the wharf because "the last 2 or 3 lots you sent came by [South]

Amboy, when your dispatch directed us to Jersey City. How does it happen?"[44]

In 1857, Jacob R. Gibbs, who had maintained a place at 59 Thompson Street to which associates who worked on Hudson River ferries directed fugitives, moved to San Francisco. There he described himself as "ex-agent of the underground Rail Road." His departure placed an even greater burden on Napoleon, who had moved uptown to 97 West Thirty-Third Street after marrying Elizabeth Seaman, a widow with two young children, in 1855. The year after Gibbs moved, Gay remonstrated to James Miller McKim, about Still's methods:

> I hate to complain, but I must state a fact. Still is in the habit of sending men on here by a train that arrives about 3 a.m. Unless it is *absolutely imperative,* . . . it should not be done. To meet such persons, Napoleon has to be out by one o'clock, go three miles, take the men the three miles back, and to keep them until late in the afternoon. This is very unnecessary labor, which all falls upon an old man [Napoleon was in his mid-fifties] who is paid a mere trifle for doing it. . . . Two or three days ago Still telegraphed late in the day. Napoleon had gone home. . . . And we have nobody in the office . . . to do that duty for him.[45]

The mention of Ray and Gibbs, both associated with the New York State Vigilance Committee, in these letters by Gay and Leonard underscores the cooperation between the two underground railroad outposts in New York City. Nonetheless, as had been the case since the days of David Ruggles, the day-to-day operations of the underground railroad in New York depended on the efforts of a small, overburdened group of dedicated activists.

IV

Sometime in 1856, Gay jotted down the names of "Agents of the U. G. R. R." It was a very partial list, consisting of only ten individuals. South of New York, it included only Jacob Bigelow, in Washington, D.C. Gay failed to mention even Thomas Garrett and William Still; because of their central role in sending fugitives to New York, he may have felt their names were superfluous. As in the 1840s, Gay continued to send fugitives to Joseph Ricketson Jr. in New Bedford and Francis Jackson in Boston, but the only person he mentioned in New England was Josephus Silliman, a black laborer living in New Haven. The majority of the agents on the list lived in Albany and Syracuse. Gay's list underscores the central role that upstate New York had assumed by the 1850s. The vast majority of runaway slaves sent onward from New York City headed to Canada via that region, where antislavery sentiment had spread rapidly and the underground railroad operated with amazing impunity. The *New York Times* reported in 1857 that a fugitive slave on his way to Canada had been welcomed in the "vestibule of the Capitol" in Albany and "received many congratulations from the gentlemen there congregated."[46]

In Albany, the key underground railroad agent was the black activist Stephen Myers, who had been aiding fugitives since the 1830s. Born in 1800, Myers worked for a time as a steward on steamboats plying the Hudson River between Albany and New York. He became a leading abolitionist, editing an antislavery newspaper and taking part in the unsuccessful campaign to repeal the property qualification limiting black voting in New York. Myers lectured widely in the capital region and western Massachusetts. But in the 1850s, most of his activity centered on assisting fugitives. Indeed, the census of 1860 lists his occupation as "agent"—Myers served as "general agent" of the twelve-man, predominantly black

Albany Vigilance Committee, whose members included, among others, a tailor, boat captain, pharmacist, lumber merchant, two barbers, a minister of the African Wesleyan Church, and a Catholic priest. Myers's wife, Harriet, worked with him, providing food and clothing for fugitives in their Albany home.[47]

In 1858, the Albany correspondent of the *Journal of Commerce* in New York City complained that he had witnessed Myers marching "six runaway negroes . . . through the streets" in broad daylight. They were headed for the offices of a local Republican newspaper, where they were "hospitably entertained." By 1860, Myers reported that since 1852 he had assisted 654 runaway slaves. In one letter to Francis Jackson of the Boston Vigilance Committee, Myers noted that he received fugitives from "three different branches of the underground road"—presumably via Boston, New York, and southern Pennsylvania. He dispatched most by rail, headed for Syracuse and Canada West (on one occasion on a train carrying Mormon migrants bound for Utah), or north to Montreal. He also found employment for some on nearby farms, where he considered them safe.[48]

Mindful that in 1842 he had been charged with fiscal malfeasance by a white-owned newspaper (a "false, wicked, low and contemptible" accusation, he insisted), Myers had his account books examined by a "committee of gentlemen" each month. He raised money via "subscriptions and agents" and received assistance not only from abolitionists but also from antislavery politicians, including Thurlow Weed, the editor of the influential *Albany Argus* (who donated $100 each year), Senator William H. Seward, and the state's first Republican governors, John A. King and Edwin D. Morgan. Myers was particularly grateful for the monetary and other assistance he received from William Jay and his son John Jay II. He informed the latter in 1860 that his new grandson had been named William John Jay Myers: "I desire to have one colored child to bear that name." Myers kept 10 percent of what he collected as a salary. "It is a wonder to all his friends," a writer in the black newspaper *Weekly Anglo-African* wrote in 1859, that Myers "raises enough money to meet his actual expenses, to say nothing of remunerating him for the industrious and sacrificing labors of himself and his family." Sometimes, he did not. "We are in debt and have not one dollar in hand," Myers lamented in January 1860.[49]

Gay directed more fugitive slaves to Syracuse, halfway between Albany and the border with Canada, than to all other destinations combined. The site of the Jerry McHenry rescue of 1851, Syracuse was known as the Canada of the United States because of its pervasive antislavery atmosphere. Ira H. Cobb, a merchant and one of the agents listed by Gay, lived in the same housing complex as the county sheriff; evidently, he did not fear arrest for his underground railroad activities. In Jermain W. Loguen, Syracuse boasted one of the most effective underground railroad operatives in the entire North. Born a slave on a small plantation in Tennessee in 1813, Loguen had escaped in 1834. His owner's family knew how to hold a grudge. Twenty-six years later, in 1860, the wife, who still held Loguen's mother as a slave, wrote to him asking for $1,000 for the horse he took while escaping, in which case she would relinquish all claim to him. Loguen replied with indignation: "You say, 'you know we raised you as we did our own children.' Woman, did you raise your own children for the market? Did you raise them for the whipping post? . . . I meet the proposition with unutterable scorn and contempt."

In 1834, after a harrowing journey, Loguen reached Canada. Seven years later he moved to Syracuse, where he became an African Methodist Episcopal Zion minister. From then on, Loguen later wrote, "scarcely a week passed" when he did not shelter fugitive slaves on their way to Canada. He himself fled across the border after taking part in the McHenry rescue; he was in danger, if arrested, of being sent back to the South. Loguen returned to Syracuse, however, in 1852, and soon became known as the city's "underground railroad king." In his autobiography, published in 1859 as a fund-raising venture, with considerable assistance from a local white abolitionist, he claimed to have aided more than 1,500 fugitives. When Loguen died, an obituary in a black newspaper declared, "With the exception of William Still of Philadelphia, he was instrumental in freeing more slaves from the American house of bondage than any other man."[50]

Loguen's operations were flagrantly public. A local Democratic newspaper complained that he "drives along his wagonloads of deluded fugitives" in open daylight. In a letter published in *Frederick Douglass' Paper,* Loguen referred to himself as "the agent and keeper of the Underground Railroad Depot" in Syracuse. Sympathetic local newspapers reported on the arrival of groups of runaways "at Loguen's" and published annual reports on the number of fugitives who had passed through the city (200 in 1855 according to one account). Loguen held "donation parties" to raise money, placed notices in newspapers seeking employment for fugitives who "would like to stop on this side" of the Canadian border, and publicized the presence of slave catchers in the city, calling on residents to run them out of town.

Loguen opened his financial records to the public. Most of the money came from bake sales and bazaars organized by Ladies' Aid Societies in upstate New York, but some funds arrived from England and Ireland. In 1857, six abolitionists published a "card" in local newspapers, stating that the work previously done by the Fugitive Aid Society would henceforth be undertaken alone by Loguen, and asked for donations to support him and his family and to maintain "this depot on the Underground Railroad." Henceforth, "all fugitives from slavery, coming this way, may be directed to him." In 1859, Loguen held a fund-raising event at his home. The house, according to a newspaper report, was "crowded with visitors and friends of the Underground Railroad," including "about thirty fugitives" who had found employment in and around Syracuse.[51]

The underground railroad agents in Syracuse with whom Gay was in contact ran the gamut of abolitionist outlooks. Loguen served on the business committee of the AASS. "Set me down as a *Liberator* man," he wrote in 1854, with the one exception that "my hands will fight a slaveholder." (Garrison, a pacifist, still hoped that Loguen would come to realize "that it is solely because of war and violence that slavery exists.") Loguen also lectured in upstate New York for the Liberty and Radical Abolition parties and worked for Lewis Tappan's American Missionary Association. Samuel J. May, to whom Gay also directed fugitives, paid for the passage of individuals to Canada out of his own pocket and was president of the Syracuse Fugitive Aid Society until it dissolved. His home served as the main reception center for fugitives until Loguen's house replaced it. May was a follower of Garrison, although he did not subscribe to the doctrine of disunion and in 1856 endorsed John C. Frémont, the Republican candidate, for president. The Reverend Lucius C. Matlack, the editor of the *True Wesleyan*, and another contact of Gay's in Syracuse, served on the executive board of the New York State Vigilance Committee, dominated by Tappanites. Ira H. Cobb, one of the underground railroad agents listed by Gay, was also connected with the American Missionary Association. As in other locales, aid to fugitives brought together Syracuse abolitionists who disagreed on other issues, and Gay worked with all of them.[52]

Harmony, however, did not always reign in the underground railroad. One name is conspicuous by its absence from Gay's Record: Frederick Douglass. Nor is there any mention of Rochester, where Douglass worked with a group of abolitionists to speed fugitives on their way from Albany and Syracuse to the Niagara

Falls Suspension Bridge. This may be because Douglass and the Garrisonians, including Gay, had experienced a bitter falling-out in the early 1850s over the former's embrace of political action and his conversion to the idea that because it did not contain the word "slave" (speaking of those in bondage as "other persons"), the Constitution could be construed as an antislavery document. Gay had earlier employed Douglass as a correspondent, helped generate subscribers for his first newspaper, the *North Star*, and corresponded with him about assistance to fugitive slaves. Now, in an editorial in September 1853, the *National Anti-Slavery Standard* condemned Douglass for "vanity and jealousy" and declared that he had "proven treacherous to his old friends and deliberately allied himself with the worst enemies" of the antislavery cause.[53]

James McCune Smith quickly weighed in on Douglass's side, accusing white abolitionists of racism. The dispute exemplified the growing strains in the 1850s between black and white abolitionists, as the former claimed that white colleagues did not do enough to combat racial prejudice. Many abolitionists were appalled by the controversy. A meeting of Chicago blacks in December 1853 condemned the "unchristian and unfeeling" articles about Douglass being published in the Garrisonian press, including the *Standard* and *Liberator*. What the Canadian abolitionist Thomas Henning called "the painful discussion" continued into 1855, which may be why Gay made no mention of Douglass in his Record. Many years later, in a letter to the historian Wilbur Siebert and again in his autobiography, both written in the 1890s, Douglass recalled his role in aiding fugitive slaves who traveled the "route to freedom" via Philadelphia, New York, Albany, Syracuse, and Rochester. He identified as the key operatives William Still, David Ruggles, Jacob R. Gibbs, Stephen Myers, and Jermain Loguen (all African Americans), but not Gay.[54]

Given the chronic problem of funding, it is not surprising that some of the controversies that embroiled the underground railroad in the 1850s revolved around money, specifically how funds collected at antislavery fairs should be allocated. Charity fairs or "bazaars" to raise money for a variety of causes sprang up on both sides of the Atlantic in the 1820s and 1830s, a natural outgrowth of the accelerating market revolution. But the abolitionist movement perfected and institutionalized the practice. Fund-raising fairs became a staple of the movement and the primary focus of female antislavery activity. Women organized these events, at which they sold goods with the proceeds going to abolitionist organizations and local vigilance committees. Generally, fairs were held just before Christmas; indeed, abolitionists helped to establish the practice of a Christmas "shopping season" when people exchanged presents bought at commercial venues. In this spirit the fairs purveyed a large assortment of dolls, toys, and other gifts for children. The items on sale also included antislavery publications and images, and goods of all kinds. The 1842 fair in Philadelphia had a "poultry stall, including a fine porker, . . . butter, cheese, chestnuts, and shellbarks," and a "refreshment table" piled high with pies, cakes, pickles, and other items "from our country friends."[55]

Fairs, the *National Anti-Slavery Standard* noted, were "among the most efficient agencies in the anti-slavery cause." In addition to raising money, "hearts are kindled, lagging sympathies wakened afresh, and new minds every year brought within the circle." However, the newspaper continued, while fairs in Massachusetts and Pennsylvania proved extremely successful, in New York City "there is no foundation for such an enterprise." This was not strictly correct; in 1851, a black group calling itself the North Star Association of Ladies organized a fair to raise money for the Committee of Thirteen. They received donations of goods from "Ladies" in Albany, Philadelphia, and Lenox and Pittsfield, Massachusetts, and netted $292. It is true, however, that New York never hosted fairs as large or lucrative as those in Philadelphia and Boston.[56]

The grandest and most successful of these fairs was the National Anti-Slavery Bazaar in Boston, which by the mid-1850s was attracting thousands of visitors and raising over $5,000 annually for the AASS. Maria Weston Chapman was the key organizer of the Boston fair, doing so from abroad between 1848 and 1855, when she lived in Paris with money inherited from her late husband, Henry, a wealthy Boston merchant. The poet James Russell Lowell paid tribute to the fashionable and talented Chapman:

The great attraction now of all
Is the "Bazaar" at Faneuil Hall . . .
There was Maria Chapman, too,
With her swift eyes of clear-steel blue . . .
The Joan of our Ark.[57]

Chapman and her Boston coworkers organized a network that extended into rural New England, New York, and Pennsylvania and across the Atlantic to Britain and France. Dozens of local societies contributed goods to the Boston fair, often items of clothing and embroidery produced by abolitionist sewing circles. Increasingly, however, the fair moved upscale, becoming a commercial extravaganza focusing on selling "fancy" goods from around the world, including items dispatched from Paris by Mrs. Chapman. (She instructed her Boston coworkers on how much to mark up each item.) British female abolitionists contributed enormously to the success of the Boston fair, sending boxes of merchandise each year. The "foreign goods" at the 1849 fair included "Afghan blankets and cushions from Edinburgh, Garden Chairs and elegant Sofa Cushions from Perth, . . . Exquisite Honiton Lace, Basket work, and dolls in costume from Bristol." Other items in the 1850s included perfumes, silks, porcelain, jewelry, and works of art. Indeed, the fair, one participant later recalled, prided itself on attracting the patronage of "the most aristocratic families," and for "having wares that were to be found in no Boston shops." Local merchants complained that the fair "undersold them and injured their business" at the holiday season.[58]

Among other things, the fairs provided a way of harnessing female domestic skills like sewing for political purposes. Their slogan, "Buy for the Sake of the Slave," offered a foretaste of later consumer activism. Of course, organizing a fair posed less of a challenge to prevailing gender norms than did public speaking or demands for women's rights. Nonetheless, some male abolitionists objected to the fairs. They criticized their commercialism and considered it unseemly for women to involve themselves in financial transactions. But the annual Boston fair was indispensable to the AASS balance sheet and became the *National Anti-Slavery Standard*'s "main dependence for funds."[59]

Lewis Tappan had spoken of the "friendly rivalry" between the New York State Vigilance Committee and Sydney Howard Gay's antislavery office, but when it came to raising money through fairs, the rivalry could become very acrimonious. Non-Garrisonian abolitionists cast a jealous eye on the flow of goods and money from Britain to the AASS. James W. C. Pennington decided to do something about it. As a minister and an official of both the American Missionary Association and the American and Foreign Anti-Slavery Society, Pennington had many reasons to dislike the Garrisonians. In 1850, while lecturing in Britain, he launched a campaign to convince abolitionists there to transfer their fund-raising largesse from the AASS to the New York State Vigilance Committee, of which he served as vice president. The Garrisonians, Pennington asserted, were "infidels" who slandered American churches for their connection with slavery.[60]

Pennington's screeds proved particularly effective in Glasgow, where a group of women abolitionists, alarmed by his account of "unorthodoxy and infidelism" in the AASS, seceded from the existing Glasgow Female Anti-Slavery Society to form the Glasgow New Association for the Abolition of Slavery. They echoed Pennington's charge that Henry C. Wright, a close associate of Garrison, had denied the divinity of the Bible in words "not surpassed in anything to be found in the coarsest pages of Tom Paine." In December 1851, the Glasgow women dispatched "a beautiful consignment of goods," not to Boston but to Pennington's church in New York, for a fair whose proceeds were earmarked for the New York State Vigilance Committee. Similar events took place in Edinburgh. The new groups held their own annual fairs "in aid of fugitive slaves." Between 1851 and 1853, the New York State Vigilance Committee received over $3,000 from Great Britain. What James Miller McKim called Pennington's "determined and unscrupulous effort" to turn British abolitionists against the AASS engendered ill will that did not dissipate. Pennington returned to the United States in 1852, to be greeted by charges forwarded from Glasgow Garrisonians that he had misused funds raised in Britain for his church. An investigating committee appointed by the New York Presbytery cleared him of fiscal wrongdoing, but in 1855 he was dismissed from the pulpit of Shiloh Presbyterian Church for drunkenness. He was succeeded by the celebrated fugitive slave Henry Highland Garnet.[61]

Another controversy within the abolitionist community centered on whether precious resources should be devoted to aiding individual fugitives in the first place. Gerrit Smith called vigilance committees "the most ultra of all abolition organizations." Others wondered if they were abolition organizations at all. Even in the 1830s and 1840s, a number of abolitionists thought that aiding fugitives diverted attention from their main goal: general emancipation. "Abolitionists," wrote Nathaniel P. Rogers, the *National Anti-Slavery Standard*'s first editor, "are more concerned in overthrowing the slave system than in helping fugitive slaves to Canada. . . . It is not the object of the anti-slavery enterprise to effect individual emancipations." His successor, Lydia Maria Child, agreed. It was "not a legitimate use of our society funds," she wrote, "to pay the expenses of runaways. . . . [O]ur energies must be concentrated on the destruction of the *system*."[62]

In the 1850s, thanks to James Pennington's campaign to have British abolitionists shift their monetary contributions to the New York State Vigilance Committee, this debate became more heated. John B. Estlin, a British abolitionist aligned with Garrison, condemned the idea of transferring aid to "so unimportant an Anti-Slavery agency" as the Vigilance Committee. That group, he hastened to add, was doing good work, "but it effects nothing . . . towards the extinction of slavery." Thomas Wentworth Higginson, in a speech at the anniversary meeting of the AASS in New York City in 1857, went so far as to claim that the underground railroad, "founded with the noblest of purposes," had outgrown its usefulness and ought to be "abolished." It was "demoralizing the conscience of our people," he claimed, allowing them to be satisfied with directing slaves to Canada rather than "making their own soil free." White abolitionists were not the only ones to raise questions about the movement's priorities. A writer in the *Weekly Anglo-African* wondered why fugitive slaves received so much more "attention and sympathy" than free blacks "who are already residents of these states" and often in dire need of financial assistance.[63]

The issue of priorities came to a head in 1857 in a dispute among female abolitionists over plans to organize a Garrisonian anti-slavery fair in New York City. Gay had previously received money from fairs organized by a ladies' society dominated by "orthodox Quakers" and other women opposed to sending money to the AASS.

In 1857, Garrisonian women, led by Abigail Hopper Gibbons and Elizabeth Gay, organized the new Anti-Slavery Fair Association. Money raised would be forwarded to the AASS, except for "one thousand dollars, which is to go to the aid of fugitive slaves passing through the city (Sydney Treasurer and A. S. Office the depot)." Mrs. Gay hoped that this arrangement would draw support from a wide circle of women while still raising money for the AASS. Setting aside some of the proceeds for fugitives, she wrote, was a "*sine qua non* with the active women in New York."

Elizabeth Gay had made baskets and other goods to be sold at the annual Boston bazaar, but she had no experience organizing a fair. She requested assistance from Maria Weston Chapman, the leading spirit in Boston, who had returned from her extended stay in Europe in 1855. Gay was stunned when Chapman refused to cooperate. "We do not feel justified," Chapman wrote, "in working where we receive only a part of what we desire." Moreover, "entangling alliances" with women only interested in fugitive slaves were not "honourable to the cause." In July 1857, when Chapman published the announcement for the "24th National Anti-Slavery Bazaar" in Boston, she included a sentence urging those who "pity the hunted fugitive . . . [to] help us everywhere awaken a stronger sentiment . . . for the millions who cannot fly." Nonetheless, New York's Fair Association pressed ahead. The fair opened on Astor Place on December 7, 1857. It "proved a failure." The weather was inclement, and because of the financial panic that had set in earlier that fall, "nobody has any money to spend." Only $700 was raised, divided between the AASS and a fund for fugitives.[64]

Soon, even stranger events unfolded in Boston. In 1858, the imperious Mrs. Chapman unilaterally decreed the end of the Boston bazaar. In its place, a system of "direct cash subscriptions" by wealthy donors would support the AASS. "I do not know of a single person amongst all our friends," wrote the Boston abolitionist Samuel May Jr., "who approves of her course." Nonetheless, the first "National Anti-Slavery Subscription Festival" opened in January 1859. It was held in the Boston Music Hall, which had been transformed into a series of drawing rooms, complete with music and refreshments, where visitors passed along donations in envelopes and received the thanks of abolitionist women. Instead of the raucous give-and-take of a commercial bazaar, money now changed hands discreetly. The event was, in the eyes of contemporaries, more ladylike. It was also more geared to Boston's elite. And it succeeded. The festival raised $6,000, $2,200 more than the last bazaar, of December 1857. In a section of her report addressed to British abolitionists, Chapman noted that Francis Jackson worked for both the AASS and the Boston Vigilance Committee. "But," she added, "five pounds paid over to him in the former capacity is, in America, worth a thousand paid to him" to aid fugitives.[65]

Despite these controversies, the underground railroad continued to flourish. And thanks to the meticulous record-keeping of Sydney Howard Gay, it is possible to construct a detailed portrait of the fugitives who passed through New York City in the mid-1850s on their way to Canada and liberty.

7

THE RECORD OF FUGITIVES: AN ACCOUNT OF RUNAWAY SLAVES IN THE 1850S

In popular memory, the individual most closely associated with the underground railroad is Harriet Tubman. Born a slave in Maryland in 1822, this remarkable woman escaped in 1849 and during the following decade made at least thirteen forays to her native state, leading some seventy men, women, and children, including a number of her relatives, out of bondage. Tubman's first rescue took place in 1850, when she received word that a niece, Kessiah Bowley, and her two children were about to be sold. Bowley's free husband purchased the family at auction, even though he lacked the money to pay the seller. He then spirited them by boat to Baltimore, where Tubman met the family and brought them to Philadelphia and then to Canada. On a later trip, in 1857, Tubman rescued her elderly parents, who had become free but were in danger of being arrested for their own efforts to help slaves escape. Her exploits were not confined to the South. In 1860, she led a crowd that rescued Charles Nalle, a fugitive slave from Virginia who had been seized by a slave catcher in Troy, New York.[1]

Tubman's fame spread quickly in abolitionist circles. She made the acquaintance of such luminaries as Frederick Douglass, Lucretia Mott, and Lewis Tappan. By the late 1850s, she had become known as the slaves' "Moses." After the Civil War, Douglass would write of Tubman, "Excepting John Brown—of sacred memory—I know of no one who has willingly encountered more perils and hardships to serve our enslaved people." Nonetheless, Tubman struggled to raise money for her undertakings. She worked in Philadelphia, New York, and Canada as a laundress, housekeeper, and cook, and solicited funds from abolitionists. On one occasion, she camped out in the antislavery office in New York City, asking visitors for donations.[2]

Tubman exhibited extraordinary courage. She "seemed wholly devoid of personal fear," wrote William Still. When Tappan asked how she would feel if she were captured and condemned to "perpetual slavery," Tubman replied, "I shall have the consolation to know that I had done some good to my people." But Tubman did not act entirely on her own. Her rescues relied on connections with slaves and free blacks in Maryland and with underground railroad networks in the mid-Atlantic states. Thomas Garrett offered assistance to Tubman as she passed through Wilmington on what he called "her very perilous adventures." He described her accomplishments at length to correspondents in Britain and passed along money they forwarded for her use.[3]

Twice in 1856, Tubman brought fugitive slaves through Sydney Howard Gay's office in New York City. In May, Gay recorded, "Captain Harriet Tubman" arrived with four fugitive slaves—Ben Jackson, James Coleman, William Connoway, and Henry Hopkins—from Dorchester County on Maryland's eastern shore, the center of slavery in the state. As young men in their twenties, the four had an "aggregate market value," Gay estimated, of $6,000. Gay took the opportunity to interview Tubman about her past deeds and the details of this escape. The group started out on foot from Maryland on May 3, 1856. When they reached New Castle, Delaware, having learned that the owners had raised a "hue and cry" and posted a substantial reward for their capture, the fugitives hid for a week in a "potato hole" (presumably a kind of root cellar) at the home of a black woman. At great risk, Tubman traveled back and forth to Wilmington by train seeking assistance; eventually she persuaded "a friend" to bring the slaves to Garrett's house in that city, where they arrived on May 11. They appeared at William Still's office in Philadelphia two days later and and then continued on by rail, reaching Gay's on May 14. Gay dispatched them all to Syracuse, from where they headed to Canada. Three of the four men appear in the Canadian census of 1861, living in or near Toronto.[4]

In November 1856, Tubman returned to Maryland, hoping to bring out her sister Rachel. Rachel, however, was not ready to leave, so instead Tubman led William Bailey, his brother Josiah, and another slave, Peter Pennington, out of Talbot County, on the eastern shore. The Bailey brothers worked in the timber business of William Hughlett, who owned thousands of acres of land and forty slaves, among them Josiah Bailey. Hughlett rented other slaves, including William Bailey, from nearby owners. He treated all of them with great cruelty. "He left his master on account of ill-treatment," Gay wrote of William Bailey, "of which lately he has received more than he could or would bear." Three weeks before the escape, Josiah Bailey had been "stripped naked" and "flogged severely" because he engaged in a dispute with another slave. Both brothers were married; they left behind their wives and a total of seven children.

Tubman and the slaves embarked for the North on November 15, 1856. With the owners in hot pursuit, Tubman led them on a circuitous journey by foot to Wilmington, ninety miles to the north. Along the way they were joined by another slave, Eliza Manokey, a forty-two-year-old woman who had escaped the previous January and hidden in the woods and then in the homes of free black families. Like the Baileys, she had experienced some of the worst horrors of slavery. "Often suffered for want of food and clothing, and often flogged," Gay recorded. Her owner had presented Manokey's four-year-old son as a gift to a nephew, who then departed for Missouri with the child; "the boy clung frantically to his mother ... but in vain." Manokey left behind a husband, their seventeen-year-old daughter, and four grandchildren.

By the time the group reached Wilmington, the owners had preceded them, posting placards offering unusually generous rewards for their return—$1,500 for Josiah Bailey, $800 for Pennington, and $300 for William Bailey. Even though local blacks tore down the notices, many persons, including the Wilmington police, were on the lookout for the fugitives. Thomas Garrett, however, managed to get black bricklayers to convey them, concealed in a wagon, to William Still's office in Philadelphia on the night of November 24. Still immediately sent them, separately, to New York, where they arrived on November 26 and 27. Gay then dispatched them to Troy and Syracuse. In Syracuse they encountered an unexpected obstacle. William E. Abbott, treasurer of the local Fugitive Aid Society, who was well acquainted with Tubman, normally forwarded runaway slaves directly to Canada via the Niagara Falls Suspension Bridge. But now, he wrote, "our funds fail us and we are obligated to send them forward to the different half way houses that are on the route." Nonetheless, Tubman got the group to Canada.[5]

I

These exploits of Harriet Tubman are related in the Record of Fugitives, a document compiled by Gay in 1855 and 1856, as well as in scattered notes on runaway slaves that he also penned. In these two years, Gay meticulously recorded the arrival of well over 200 fugitives in New York City: 137 men, 44 women, 4 adults whose sex he failed to mention, and 29 children. Gay set down information about their owners, motives for leaving, mode of escape, who assisted them, where he sent them, and how much money he expended. Gay's Record is the most detailed account in existence of how the underground railroad operated in New York City, and of the fugitives who passed through the city. He chronicled the experiences of slaves who escaped individually and in groups, by rail, by sea, on foot, and in carriages appropriated from the owners. Some reached the free states within a day or two of their departure; others hid out for weeks or months in swamps or woods before moving on. Most of those whose tales Gay transcribed then disappeared from the historical record. But when supplemented with information compiled about many of the same individuals by William Still in Philadelphia, Gay's Record is a treasure trove of riveting stories and a repository of insights into both slavery and the underground railroad.

Gay's account of Tubman's passage through the city in May 1856 is the longest entry in his journal, a reflection of the high regard in which he held her. Gay also seems to have been the only person at that time who referred to her as "Captain" Tubman, which suggests that he knew her, or of her activities, before 1856.[6] In many ways, Tubman's activities were unique. But in others, the escapes she engineered were typical of many in these years. Like Tubman's charges, nearly half the slaves who appear in Gay's Record originated in Maryland and Delaware, the eastern slave states closest to free soil (see table). The Maryland fugitives mostly came from Baltimore, with its railand sea connections with the North; the northern counties of the eastern shore; or the region of the state farther

ORIGINS OF INDIVIDUALS IN THE RECORD OF FUGITIVES

Maryland	94
Virginia	66
North Carolina	19
Delaware	11
District of Columbia	10
Kentucky	3
South Carolina	2
Georgia	2
Unknown	7
Total	214

west that bordered on Pennsylvania. Ten of the eleven from Delaware hailed from New Castle, the county closest to Pennsylvania. Here, slavery was all but extinct; on the eve of the Civil War, 97 percent of its black population was free. Perhaps more surprising is the number of fugitives who arrived in New York City from Virginia and North Carolina, states considerably more distant (although most of those who escaped over land, rather than by boat, from Virginia originated in the northernmost part of the state, closer to free soil than Washington, D.C.). Slaves of every age absconded, but most were in their twenties (the average age of the adults was 25.5), their prime working years, when their economic value to their owners was at its peak. Only a handful were above the age of forty. Three-fourths of the adult fugitives were men, a figure in line with previous studies of runaway slaves.[7]

In occupation, the fugitives who passed through New York City reflected how slavery permeated every corner of the southern economy. They ran the gamut from plantation hands and laborers on small farms to household domestics, hotel porters and cooks, and skilled urban craftsman—carpenters, blacksmiths, and William Bailey himself, who operated a steam engine. Among one group of fugitives, William Still commented, "were some good mechanics—one excellent dress-maker, some 'prime' waiters and chambermaids—men and women with brains, some of them evincing remarkable intelligence and decided bravery, just the kind of passengers that gave the greatest satisfaction to the Vigilance Committee."[8] Many of the slaves had "hired their own time," living apart from their owners in urban centers and passing along their earnings, while usually being able to keep some money for themselves. This was a growing practice in the Upper South. Such slaves clearly had greater opportunities to learn of possibilities for escape than those on isolated farms and plantations. Many were able to pay for assistance in departing.

The owners of these fugitives also illustrated how every kind of enterprise in the South employed slave labor. A few were men of considerable prominence and wealth, notably John Branch, the son of a revolutionary war hero and a former governor of North Carolina and Florida who owned large plantations in both states and more than 100 slaves. Other well-to-do owners included Freeman Woodland of Chestertown, Maryland, who possessed $40,000 worth of real estate and nineteen slaves; Joshua Pusey of Leesburg, Virginia, a farmer with nine slaves and land valued at over $100,000; William Brisbane, a South Carolina planter with thirty-one slaves; and Thomas Warren, a physician and farmer in Edenton, North Carolina, whose holdings included fifty slaves and $162,000 in real estate. A larger number of owners were small farmers with only a handful of slaves, for whom the escape of even one would be a significant financial loss. And many had nonagricultural occupations, including the proprietors of Haxall and Company (one of Richmond's two flour mills), the president of the Chestertown Bank, merchants, ministers, lawyers, an employee of the U.S. Treasury

Department, a U.S. naval officer, a tailor, and a tavern keeper. Even slave traders suffered the loss of absconding slaves. George Sperryman, who escaped from Richmond, had been owned by H. N. Templeman, whose account book notes handsome profits derived from slaves, including children, "taken South" for sale.[9]

To a Glasgow audience in 1853, the abolitionist James Miller McKim described the fugitives who arrived at the antislavery office in Philadelphia, many of them headed for New York: "These were not ill-treated slaves who had braved death and suffered so much to get their liberty.... It is those which have indulgent masters... that escape from slavery." McKim's point was that the desire for freedom, not the brutality of individual owners, led to escapes. "He wanted to be free, he says," Gay recorded of one fugitive, "and has wished to be for years." Several runaways mentioned to Gay that they had tried unsuccessfully to escape and were severely punished, but nonetheless they tried again and managed to reach the North.

Some fugitives who passed through New York fit McKim's description, such as James Jones of Alexandria, who, Gay recorded, "had not been treated badly, but was tired of being a slave." Charles Carter, the slave of a flour inspector in Richmond, spoke of his owner "rather favorably in comparison with slaveholders generally ... he has not been so badly abused as many others." But these were exceptions. Few fugitives interviewed by Still and Gay had anything good to say about their treatment. Even if the desire for freedom was the underlying motive, the decision to escape usually arose from an immediate grievance. And among the causes mentioned for running away, by far the most common was physical abuse.[10]

The fugitives who arrived in New York told stories replete with accounts of frequent whippings and other brutality; their words of complaint included "great violence," "badly treated," "ruff times," "hard master," "very severe," "a very cruel man," and "much fault to find with their treatment."[11] Frank Wanzer called his owner Luther Sullivan, who operated a plantation in Fauquier County, "the meanest man in Virginia." Franklin Wilson, who escaped from Smyrna, Delaware, had "plenty of scars" from whippings by his owner, a physician. Samuel Hill reported that John Appleton, a farmer in Duck Creek, Delaware, "worked him hard, clothed him poorly, and beat him." John Haywood related how his brother had been shot dead by owner after physically resisting a whipping, and another slave was hanged after being discovered "playing soldier . . . with a parcel of other boys in the woods." James Morris of Norfolk, who referred to his owner, Ann McCourt, as "a heel of a woman," wrote a brief account for Gay of the sadistic treatment to which he had been subjected: "One meal a day for 8 years. . . . Sold 3 times and threten to be sold the fourth. . . . Struck 4 hundred lashes by overseer choped cross the head with a hatchet and bled 3 days. Tied hands and feet and knocked down with a stick, made to stand out in the cold 4 ours for punishment without shoes on."[12]

Second only to physical abuse as a motive for escape was the ever-present threat of sale. The marketing of slaves to the Lower South had long since become a lucrative enterprise for Upper South owners. Many of the slaves mentioned by Gay ran away to avoid being placed on the auction block or fled after members of their families had been sold. In an advertisement seeking his capture that ran six times in the *Baltimore Sun*, William Elliott claimed that his slave William Brown had run off "without the slightest provocation." Brown, however, told Gay that he absconded because "he was to have been sold to go to Georgia." Nathaniel Bowser, a slave in North Carolina, decided to escape after hearing his owner talk of buying a plantation in Louisiana and "selling all of his negroes who were not willing to go with him." Despite a history of harsh treatment, Franklin Wilson told Gay, he left Delaware only after he "overheard his master chattering with a stranger for his sale."

Phillis Gault, a widow who worked for a Norfolk woman as a dressmaker, "had witnessed the painful sight of seeing four of her sister's children sold on the auction block, on the death of their mother," and feared that she herself would soon be sold.[13]

Slave sales could take place for all sorts of reasons. Thomas Jones, a Virginia house servant, decided to abscond after his wife and four children "were all sent to Richmond to be sold" because, he told William Still, "she had resisted the lustful designs of her master." After fighting back against a whipping, Charles Hall, the slave of the wealthy Maryland farmer Atwood Blunt, was handcuffed and incarcerated in Blunt's house, to be taken to Baltimore for sale the following day. He somehow managed to "tear up the hearth" and escape. Blunt placed an advertisement in successive issues of the *Baltimore Sun*:

> One Hundred Dollars Reward. Ran away from the subscriber, living in Baltimore county, Md., during the night of the 24th inst., his servant man Charles Hall, aged about 25 or 30 years; of dark color, nearly black; about 5 feet six inches, and well set. He has a fresh wound over the left eye—other marks or clothing not known. I will give the above reward if arrested and delivered to me, or secured in jail so that I get him.[14]

The fugitives' experiences also made clear the danger of relying on an owner's promises, even if well intentioned. Three related how a will providing for manumission had been disregarded by heirs or creditors. Laura Lewis of Kentucky told Gay that her owner, who died twenty-five years previously, provided for the emancipation of his slaves on the death of his wife. The widow passed away in March 1855, but her creditors moved to have the will set aside and the slaves sold to satisfy her debts. Jacob Hall of Maryland had been verbally promised his freedom when he reached the age of twenty-one, but when his owner died before that date the heirs reneged on the commitment and sold him. Joseph Rittenham, a fugitive from Maryland's eastern shore, "was always promised by his master to be emancipated at his death; but believing that his heirs would not carry this intention into effect, ran away."[15]

In powerful, contradictory ways, family ties affected slaves' decisions about running away. Escape from slavery generally involved wrenching choices about whether family members should leave or stay. As in the case of Tubman's rescues, when slaves escaped in groups, these frequently included relatives—husbands and wives, brothers and sisters, even, as in the case of eleven women or married couples and one man in Gay's records, small children. Nonetheless, most of the fugitives listed by Gay left relatives behind in the South. William Henry Larrison abandoned his wife of one month; Major Latham, his wife and three children (he later married an Irish-born woman and was living with her in Etobicoke, a town adjacent to Toronto, in 1861). On one of Captain Albert Fountain's voyages, four young fugitives had each left a wife in slavery. Most of the women on Gay's list were either unmarried or brought children with them, but occasionally, mothers left children behind when they escaped. Even when children were not involved, escape often meant severing ties with an extended family. William Brown, who ran away because he feared being sold, left in Maryland his grandmother, father, four sisters, and two brothers; Anna Scott, also from Maryland, her father and nine brothers and sisters.[16]

Some fugitives reunited with relatives who had previously run away. Elizabeth Harris, who arrived at Gay's office from Delaware in December 1856, was the wife of James Harris, a fugitive who had passed through the city a month earlier. Shortly after Gay dispatched Mrs. Harris to upstate New York, William Still received a letter from Auburn, announcing that the couple would remain there, working for an abolitionist family. Rebecca Jones, who

Gateway to Freedom

UNDERGROUND RAILROAD SITES AND ORIGINS OF FUGITIVE SLAVES

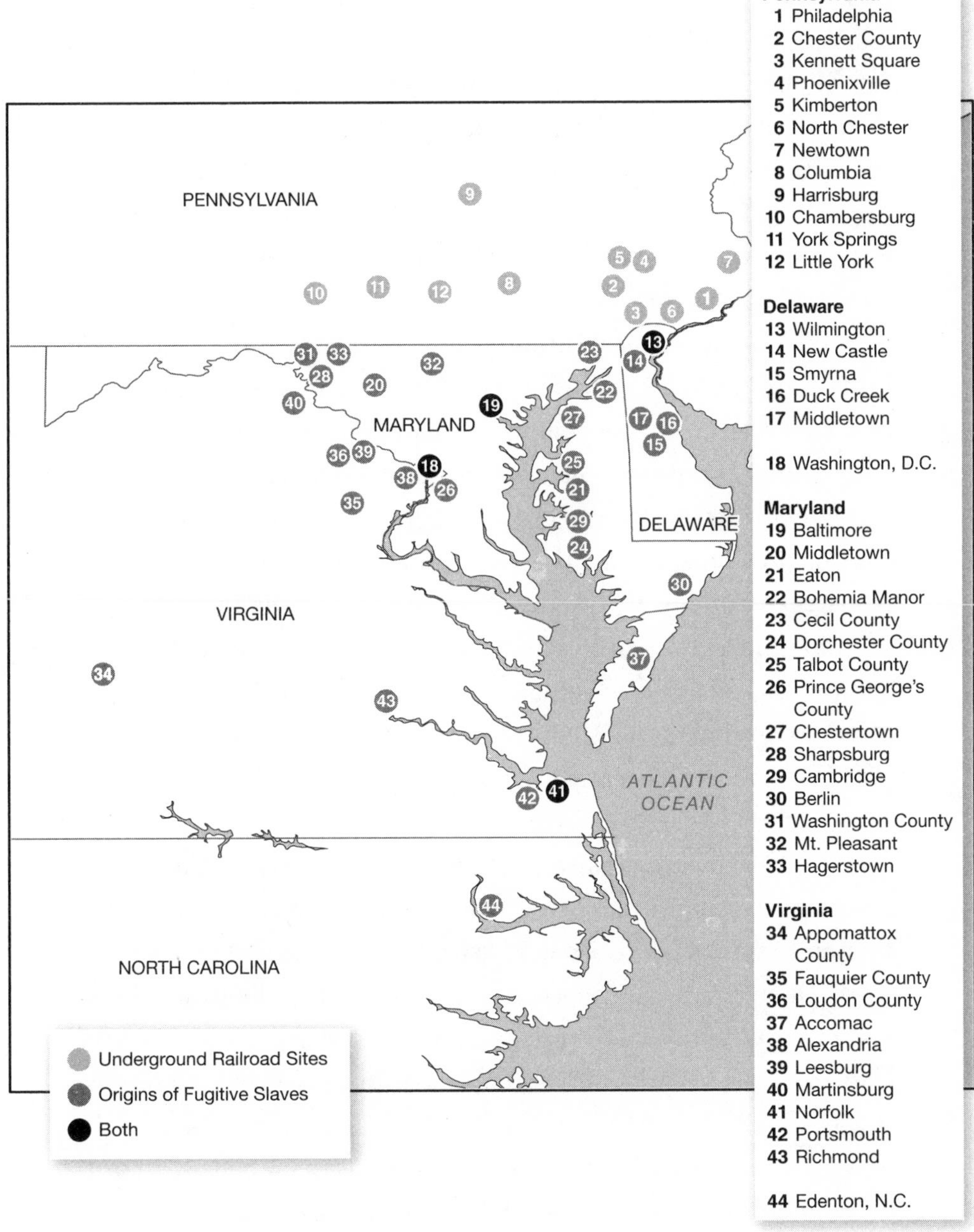

reached New York from Norfolk with her three children in April 1856, was heading for Boston, where she hoped to find her husband, who had escaped six years earlier "in company with the noted slave Shadrach." (Their reunion proved unsuccessful. Six months later, Jones notified Still that she was heading for California and had no intention of resuming the relationship.) Frances Hilliard, a slave from Richmond who had been sold a number of times by slave traders as a "fancy article," arrived in New York via Philadelphia in August 1855, a year after helping her husband escape from a private jail operated by his owner, the slave trader Bacon Tait. The husband had hidden on a British vessel and made his way to Liverpool and then Canada where, Hilliard told Gay, she was "anxious to join him." Caroline Taylor's free husband William was at sea, employed as a coal heaver on the U.S. naval vessel *Saranac*, when the couple planned her escape. She was able to pay Albert Fountain $100, "drawing the money from the Navy Agent on her husband's order," to transport herself and two young daughters out of Virginia. Gay dispatched them to New Bedford, to await the husband's return.[17]

A few fugitives, like Frederick Douglass before them, had free spouses or fiancés, who could readily join them on free soil or had already traveled there. Albert Hennison of Richmond, who arrived at Gay's office in March 1856, had previously sent his free wife to New York, "thinking he might get away." Isaiah Robinson, who escaped by boat from Norfolk along with his sister and her three children, was married to a free woman who planned to meet him in Boston, where other relatives already lived. David Cale, of Middletown, Delaware, sent his free wife ahead by rail while he walked to Wilmington, where he boarded a train and met her in Philadelphia. Daniel Johns, a blacksmith and minister in the African Methodist Episcopal Church, fled Cambridge, Maryland, leaving behind his wife Ann and five children, all free. The 1861 Canada census records him under his new name, Joseph Cornish, living in the black settlement St. Catherine's, near Niagara Falls, with Ann, but makes no mention of their children.[18]

Most fugitives' relatives, of course, were slaves and could not simply pick up and leave the South. Even so, many runaways hoped that family separations would not prove permanent. Charles Carter told Gay that he was "determined to get" his wife and four children "somehow." Emeline Chapman escaped from Washington, D.C., in September 1856, leaving her two small children with "free people who promised to bring them north." Catherine Pitts, who absconded from Berlin, Maryland, with an infant in her arms, related that her husband and brother had advised her to "cut sticks" (escape) because she was about to be sold. Pitts's husband took his wife and child in a wagon to Delaware, where they managed to board a steamboat headed for Philadelphia. "Expects her husband and brother to follow her with a child she left behind," Gay noted when she arrived at his office in New York.[19]

Although unusual in the number of forays, Tubman was not the only fugitive to return to the South in an effort to bring out family members. Otho Taylor escaped from Washington County, Maryland (on the Pennsylvania border), in April 1856 with his wife, two children, and four other slaves, and soon reached Canada via Philadelphia and New York. He turned up again at Gay's office the following September. Gay recorded what had happened: Taylor "went to Canada, and earned about $80, and then returned to bring away his parents, and brother and sister, but did not succeed. They had been promised their freedom and preferred to remain till the time was up."[20]

After Gay's account of Harriet Tubman's exploits, the next longest entry in the Record of Fugitives relates the dramatic escape of twenty-five-year-old Frank Wanzer, his fiancée Emily Foster, and a married couple, Barnaby and Mary Elizabeth Grigby, and Wanzer's subsequent return to bring out relatives still in slavery.

Having hired a carriage and pair of horses, the group departed on Christmas Eve, 1855, from Loudoun County, Virginia, northwest of Washington, accompanied by two other men on horseback. They traveled day and night, braving frost, hunger, and "very severe weather." They barely avoided recapture. After covering 100 miles, they lost their way in Maryland and inquired at a mill for the road to Pennsylvania. The miller realized they were fugitive slaves, and the party soon found itself surrounded by seven white men on horseback, who "demanded of them to give account of themselves." The fugitives, however, including the women, were heavily armed; when they brandished knives and double-barreled pistols, their pursuers decided not to "meddle" with them. To increase their speed, the group abandoned the carriage and continued on horseback, followed by the mounted whites. They decided to disperse, and the whites took off after the two single men, while the couples hid in the woods until nightfall, when they resumed their journey. At one house, they were "fired upon but fortunately were not hit." Eventually, they proceeded on foot; the feet of one of the men "were frozen from the exposure." They finally reached Philadelphia, by way of Columbia, Pennsylvania, on January 16, 1856, and New York two days later. Gay forwarded them to Syracuse, where Frank and Emily were married, and they then proceeded to Toronto.

Wanzer, however, was determined to return to Virginia. In July 1856, armed with three pistols, he traveled by train from Toronto to Columbia and walked the rest of the way. A dozen slaves agreed to leave with him, but only three kept the appointment—his sister, her husband, and another man. The party turned up at William Still's office on August 18 and at Gay's the following day, and were dispatched to Canada.[21]

Such return journeys, of course, were unusual and extremely dangerous. More frequently, those who reached free soil tried to enlist friends or underground railroad agents to rescue relatives.

By the 1850s, many escaped slaves appear to have been able to communicate with loved ones in the South. "There is an underground telegraph," the abolitionist Thomas Wentworth Higginson observed, "as well as an underground railroad." Winnie Patsy arrived at Gay's office in May 1856 from Norfolk via Wilmington and Philadelphia with her three-and-a-half-year-old daughter. Her husband had escaped by boat a few months earlier and ended up in New Bedford, from where he arranged for the same captain to bring out his wife and child. Many fugitives sought William Still's assistance for such endeavors. Phillis Gault, who ended up in Boston with her son Dick after escaping from Norfolk in 1855, wrote Still two and a half years later, asking if he could arrange to "steal little Johny." Still's response, if any, does not survive; most of the time, however, there was little he could do. Lewis Burl, who escaped from Virginia in 1856 and made his way to Philadelphia, New York, and Canada, wrote to Still in 1859 that his wife, who was now living in Baltimore, was ready to abscond if she could "find a friend to help her." Burl implored Still to act, adding, "I will pay you for your trouble." "As in the case of many others," Still later wrote, "the way was so completely blocked that nothing could be done for the wife's deliverance." From Toronto, James Morris begged Still to help his "dear wife and child" escape from Norfolk. "I have received two letters from my wife since I saw you," he related, "and the second was awful. I am sorry to say she says she has been treated awful since I left." Still could do nothing: "This sad letter made a mournful impression, as it was not easy to see how her deliverance was to be effected."[22]

While the popular image of the underground railroad tends to focus on lone fugitives making their way north on foot, in fact more slaves who passed through New York in the mid-1850s escaped in groups than on their own. Many absconded on Captain Albert Fountain's ship, the *City of Richmond,* or other vessels. One locale that seemed particularly vulnerable to mass escapes was Chestertown, in the heart of Maryland's eastern shore. No fewer than twenty-two of the slaves noted by Gay hailed from this town or its immediate vicinity. In two months in 1855, the *Chestertown News* reported parties of seven, ten, and eleven slaves escaping to the North; the following year a group of eight departed, taking with them $300 worth of silks and jewelry. Many of these slaves passed through New York, including seven men and two women in October 1855, and a woman and her five children the following month, part of a group of eleven fugitives who had reached Pennsylvania and been sent northward by various routes. Not surprisingly, these "stampedes" alarmed Chestertown slaveowners. In 1858, a public meeting there warned anyone "detected in interfering with slave property" and "all who aid, abet, or sympathize with them" of dire consequences if they did not desist.[23]

Gay's records offer a glimpse of the many methods slaves employed to flee their owners and the ingenuity their escapes involved. In addition to the groups who secured passage on boats like the *City of Richmond*, many fugitives arranged individually with captains for their passage (often for a sizable fee), were hidden on ships by sympathetic crew members, or stowed away without anyone's knowledge. A few fugitives traveled openly by boat. Albert McCealee, owned by a merchant tailor in Charleston, booked passage to Savannah, "disguising himself as a Spaniard." When he arrived in that city, Gay related, "he enjoyed the largest liberty as a foreigner unacquainted with the rules of the place such as smoking cigars. He visited all the principal taverns and was suspected by no person." Then he and another slave of the same owner boarded a ship for New York, with McCealee's light-skinned companion "easily pass[ing]" for white.[24]

Some fugitives emulated Frederick Douglass and departed from Baltimore or other cities by train. Charles Holliday left Baltimore

CAZENOVIA CONVENTION. A photograph from August 1850, with some of the participants in a convention in upstate New York that protested the Fugitive Slave Bill then under consideration by Congress. Some fifty fugitive slaves were present, a fact that enraged supporters of slavery. Among those pictured are Frederick Douglass, at the table, on the left, and Gerrit Smith, standing to Douglass's left. (Madison County Historical Society)

A fund-raising broadside issued by the Albany Vigilance Committee in 1856. The Committee's activities, including its participation in the underground railroad, were quite public. (American Antiquarian Society)

Vigilance Committee Office,

198 *Lumber Street, Albany, N.Y.*

At a meeting of the Vigilance Committee of Albany held on the evening of the 27th of April, 1856, it was

Resolved, That we, the Vigilance Committee, appreciate the untiring efforts of our Chairman, Stephen Myers, in behalf of the Fugitive for the last three years.

The following resolution was offered by the Rev. John Sands of Albany:

Resolved, That we tender to Mr. Stephen Myers our sincere thanks for his faithfulness in the proper expenditure of all funds placed at his control for the benefit of the Fugitive, and in accordance with the instructions of the Committee.

From the 12th day of September, 1855, to July 15th, 1856, two hundred and eighty-seven Fugitives passed through Albany. Paid for passage, $542.36; board, $76.60.

T. ELKINS, *Secretary.* **C. BROOKS,** *Chairman.*

We call on our fellow citizens, here and elsewhere, to aid us in funds to help the poor, unfortunate Fugitives who come to us daily---in many cases destitute of clothing, weary of traveling, and hungry. No one is so poor as to be unable to give a little to this down-trodden class.

We appeal to the sympathy of ladies and gentlemen everywhere. We are in want of material aid and cast-off clothing.

All funds forwarded to Stephen Myers, William H. Topp, or any gentleman of the Committee, will be faithfully applied. All letters directed to this Office will be duly answered.

Rev. J. J. KELLEY, *Agent.* **STEPHEN MYERS,** *Gen'l Agent and Sup't.*

COMMITTEE:

Rev. JOHN SANDS,	RICHARD WRIGHT,	MINOS McGOWAN, Lumber Merchant, North Pearl St,
A. JOHNSON,	STEPHEN MYERS,	JAMES WOOD,
IAM GARDNER,	WILLIAM MATTHEWS,	Dr. T. ELKINS.

BY THE UNDERGROUND RAILROAD.

last week a party of sixteen escaped slaves arrived in Canada, and found quarters in Stamford township. ters at the Clifton House, near the Suspension Bridge, who escaped two or three years ago from bondage apprised of the coming of the party and exerted himself to procure them a resting place. It so happened tale to a gentleman at the hotel who was his master's neighbor in Virginia. The recognition was mutual

ssed through Albany on the 13th July.

ANY, July, 1856.

STEPHEN MYERS, the leading spirit of the Albany Vigilance Committee. (*The Autobiography of Dr. William Henry Johnson*)

JERMAIN LOGUEN, a fugitive slave and the "underground railroad king" of Syracuse. Most of the fugitives dispatched from New York City in the mid-1850s were headed to Canada via Syracuse. (Onondaga Historical Association)

HARRIET TUBMAN, who made several forays into the South after her own escape and led some seventy slaves to freedom. She passed through New York with groups of fugitives twice in 1856. The titles beneath her name refer to her service with the Union army during the Civil War. (Library of Congress)

will only, however, have to go Canada. It is not,
to-be-sure so far, but ye difficulties would hardly
be greater, as in ye other place, a slave-catcher
would be sure of aid & sympathy.
They left on ye night of ye 16th. inst. reached
Wilmington before morning & were received by
Thos. Garrett. Forwarded to Still, who sent them
here. Sent on to Syracuse. $8.50

May 14th. A party of four arrived from Phila. It was
headed by Captain Harriett Tubman, ye subordinates
being Ben. Jackson & Jas. Coleman who belonged
to Henry Hight of Dorchester Co. Md. Wm. A. Connoway, Laban Hudson, master, & Henry Hopkins
John Houston master, of ye same neighborhood. They
are all young men, of an aggregate market value
probably of $6000.
Harriett Tubman seven years ago was ye slave
of Edward Brodhurst of Bucktown, Md. Her
master dying, & ye estate to be settled, & two of her
sisters having been sold into a 'chain-gang,' she determined to run away. She did so, & made her way
to Canada. In a few months, however, she conclude
to return. She went back, & sought concealment in

A page from the Record of Fugitives compiled by Sydney Howard Gay. The entry dated May 14 [1856], begins Gay's long account of the arrival of Harriet Tubman and three fugitives. (Sydney Howard Gay Papers, Rare Books and Manuscripts Library, Columbia University)

Two fugitive slave ads for runaways who passed through New York City and are mentioned in Gay's Record of Fugitives.

Top: *Baltimore Sun,* September 3, 1855, describing the escape by boat of four men, adding "supposed they may aim for New York." (Maryland State Archives)

EIGHT HUNDRED DOLLARS REWARD.—Ran away from the Farms of J. & H. Holland and W. H. Talbot, Tanner's Creek, near Norfolk, on or about the 24th ult., FOUR NEGRO MEN—"Anthony," "Isaac," "Albert" and "James." Isaac is very dark, about 5 feet 4 inches high, and heavy set; Albert is about 5 feet 4 inches James 5 ft. 6 inches; both a shade lighter than the other two.—James wears a truss for hernia. They were last seen about Old Point, in a Jenny Lind Boat of 3 or 4 tons, with a white bottom, 22 feet long. The boat has no deck, has a centre-board and white zinc bottom; her boat-topping is of green and yellow streaks. Supposed they may aim for New York.

The above reward will be paid for their arrest, or $150 for either man.

P. F. SCHLIECKER & CO.,
105 Smith's Wharf.

s8 tf

$100 REWARD.—RAN AWAY from the subscriber on Saturday, the 30th of August, 1856, a NEGRO WOMAN named EMELINE CHAPMAN, aged about 26 years; 5 feet 4 inches high; rather slender; quite dark-colored; speaks quick and short when spoken to and stammers some; with TWO CHILDREN—the eldest a female, about 2 years and 4 months old, the same color of the mother; the other a male, about 6 or 7 months old, quite bright colored. I will give the above reward if taken outside the District of Columbia, or $50 if taken withint he limits of the District—in either case to be secured in jail or brought home to me, so that I get them again.

MRS. EMILY THOMPSON,
Capitol Hill, Washington, D. C.

s6-3t

Bottom: *Baltimore Sun,* September 6, 1855, offering a reward for Emeline Chapman and her two infant children. (Maryland State Archives)

THE RAILROAD SUSPENSION BRIDGE NEAR NIAGARA FALLS, a print by Currier and Ives from 1857. The opening of the bridge in 1855 made it easier for fugitives to travel via upstate New York to Canada. (Library of Congress)

860

FUGITIVE SLAVES IN CANADA.

THE ELGIN SETTLEMENT.

THERE WILL BE A PUBLIC MEETING IN

FREE SOUTH LEITH CHURCH,

ON

THURSDAY EVENING NEXT, AT 7 O'CLOCK,

TO HEAR STATEMENTS FROM

THE REV. WILLIAM KING,

formerly a Slave Owner in Louisiana, United States, and

WILLIAM H. DAY, ESQ. M.A.,

A Deputation from Canada, whither the Thirty Thousand have fled, escaping from American Slavery.

The Rev. WILLIAM KING liberated his own Slaves, and in this respect is mentioned in Mrs Harriet Beecher Stowe's work, "Dred," as "Clayton."

As this is a work of general benevolence—simply to give the Bible to those in Canada who have heretofore been deprived of it—it is hoped that there will be a large attendance at the Meeting.

[illegible] h November 1859. Burrell & Byers, Printers, Leith.

An 1859 broadside advertising a public meeting in Scotland to raise funds for the Elgin Settlement, one of several communities established by Canadian abolitionists for fugitive slaves and free blacks from the United States. (Library and Archives Canada)

FUGITIVE SLAVES FORDING THE RAPPANHANNOCK RIVER. An 1862 photograph depicts a family of slaves seeking refuge with the Union army in Virginia. As the Civil War progressed, more and more slaves were able to enjoy freedom by heading for Union lines within the South, and the number escaping to the North dwindled. (Library of Congress)

"by the cars" (as Gay referred to the railroad) and "came through immediately" to Philadelphia. Nathaniel West, who worked in Barnum's City Hotel in Baltimore, "bought a ticket at the depot, and came off in the cars like a gentleman." Harriet Eglin and her cousin Charlotte Giles of Baltimore borrowed five dollars "on the credit of Charlotte's mistress" and arranged for a white man, who had been told they were free, to buy their train tickets to Little York, Pennsylvania. Eglin and Giles traveled wearing large mourning hats and veils to conceal their appearance. Their owners placed several notices in the *Baltimore Sun* offering rewards for their recapture and later unsuccessfully sued both the individual who had helped them and the railroad company itself for damages. In May 1856, seven fugitives boarded a train in Mt. Pleasant, Maryland, hoping to reach Wilmington. They "were questioned but not stopped" and soon made their way to Philadelphia and New York.[25]

Another common mode of escape involved appropriating horses or carriages. John T. Jones left Chestertown in December 1855 in a buggy owned by his owner's niece and soon arrived in Wilmington, from which Thomas Garrett sent him to Philadelphia. Mary Cummens, her adult son James, eleven-year-old daughter Lucy, and another slave, all owned by the wealthy planter Jacob Hollingsworth of Hagerstown, Maryland, rode off in his horse-drawn carriage to Shippensburg, where they boarded a train to Harrisburg and Philadelphia. Gay forwarded the Cummens family to Canada, where Mary and Lucy were living in Hamilton, just south of Toronto, in 1861. Thomas Jones, a house servant in Martinsburg, Virginia, hired a horse and departed on Christmas night, 1855. He crossed the Potomac, then turned the horse loose and walked two days and nights to Harrisburg, his clothing "frozen to his body." He arrived in Philadelphia on New Year's Eve and in New York on January 4.[26]

Many slaves had no alternative but to try to escape on foot, sometimes over very long distances. Simon Hill, a slave in Appomattox

County, Virginia, told Gay that he "took . . . to the woods, and bent his steps northward and in about two weeks reached Philadelphia," a distance of well over 200 miles. John Richardson walked over fifty miles from Baltimore to Columbia, Pennsylvania, from where he "took the cars to Philadelphia." Even those who initially escaped by other means ended up having to walk significant distances. The brothers Albert and Anthony Brown, owned by a Virginia oysterman, appropriated one of his boats and sailed up Chesapeake Bay until head winds forced them to make landfall just north of Baltimore. From there, they walked by night, following railroad tracks. They traveled with the aid of a compass, but abandoned the instrument at some point "lest it should excite the suspicions of two white persons whom they saw approaching." When they arrived in Wilmington, "friends" sent them on to Philadelphia and New York. William Brown walked for five weeks from Prince George's County, Maryland, just outside Washington, D.C., to Columbia, Pennsylvania. His journey took place in November and December 1855, and as Gay recorded, "he suffered severely . . . from cold and wet, being often obliged to ford ponds and streams. His clothes sometimes froze to him, and he would lie all day in the sun to thaw and dry them." Most of those who escaped on foot were men, but Emeline Chapman walked the 120 miles from Washington to Harrisburg.[27]

The story of Peter Matthews, a fugitive who took two weeks to walk by night from Accomac, Virginia, to Pennsylvania, a distance of 200 miles, illustrates the perils slaves escaping on foot encountered. Motivated by the "hard treatment" dispensed by a man to whom he had been hired—he was beaten severely for "allowing an ox into a vegetable patch"—as well as the belief that "he had better work for himself for wages than for another man for nothing," Matthews planned his escape for nearly two years. At a religious camp meeting, he "earned a few dollars," which he used to buy a pistol and flour for "cakes to support him on his journey." At one point,

Matthews encountered a man to whom he had once been hired, riding in a buggy. When the buggy passed, he leaped over a hedge and "ran 'he couldn't tell how fast.' " Soon he heard the sound of a dog, accompanied by two men with guns. He "gave himself up for lost," but managed to hide until nightfall, when he resumed his journey, eventually reaching Philadelphia. William Still "started him on Canada-ward," via New York. Matthews left his weapon with Still, who kept it as "a relic of the Underground Railroad."[28]

Not every fugitive who passed through New York had traveled directly to the North after escaping. Many who planned to flee by boat hid out in the South for some time until a vessel was ready to take them. Twenty-two-year-old Winnie Patsy, whose husband had arranged for a ship to carry her north from Norfolk, absconded from her owner with her young daughter in October 1855. The two hid under a house just outside the city, in a space that had been "excavated by the slave who lived there, for the concealment of fugitives." "It had no window," Gay recorded, "and no means of light or ventilation. . . . That has been their home for the last five months." Maria Joiner was secreted for eight months "in private quarters where she suffered severely from cold," before boarding Albert Fountain's schooner, which took her to Philadelphia. Several fugitives hid in woods and swamps until being able to board ships that would carry them to freedom. William Jordan "lived for ten months in woods, three in a cave, surrounded by bears, wild cats, snakes etc.," until a friend finally arranged passage on Fountain's vessel. Despite the dangers that surrounded him, he told William Still, he "feared nothing but man."[29]

Some of the fugitives aided by Gay had lived in the North for a time but suddenly confronted the prospect of being returned to slavery. Elizabeth Banks had worked in Philadelphia since escaping from Easton, Maryland, in 1853. She "felt herself secure," but in August 1855, "being informed that her owner was in pursuit she became alarmed and anxious to leave for Canada." Eighteen-year-old Alexander Munson, who arrived at Gay's office in January 1856, had escaped from Chestertown, Maryland, a year earlier and lived "in various places in Pennsylvania." But his father, a free man in Delaware, learning that the owner was "in search of him . . . came for him a few days since to send him Northward." Mary Jeffers, who arrived in New York with two young daughters, had been living in Philadelphia for six years with the permission of her owner, Joshua Craig of Bohemia Manor, Maryland. But after the death of Craig and his wife, title passed to their children, and the son arrived at Jeffers's home with a policeman, "saying that Mary and the daughters were his property, and meant to take them." Fortunately, the family was not at home. Legally, Jeffers and her children were no longer slaves, since they had entered Pennsylvania with the permission of their owner. For a week, nonetheless, they "remained in concealment" at the home of a friend, with Jeffers petrified of being "taken with the children to the South, reduced again to slavery." Finally, they got word to Still, who put them on a train to New York. Gay sent them all to Syracuse.[30]

II

In 1858, after fourteen years as editor, Sydney Howard Gay resigned from the *National Anti-Slavery Standard* to assume a position, at a considerably higher salary, with Horace Greeley's *New York Tribune*, the nation's most important antislavery newspaper. Gay continued to assist fugitives; his letter, quoted in the preceding chapter, to James Miller McKim complaining of runaways arriving by train at three in the morning, was written six months after he joined Greeley's staff. Into 1860, Gay continued to keep an account of expenses related to the underground railroad, but he no longer maintained his Record of Fugitives. Thus, it is difficult to know how many fugitives passed through New York in the years immediately preceding the Civil War. But there is no question that they continued to come.[31]

The New York State Vigilance Committee—"the old Tappan and Gerrit Smith organization," as the *New York Herald* described it—although not as active as in the past, still operated out of the American Missionary Association's office, now located at 48 Beekman Street. In one instance, Tappan helped to secure the freedom of James Stead (or Steele), a "nearly white" slave who had worked in a billiards parlor in Augusta and a coffeehouse in Charleston. Stead absconded in November 1857 to Savannah, where he "put up as a free and easy gentleman at a first class hotel . . . and dressed in the last mode de Paris." Soon afterward, he purchased a ticket on a steamship sailing to New York City. Alerted by the owner, Savannah's sheriff notified Mayor Fernando Wood in New York by telegram. Two policemen boarded the ship when it arrived, arrested Stead, and took him to a boardinghouse in Red Hook, Brooklyn, where he was held for shipment back to the South. Tappan and Theodore Tilton, the editor of the reform magazine *Independent*, somehow discovered Stead's whereabouts. They asked Erastus D. Culver, the antislavery lawyer who had been elected to a judgeship in Brooklyn in 1854, to issue a writ of habeas corpus. Culver directed a constable, deputy sheriff, and deputy clerk of court to bring Stead to his home. When they did, Culver immediately discharged him. The *Brooklyn Eagle* reported that Stead was "now thought to be on his way to Canada via the underground railroad."[32]

In the late 1850s, the *Standard*'s antislavery office, now headed by the new editor, Oliver Johnson, remained the "regular depot of the underground railroad" in New York. Johnson himself was far less involved in its activities than Gay had been. As he explained to McKim in 1860, "I am compelled to shirk the whole business of fugitives. . . . My editorial cares . . . use up every iota of my strength."

William H. Leonard and Louis Napoleon, he added, "do all that is done." They communicated with William Still, met runaway slaves, arranged for shelter, and sent them northward.[33]

Slaves brought to the city from the South by their owners continued to claim their freedom. In defiance of state law, Aaron Cohen, a merchant operating a business in Charleston but living in New York, brought his thirty-year-old slave Lena Fields to the city in January 1860 as a nurse for his infant child. A few weeks after their arrival, Fields disappeared, along with her bedding. In October, Cohen's wife encountered her on the street and had her arrested for theft. Fields insisted that a "custom in the South" allowed slaves to acquire "a certain amount of personal property," and that the bedding belonged to her. A jury acquitted Fields of theft, and, the *Herald* reported, she was "borne triumphantly from the court" by "a number of colored individuals, among whom Louis Napoleon and his wife were quite prominent." New York, though, remained a dangerous place for blacks, fugitive or otherwise. As late as 1858, the press reported two attempted kidnappings of black children, including a "colored lad" abducted from a city street and imprisoned on a ship bound for Virginia who managed to escape and reach shore before the vessel sailed.[34]

The underground railroad, James Miller McKim quipped, was the "only branch of industry" that "didn't suffer" during the Panic of 1857: "Other railroads are in a declining condition and have stopped their semiannual dividends, but the *Underground* has never done such a flourishing business." In the late 1850s, hundreds of fugitives entered Canada via upstate New York, and from Detroit, Cleveland, and other cities. Escapes, McKim reported from Philadelphia late in 1857, were "100 per cent more numerous than they were this time last year." Fifty fugitives had "passed through the hands of the Vigilance Committee" in the past two weeks. Early in 1860, Stephen Myers declared that more fugitives had arrived in

Albany in the past three years than in the previous six.[35]

In sharp contrast with other parts of the North, New York City's ties with the slave South seemed to solidify as the sectional conflict deepened. In 1860, for the first time since 1854, the Fugitive Slave Act was successfully enforced in the city. Allen Graff and Josiah Hoy escaped from Maryland in April of that year and made their way to Philadelphia. William Still sent them to New York and notified the antislavery office, but they did not appear on the designated train. Graff and Hoy did manage to reach the city, but before they made contact with anyone who could help them, federal marshals, alerted by their owners, arrested the pair and brought them before a U.S. commissioner. The case proceeded in secrecy; no one knew of it until the following day, by which time the fugitives were on their way back to "a locality in Maryland called 'Liberty.'"[36]

In a letter to James Miller McKim, William H. Leonard of the antislavery office refused to accept blame for the outcome:

> The idea of them having been in this city 8 or 10 days without reporting themselves here don't look feasable, and if they were, it shows quite a disregard for their own personal safety. . . . That they could have been taken from any one of our piers, is all nonsense, as there are always more or less colored men around them. . . . There are always plenty ready and willing to show them hence with the usual directions given in such cases. . . . This is the first case in over six years I have been actively engaged in the business I have failed to receive and safely dispose of and I sincerely hope it may be the last.

Almost as disturbing as the rendition itself was that it took place "without causing a ripple in public opinion," a sad reflection, observed the *National Anti-Slavery Standard*, on "the public sentiment of this great city." Two months later a Virginia slaveholder seized a fugitive named Jim on the streets of New York. Accompanied by a U.S. marshal, Jim was returned to Virginia without any legal proceeding and sold at auction in Richmond for $1,330.[37]

The last rendition of a fugitive slave from New York City took place three weeks before South Carolina severed its ties with the American Union. In the fall of 1860, John M. Winter of Louisville sent his twenty-five-year-old slave John Thomas to Evansville, on the Indiana side of the Ohio River, to seek employment. For a few weeks, Thomas worked as a riverboat steward, passing the money he earned along to Winter. He then absconded to Canada and soon decided to make his way to New York City, where he found a job in a local store. In November, a group of men seized Thomas on a city street and hustled him before a judge (not, as the Fugitive Slave Law required, a U.S. commissioner), who ordered him remanded to the South. Two deputy federal marshals brought Thomas to Richmond, where Winter, who had traveled from Kentucky, sold him at a slave market for $700.

Thomas's return to slavery, a Richmond newspaper declared, offered a gratifying example of "good faith and observance of a constitutional obligation." New York's antislavery activists, however, saw the rendition as an egregious case of kidnapping. Justice Joseph Mullin, a Republican member of the New York Supreme Court, declared the proceedings an affront to "the dignity of the law" and asked a grand jury to look into the matter. Nothing, however, seems to have come of this. The entire episode, the *Tribune* claimed, demonstrated that "certain officers of the United States in this city . . . are actively and successfully engaged in man-stealing." Three months later, in early March 1861, a group of men seized and handcuffed John Bell, who had recently escaped from Virginia with his wife and child, and transported him to a wharf, intending to place him on a vessel about to embark for the South. Bell protested so loudly that a crowd gathered and the slave catchers fled. Nonetheless, on the eve of the Civil War, the situation of fugitives in New York City clearly remained precarious.[38]

As the number of fugitives increased in the late 1850s, articles in the southern press about the underground railroad became more and more frequent. Some slaveowners feared these reports actually encouraged escapes. The South's slaves, the *Richmond Whig* insisted, "are the happiest and best cared for laboring population in the world." But, it warned, the "weak mind of the slave" might be adversely affected by accounts of the "operations of the underground railroad." "Is there no way to break up this 'railroad'?" wondered another Virginia newspaper. The fugitive slave issue continued to roil national politics as the irrepressible conflict careered toward its final crisis.[39]

8

THE END OF THE UNDERGROUND RAILROAD

I

As slaves made their way to freedom in the late 1850s, the fugitive slave issue not only continued to intensify the sectional conflict over slavery, but also produced divisions within the North. The Kansas-Nebraska Act of 1854, which repealed the Missouri Compromise of 1820 and opened most of the Louisiana Purchase to the spread of slavery, produced a political earthquake. In its aftermath, the Whig party disintegrated, and the Republican party emerged as a northern sectional organization committed to preventing slavery's westward expansion. The Fugitive Slave Act became a point of controversy within the new party. Many Radical Republicans demanded the law's repeal and sought to obstruct its operation. Moderate Republicans disliked the statute but were reluctant to embrace open defiance of the law.

Between 1855 and 1860, legislatures in New England, Ohio, Michigan, and Wisconsin enacted new personal liberty laws that authorized the state to provide counsel for accused fugitives, required that their status be determined by a jury trial, and increased the penalties for kidnapping free blacks. Wisconsin and Ohio Republicans went even further. The Wisconsin Supreme Court overturned the conviction of Sherman Booth, an abolitionist who led a crowd that rescued a fugitive slave from jail, and declared the federal statute unconstitutional (a ruling reversed by the Supreme Court in 1859 in *Ableman v. Booth*). In Ohio, after a widely publicized fugitive slave rescue and the subsequent trial and conviction of some of those involved, the state Republican platform in 1859 called for the repeal of the Fugitive Slave Act. Ironically, by making the return of fugitives a national responsibility, Congress, in the words of the *New York Times*, had made "the doctrine of state rights, so long slavery's friend, . . . its foe." One Republican leader in Ohio even called for the party to "come to Calhoun's ground"—to affirm the right of states to nullify federal legislation.[1]

Many Republicans found these developments legally indefensible and a threat to the party's electoral prospects. Even in radical Wisconsin, Senator Timothy O. Howe observed that since "almost the whole country has declared *nullification* to be an unconstitutional remedy," it would be suicidal for Republicans to become associated with that doctrine. During the 1850s, New Jersey, Pennsylvania, Illinois, and Indiana—the more moderate states of the Lower North—enacted no new laws relating to fugitives. Nor did New York, although its personal liberty laws from 1840 remained on the books. Moderate Republican newspapers, including the *New York Times*, criticized the Fugitive Slave Act but insisted on adherence to the rule of law.[2]

Abraham Lincoln, who on this and other issues sought to find common ground among the party's factions, urged Republicans in each state to avoid taking positions that alienated voters in others. Lincoln acknowledged that under the Constitution, the South had a right to recover fugitive slaves, but he favored modifying the 1850 law to provide guarantees that free persons would not be "carried into slavery." "The cause of Republicanism in Illinois," Lincoln wrote to Salmon P. Chase, the governor of Ohio, "is hopeless, if it can be in any way made responsible" for demands to resist or repeal the federal statute. After Lincoln's nomination for president in 1860, some abolitionists cited his commitment to enforcing the Fugitive Slave Act as evidence of a lack of antislavery conviction. Wendell Phillips went so far as to call Lincoln "the Slave-Hound of Illinois." To preserve party unity, the Republican national platform of 1860 made no mention of fugitive slaves or the 1850 statute. Nonetheless, as the decade drew to a close, enforcement of the federal law was becoming more difficult in many parts of the North. In 1859, a U.S. commissioner in Philadelphia discharged an accused fugitive with the resonant name Daniel Webster. Every previous case of this kind, wrote James Miller McKim, had "gone against us. ... The day of Pennsylvania's redemption draweth nigh."[3]

The fugitive slave issue affected the secession crisis that followed Lincoln's election in contradictory ways. The eight states of the Upper South, where most fugitives originated, rejected secession until after war broke out, and the four northernmost—Delaware, Maryland, Kentucky, and Missouri, which bordered the free states and whose owners suffered the most from slaves running away—never left the Union. But in the Lower South, what the *New York Herald* called the underground railroad's "fanatical warfare on the constitutional rights of property" figured prominently in enumerations of secessionists' grievances. In October 1860, the *Charleston Mercury* warned that in the event of Lincoln's election, enforcement of the Fugitive Slave Act would cease and the underground railroad would operate "*over*-ground."[4]

Even though few fugitive slaves reached the North from South Carolina, the longest paragraph in that state's "Declaration of the Immediate Causes" of secession, adopted on Christmas Eve in 1860, related not to the territorial issue that had dominated national politics but to northern obstruction of the rendition of fugitives. "An increasing hostility on the part of the non-slaveholding states to the institution of slavery," the document maintained, had led the free states to render "useless" the fugitive slave clause, without which the Constitution would never have been ratified. With the North having "broken" the constitutional compact, South Carolina, in turn, was "released from her obligation" to it. Alluding to the *Lemmon* case in New York, the declaration also assailed northern states' abrogation of the right of slave transit. The Confederate Constitution, approved in March 1861, copied virtually word for word its U.S. counterpart's fugitive slave clause, although unlike its predecessor it explicitly referred to an escaped "slave," not simply a "person held to service or labor." Even though there were no free states in the Confederacy, its constitution took no chances about the right to bring slaves from one state to another. It explicitly guaranteed that slaveholders would enjoy "the right of transit and sojourn in any State . . . with their slaves and other property."[5]

Rarely was the pro-southern orientation of New York City's political and commercial leaders more evident than during the secession crisis. Anxious to retain the city's economic ties with the South, prominent New Yorkers of both political parties pressed for northern concessions that might avert disunion. Mayor Fernando Wood even proposed that the city itself secede. New York, he declared, had no quarrel with the South. It should reconstitute itself as a "free city" so that it could enjoy "uninterrupted intercourse" with the cotton states. The *Journal of Commerce*, which had supported John C. Breckenridge, the presidential candidate of proslavery southern Democrats, called for repeal of the personal liberty laws and abandonment of the "new-fangled doctrine, that to rob our neighbor of his slave . . . is a Christian duty." In January 1861, a special train brought thirty prominent New York capitalists to Washington, including the iron magnate Peter Cooper and William H. Aspinwall of the Union Safety Committee, which a decade earlier had promoted enforcement of the Fugitive Slave Act. They bore a petition for compromise signed by 40,000 businessmen.

Hamilton Fish, a conservative Republican, expressed surprise at the "extent of concessions" New York merchants were willing to make to the South, including acceptance of the *Dred Scott* decision allowing slavery to spread throughout the West.[6]

In Washington, compromise proposals abounded during the secession winter, and most included provisions relating to fugitive slaves. Nearly sixty plans to resolve the sectional conflict came before Congress, the most prominent being a series of unamendable constitutional amendments proposed by Senator John J. Crittenden of Kentucky. One amendment provided for federal compensation to the owners of fugitive slaves (an idea, it will be recalled, the Lower South had rejected ten years earlier). Crittenden also presented resolutions calling for faithful execution of federal laws relating to fugitives, declaring the personal liberty laws unconstitutional, and, to meet one northern objection to the Fugitive Slave Act, equalizing the fee awarded to U.S. commissioners for discharging or returning an accused runaway.

None of these proposals managed to soothe secessionists' fears, and none won congressional approval. "It is not your personal liberty bills that we dread," declared Senator Alfred Iverson of Georgia. "Those personal liberty bills are obnoxious to us not on account of their practical operation . . . but as an evidence of deep-seated, widespread hostility to our institutions." Without a "change of public sentiment" in the North, his colleague James S. Green of Missouri agreed, the repeal of such laws "would not amount to a straw." Nonetheless, Republicans demonstrated far more willingness to make concessions on the fugitive question than on their party's core principle of halting the westward expansion of slavery. Governor Edwin D. Morgan urged the legislature to demonstrate the North's good faith by repealing New York's 1840 law requiring a trial by jury for accused fugitives. Senator Lyman Trumbull, who as an Illinois lawyer had represented fugitive slaves and blacks illegally held to long-term indentures, insisted that Republicans must recognize "the right of a slave owner to a reasonable law to recapture his runaway slaves."[7]

Lincoln, who vehemently opposed compromise on the territorial issue during the secession crisis, urged congressional Republicans to abandon "all opposition, real and apparent, to the fugitive slave [clause] of the constitution," while continuing to insist that federal law ought to include the "usual safeguards . . . securing free men against being surrendered as slaves." In his inaugural address, on March 4, 1861, Lincoln reaffirmed the constitutional obligation to return fugitives but added that "all the safeguards of liberty known in civilized and humane jurisprudence" ought to be respected, "so that a free man be not in any case surrendered as a slave." Lincoln must have known that this discussion was unlikely to conciliate the South. Abolitionists, nonetheless, excoriated his acknowledgment of a duty to return fugitives. Frederick Douglass praised parts of the speech but added that on this question, Lincoln "stands on the same moral level" with slaveholders.[8]

Whatever Lincoln's stance, his election seems to have inspired an increase in the number of slaves seeking freedom in the North. "During the last eight weeks," Stephen Myers reported from Albany on December 17, 1860, more fugitives had escaped from the South than "in any four months before." Myers was particularly impressed by the growing number who had "come away in vessels this season . . . and have landed in eastern ports." The outbreak of the Civil War accelerated the process. In April 1861, three days after the firing on Fort Sumter, the *New York Tribune* observed that fugitives were passing through Philadelphia on the underground railroad "in far larger numbers than usual." Throughout 1861, slaves from Maryland and Delaware continued to escape into Pennsylvania, although, as one underground railroad operative remarked, the organization was no longer needed, since "nearly every northern man" was now willing to offer assistance. Runaway slaves, James Miller McKim reported from Philadelphia in December 1861, now traveled "fearlessly by daylight . . . and by a variety of routes heretofore closed to them." Anyone "who would now undertake to catch and return a fugitive slave," he added "would be a fool."[9]

The Civil War fundamentally transformed the opportunities available to slaves seeking freedom. As soon as federal troops entered a locality, which in Maryland meant from the very beginning of the war, slaves sought refuge with the Union army. Others flocked to Washington, D.C., now the capital of an antislavery government. Eager to conciliate what it imagined to be a host of pro-Union southerners within the Confederacy, and desperate to prevent the secession of the northernmost slave states, the Lincoln administration at first enforced the Fugitive Slave Act, and Union commanders issued strict orders to their troops to respect private property and return runaway slaves. Three months into the conflict, a Maryland newspaper pointed out that more escaped slaves had been remanded to their owners under Lincoln "than during the whole of Mr. Buchanan's presidential term." Ward Hill Lamon, a friend from Illinois whom Lincoln had appointed marshal of the District of Columbia, filled the city's jails with runaway slaves, leading to a power struggle between Lamon, army officers in need of black labor, and antislavery members of Congress. But, especially after the abolition of slavery in the District in the spring of 1862, it became very difficult for owners, even if they hailed from Maryland, which remained in the Union, to retrieve fugitives there. As late as mid-1863, however, a few fugitives whose owners were able to demonstrate loyalty to the Union were remanded to Maryland from the nation's capital.[10]

In the fall of 1860, when it became clear that Lincoln would be the next president, Oliver Johnson, who had succeeded Sydney Howard Gay as editor of the *National Anti-Slavery Standard,* heralded "the beginning of a new and better era." Little could he imagine how quickly the new era would arrive. Many soldiers ignored orders forbidding them to harbor runaways. In May 1861, the president's cabinet approved the decision of Benjamin F. Butler, who commanded Union forces at Fortress Monroe, Virginia, not to return slaves who arrived at his outpost. That July, the House of Representatives adopted a resolution introduced by Owen Lovejoy, a Radical Republican from Illinois, stating that it was not "part of the duty of the soldiers of the United States to capture and return fugitive slaves." The resolution did not come before the Senate, but it indicated widespread Republican dissatisfaction with military commanders who returned runaway slaves. By the end of 1861, as slaves by the hundreds, then thousands, sought refuge with the army, Lincoln declared that those who reached Union lines had become free. Early in 1862, the press reported Lincoln's view that the government had no obligation to return fugitive slaves and that in any event public opinion would not allow it to do so. That March, just as federal forces were entering the Mississippi Valley, leading to a flood of slaves to the army, Congress forbade military officers from returning fugitives.[11]

Before the war, the actions of runaway slaves had powerfully affected the national debate over slavery. Now, fugitives were helping to propel the nation down the road to emancipation. As the *New York Herald* noted, the question of the fate of slavery had been "forced upon the administration by these . . . negroes in our army camps." By 1862, one historian has written, the federal government had "undertaken the work of the underground railroad." No longer did slaves have to reach the North or Canada to escape from bondage. As new gateways to freedom opened within the South, what the *Liberator* called the "National Underground Railroad" superseded its predecessor. Far more slaves—men, women, and children, of all ages—escaped to Union lines than had reached the free states and Canada during the preceding thirty years. "An end is put . . . to the Underground Railroad," wrote McKim. "I take this opportunity . . . to thank the contributors to the treasury of the Philadelphia Vigilance Committee, . . . and to notify them that in all probability we shall have no further call for their aid in this particular line of business." As for New York City, in 1863 a writer in *Principia*, an abolitionist newspaper published irregularly there during the Civil War, jested that because of wartime prosperity, all the railroads in the North were "doing a flourishing business" except one—the underground railroad "now does scarcely any business at all . . . scarcely a solitary traveler comes along." Many of the fugitives who had found refuge in Canada now returned to the United States; some enlisted in the Union army. Indeed, reversing the historic pattern, during and after the war black northerners began to seek their fortunes in the South as teachers, employees of the Freedmen's Bureau, aspirants for political office, or simply individuals in search of economic opportunity. The overthrow of Reconstruction put an end to this North-South black migration; it would not resume until late in the twentieth century.[12]

Although increasingly impossible to enforce, the Fugitive Slave Act incongruously remained on the books until its repeal in 1864, more than a year after Lincoln issued the Emancipation Proclamation. During Reconstruction, it enjoyed an ironic afterlife. Lyman Trumbull, now chair of the Senate Judiciary Committee, used the infamous 1850 statute as a model for the Civil Rights Act of 1866, which revolutionized American jurisprudence by establishing the principle of birthright citizenship and extending to black Americans many of the rights previously enjoyed exclusively by whites. To do so, Trumbull drew on the Fugitive Slave Act's enforcement mechanisms and civil and criminal penalties, and the way it superimposed federal power on state law in order to establish a national responsibility for securing constitutionally protected rights. "The act that was passed that time for the purpose of punishing persons who should aid Negroes to freedom," Trumbull declared, "is now to be applied . . . to the punishment of those who shall undertake to keep them in slavery." Thus, as James Wilson of Iowa put it, in the aftermath of the Civil War Congress turned "the arsenal of slavery upon itself," wielding "the weapons which slavery has placed in our hands . . . in the holy cause of liberty."[13]

II

As the underground railroad faded into history, the men and women who had devoted themselves to its operations followed divergent paths into the future. Some disappeared from the historical record. Albert Fountain, who had transported dozens of slaves to freedom on his ship *City of Richmond,* was last heard of in 1862, when Confederate authorities burned his vessel and he was reported by Thomas Garrett to have joined the Union army. Garrett himself, who claimed to have helped nearly 3,000 slaves reach the North and Canada, died in 1871 at the age of eighty-one. The previous year, as part of a celebration of the ratification of the Fifteenth Amendment, which granted black men throughout the nation the right to vote, the black community led Garrett through the streets of Wilmington in a carriage bedecked with a sign reading, "Our Moses."

Another "Moses," Harriet Tubman, secured a position with the Union army on the South Carolina Sea Islands. Officially a cook and nurse, she also served as a spy gathering intelligence behind enemy lines. In 1863, Tubman guided two Union gunboats carrying black soldiers up the Combahee River on a raid that disrupted Confederate supply lines and liberated over 700 slaves. For decades, Tubman fought to receive a veteran's pension for her wartime services, only to be denied. She eventually was awarded a pension, but only as the widow of a Civil War soldier she married after the war. Tubman died at ninety-one in 1913, the fiftieth anniversary of the Emancipation Proclamation.[14]

Many prominent underground railroad operatives continued their efforts to improve the lot of black Americans. In 1862, William Still became head of an employment office established by Philadelphia's black leaders to assist slaves who had escaped to Union lines. After the Civil War, Still prospered as the proprietor of a coal yard; he was so successful that he was invited to join the Philadelphia Board of Trade. Still took part in the fight to integrate the city's streetcars and secure for blacks the right to vote, as well as helping to organize a home for orphans of black soldiers and sailors and the city's first YMCA for black youth. Determined to boost sales of his book *The Underground Railroad* (1872), a vast compilation of information about runaway slaves and their escapes, he hired a bevy of agents to market it and arranged for it to be displayed at the Philadelphia Centennial Exposition of 1876. When Still died in 1902, a black businessman wrote to his son, "There are costly monuments towering toward the sky to men of the Caucasian race for deeds not so great nor so dangerous as his acts in the under-ground Rail Road."[15]

Still's coworker in the Philadelphia antislavery office, James Miller McKim, pioneered northern efforts to assist the freedpeople in the South. In 1862, he organized a committee to aid blacks on the Union-occupied Sea Islands. After the war, McKim was instrumental in the creation of the American Freedmen's Aid Commission, as well as the founding of the *Nation*, a weekly that, initially at least, promoted the cause of the former slaves. Robert Purvis, the former head of the Philadelphia Vigilance Committee, devoted himself to a wide range of issues, including home rule for Ireland, the rights of Native Americans, and women's suffrage. Purvis was one of the few black men to support Susan B. Anthony and Elizabeth Cady

Stanton in repudiating the Fifteenth Amendment for failing to secure women's right to vote. "He would rather that his son never be enfranchised," Purvis declared at a women's rights convention, "unless his daughter could be also." Purvis died in 1898, the last surviving founder of the American Anti-Slavery Society.[16]

During the Civil War, Stephen Myers, head of the Albany Vigilance Committee, raised a company of black soldiers, but when New York's governor, Edwin D. Morgan, refused to accept them, they served instead in the famous Fifty-Fourth Massachusetts Infantry. After the war, Myers worked as a hotel steward in Albany and Lake George, and as janitor for the postmaster of New York City. At his death in 1870, an Albany newspaper lauded him as a person who "did more for his people than any other colored man living, not excepting Fred. Douglass." Jermain W. Loguen, the "underground railroad king" of Syracuse, also recruited black troops. After the war, Loguen returned to Tennessee in search of long-lost family and friends. Increasingly, he devoted himself to church work. Elected as a bishop to the African Methodist Episcopal Zion church in 1868, he established congregations among freedpeople in the South. Loguen died in 1872, as he was about to leave on a missionary expedition to the West Coast.[17]

Of the New Yorkers most closely associated with the underground railroad, Lewis Tappan, although well into his seventies, helped to shape the efforts of the American Missionary Association to establish schools and colleges for blacks in the South. Charles B. Ray continued his work as a missionary among the city's black poor until his death in 1886. He also helped to organize a black labor convention and aided former slaves who emigrated to Kansas during the "Exodus" of 1879. James W. C. Pennington helped raise black troops during the war and then established black churches and schools in the South during Reconstruction. He died in Florida in 1870. Abigail Hopper Gibbons worked as a nurse in a camp for runaway slaves and wounded Union soldiers in Maryland during the Civil War, and afterward she engaged in activities including finding jobs for war widows, working to reform prisons, and participating in the "purity crusade" that sought to rid New York City of prostitution. At the age of ninety-one, she addressed the state legislature on behalf of a bill establishing a women's reformatory in the city. During the New York City draft riots of July 1863, while she was away working as a nurse, the Gibbons' home on West Twenty-Ninth Street was sacked by the mob. Her husband, James, and two of their daughters had to escape over rooftops to safety. The riots demonstrated once again the powerful hold of racism and pro-southern sentiment in New York City.[18]

Sydney Howard Gay's career in journalism flourished after he left the *National Anti-Slavery Standard.* During the Civil War, he served as managing editor of the *New York Tribune.* With the editor, Horace Greeley, often away, Gay essentially ran the newspaper, offering strong support to the war effort, pressing the Lincoln administration on emancipation and the enlistment of black soldiers, and trying to moderate the mercurial Greeley's unpredictable enthusiasms. He resigned in 1865 and later worked briefly on the *Chicago Tribune* and *New York Evening Post.* In the 1870s, when the publisher Charles Scribner engaged the renowned poet William Cullen Bryant to write a "centennial history" of the United States, Bryant, then in his eighties, asked Gay to become his "associate" on the project. Gay did "the real hard work of writing" the four-part history, while Bryant made editorial corrections to the two volumes that were completed before he died in 1878. To Gay's annoyance, however, the publisher listed Bryant as coauthor on all four, and continued to advertise the work as *Bryant's Popular History of the United States.* In 1882, when Gay penned an autobiographical sketch, he dwelled at length on the publisher's "mistake" of "attempting to persuade the public that [Bryant] was the author of a work, of one half [of] which not a word was written till after his death." Nonetheless, along with a subsequent biography of James Madison, the series gave Gay a reputation as a historian. In 1885, three years before his death, the newly founded American Historical Association invited Gay to become a member.[19]

Because of excessive detail in the first three volumes, the fourth and final part of the centennial history, which appeared in 1880, had to cover the entire period from 1780 to 1876. Gay used it to fight the battle against slavery one last time. He placed the blame for the Civil War squarely on the leaders of the South, who believed that "the best and truest government was an oligarchy founded upon property in man," and made the abolitionists, progenitors of a "new era in American history," the heroes. While remaining silent on his own role, he lauded the underground railroad and estimated that 30,000 slaves had reached "a safe refuge in Canada" in the three decades before the Civil War. Yet signs of disillusionment, or perhaps exhaustion, crept in. Gay said nothing about Reconstruction, except that it was "a work badly begun, unwisely carried on, and . . . still unfinished." His treatment of aid to fugitive slaves and of abolitionism more generally focused almost entirely on whites. Gay's idol and sometime tormenter William Lloyd Garrison received his due, as did Isaac T. Hopper, but William Still, Charles B. Ray, even Frederick Douglass, went unmentioned. "The African in America, whether bond or free," Gay concluded, had learned "the habit of submission" and had "rarely shown any spirit of revolt." *Bryant's Popular History*, as Gay proudly insisted, helped to stimulate public interest in the American past, but it offered an early iteration of the myth of the underground railroad, indeed the entire crusade against slavery, as a white humanitarian enterprise in aid of helpless blacks.[20]

Actually, as Gay well knew, the heroic work of white New Yorkers like himself, Hopper, Lewis Tappan, and James and Abigail

Gibbons on behalf of fugitive slaves would not have been possible without the courage and resourcefulness, in a hostile environment, of blacks, from the members of the original Vigilance Committee to the black churches that sheltered runaway slaves and the ordinary men and women who watched for fugitives on the docks and city streets and took them into their homes. Not to mention the two black men who had labored alongside Gay in the antislavery office. Information about their subsequent lives is not easy to come by. William H. Leonard continued to work as a printer until his death in 1873. His son William Jr., who followed the same craft, headed a black Republican club in Brooklyn in the 1880s. He later moved to New Jersey, where he became the leader of a black volunteer fire company in Asbury Park, the only one in the state until 1907, when white firemen threatened to "refuse to perform fire duties" unless it were dissolved.[21]

As for the indispensable Louis Napoleon, thanks to Gay he worked for a number of years as a messenger and janitor for the *New York Tribune*. He retired after the war, living on contributions from old friends in the abolitionist movement. In the 1870s, Napoleon finally achieved a certain notoriety. The *Brooklyn Eagle* included him in a list of the "Memorable Men" of that city, where he now lived. In 1875, the *New York Tribune* published a brief sketch of Napoleon, in a series on "New-York Characters." "The old man," it reported, "hobbles painfully" with the aid of a walking stick; "few would have suspected . . . that he had ever been the rescuer of 3,000 persons from bondage." Napoleon, the writer added, "loves to talk of these exploits of a past era."

Louis Napoleon died in 1881, four days shy of his eighty-first birthday. On his death certificate, enshrined for posterity, is recorded his occupation: "Underground R. R. Agent."[22]

ACKNOWLEDGMENTS

Like all works of history, this book rests on a foundation created by others. My greatest debt is to the numerous scholars who have come before me studying fugitive slaves, the underground railroad, and the origins of the Civil War. But I am delighted to be able to take this opportunity to thank those individuals who directly assisted this project.

I begin with Madeline Lewis, a history major at Columbia College, who in 2007 was employed part-time to walk my family's dog, the celebrated cocker spaniel Sammy. She was writing her senior thesis about Sydney Howard Gay's journalistic career and one day mentioned that I might find interesting a document relating to fugitive slaves that she had seen in the Gay Papers at Columbia University. I filed this away for future reference as I was then engaged in work on a book about Abraham Lincoln and slavery. But one day, many months later, when I happened to be at Columbia's Rare Book and Manuscript Library, I asked to see the relevant box. I found the Record of Fugitives so riveting that it led me to embark on the research project that resulted in this book. Thank you, Madeline, and I wish you every success in your career as a lawyer. Thanks also to Sarah Bridger, then a graduate student in history at Columbia, who transcribed the manuscript, and to the Rare Book and

Manuscript Library staff, who accommodated my many requests, especially Eric Wakin, who provided me with a photographic reproduction of the Record of Fugitives and in other ways aided my research in the Gay, Jay Family, and other collections.

I also thank the historians who generously shared insights and the results of their own research. Tom Calarco and Don Papson, who are engaged in their own project relating to Gay, generously shared ideas and information. Prithi Kanakamedala passed along the impressive study she compiled on black abolitionism in Brooklyn for a major exhibition at the Brooklyn Historical Society. David Blight allowed me to read a draft of the chapter on Frederick Douglass's escape from slavery in his forthcoming biography of Douglass. Jeffrey Bolster helped unravel the story of a fugitive's husband who worked for the U.S. Navy. Kate Larson shared her deep knowledge of the career of Harriet Tubman and helped me make sense of the entries related to Tubman in Gay's records. Graham Hodges provided insights derived from work on his important biography of David Ruggles. Other scholars who responded to my requests for information and advice included Richard J. Blackett, Andrew Cohen, Norman Dann, Paul Finkelman, David Gellman, Kathryn Grover, W. Caleb McDaniel, Dwight Pitcaithley, Paul Stewart, Marie Tyler-McGraw, and Judith Wellman.

Librarians and archivists provided valuable assistance in locating and utilizing material, especially Bruce Abrams and Kenneth Cobb of the Municipal Archives, New York City; Christopher Densmore of the Friends Historical Library, Swarthmore College; and Allan Weinreb of the John Jay Homestead. Thanks, too, to researchers who located materials in other repositories: Julia Moser at Cornell University; Elizabeth Skilton at the Amistad Research Center; Matthew Spooner at the Virginia Historical Society; and Ashley Towle at the National Archives.

I am deeply indebted to five outstanding scholars who took the time to read the entire manuscript of this book and offered valuable corrections and suggestions: Elizabeth Blackmar, Graham Hodges, James Oakes, Matthew Pinsker, and Manisha Sinha. Portions of the book were presented as the Littlefield Lectures at the University of Texas, Austin, and as the Nathan I. Huggins Lectures at the Hutchins Center for African and African American Research, Harvard University.

As always, I thank my literary agent and all-around advocate Sandra Dijkstra, and the staff at W. W. Norton & Company, especially Steve Forman, an insightful and supportive editor, and his colleagues Justin Cahill and Penelope Lin.

My greatest debt is to my wife, Lynn Garafola, and daughter, Daria Rose Foner, who displayed remarkable patience and fortitude in listening to stories and ideas about the underground railroad. Lynn, a writer and editor extraordinaire, read the manuscript and improved it immensely.

In a few years I will retire after a long career of teaching. I dedicate this book to my students, past and present, undergraduate and graduate, from whom I have learned so much.

NOTES

Abbreviations Used in Notes

AC Antislavery Collection, Boston Public Library

AMA American Missionary Association Archives, Amistad Research Center, Tulane University

ANHS American Negro Historical Society Collection, Historical Society of Pennsylvania, Philadelphia

BAP C. Peter Ripley, ed., *The Black Abolitionist Papers* (5 vols.; Chapel Hill, 1985–92)

BE *Brooklyn Eagle*

BS *Baltimore Sun*

CA *Colored American* (New York)

CG *Congressional Globe*

FDP *Frederick Douglass' Paper* (Rochester)

FHL Friends Historical Library, Swarthmore College

FJ *Freedom's Journal* (New York)

FOM *Friend of Man* (Utica)

GP Sydney Howard Gay Papers, Rare Book and Manuscript Library, Columbia University

HSPa Historical Society of Pennsylvania, Philadelphia

JFP Jay Family Papers, Rare Book and Manuscripts Library, Columbia University

JJH John Jay Homestead, Bedford, N.Y.

JL Oliver Johnson Letters, Miscellaneous American Letters and Papers, Schomburg Center for Research in Black Culture, New York Public Library

JP	John Jay Papers, Rare Book and Manuscript Library, Columbia University
MAC	Samuel J. May Anti-Slavery Collection, Cornell University
MB	Minute Book, American and Foreign Anti-Slavery Society, Amistad Research Center, Tulane University
MC	Maloney Collection of McKim-Garrison Family Papers, New York Public Library
MOL	*Mirror of Liberty* (New York)
NAS	*National Anti-Slavery Standard* (New York)
NS	*North Star* (Rochester)
NYE	*New York Evangelist*
NYEP	*New York Evening Post*
NYH	*New York Herald*
NYHS	New-York Historical Society
NYO	*New York Observer*
NYPL	New York Public Library
NYS	*New York Spectator*
NYT	*New York Times*
NYTrib	*New York Tribune*
PF	*Provincial Freeman* (Toronto)
PL	Elijah Pennypacker Letters, Friends Historical Library, Swarthmore College
PP	Wendell Phillips Papers, Houghton Library, Harvard University
RG 21	Records of the Clerk of the Court, 1746–1932, and of the U.S. Commissioners, 1837–1860, of the U.S. District Court for the Southern District of New York, Record Group 21, National Archives
SC	Wilbur H. Siebert Collection, Ohio Historical Society, Columbus
SP	Gerrit Smith Papers, Syracuse University
TP	Lewis Tappan Papers, Library of Congress

1. Introduction

1. *Life and Times of Frederick Douglass Written by Himself* (rev. ed.: Boston, 1892), 97, 153; David Blight, *Frederick Douglass: A Life* (forthcoming), ch. 5.
2. *Life and Times of Frederick Douglass*, 249; Blight, *Frederick Douglass*, ch. 5; William G. Thomas, *The Iron Way: Railroads, the Civil War, and the Making of Modern America* (New Haven, 2011), 17–20.
3. Solomon Northup, *Twelve Years a Slave: Narrative of Solomon Northup, a Citizen*

of New-York, Kidnapped in Washington City in 1841, and Rescued in 1853 (Auburn, N.Y., 1853).

4. *Life and Times of Frederick Douglass,* 253; Graham Russell Gao Hodges, *David Ruggles: A Radical Black Abolitionist and the Underground Railroad in New York City* (Chapel Hill, 2010), 1–2; Blight, *Frederick Douglass,* ch. 5.
5. Pennington's account of his life in slavery and his escape takes up most of his memoir, *The Fugitive Blacksmith* (London, 1849); see also Christopher Webber, *American to the Backbone: The Life of James W. C. Pennington, the Fugitive Slave Who Became One of the First Black Abolitionists* (New York, 2011), 1–40.
6. *Life and Times of Frederick Douglass,* 253–55; Kathryn Grover, *The Fugitive's Gibraltar: Escaping Slaves and Abolitionism in New Bedford, Massachusetts* (Amherst, Mass., 2001), 1–28.
7. Louis A. Chamerovzow, *The Slave's Underground Railroad to Freedom* (Edinburgh, n.d.), 1; J. Blaine Hudson, *Encyclopedia of the Underground Railroad* (Jefferson, N.C., 2006), 9, offers a highly speculative estimate of 135,000 slave escapes in the half century before the Civil War.
8. Stanley Harrold, *Border War: Fighting over Slavery before the Civil War* (Chapel Hill, 2010), 39–40; *De Bow's Review,* 11 (September 1851), 331; Frederick Law Olmsted, *A Journey in the Seaboard Slave States* (New York, 1856), 226; John Hope Franklin and Loren Schweninger, *Runaway Slaves: Rebels on the Plantation* (New York, 1999), 210; Pennington, *Fugitive Blacksmith,* 11.
9. Harrold, *Border War,* 47–49; Fergus M. Bordewich, *Bound for Canaan: The Epic Story of the Underground Railroad, America's First Civil Rights Movement* (New York, 2005), 109–13; *Narrative of the Life of Frederick Douglass, an American Slave, Written by Himself* (Boston, 1845), 85, 106.
10. *Life and Times of Frederick Douglass,* 253–54; Eber M. Pettit, *Sketches in the History of the Underground Railroad* (Fredonia, N.Y., 1879), 35–36; *Tocsin of Liberty* (Albany) in *NYO,* September 28, 1842; *NYT,* September 7, 1853; *Raleigh Daily Register,* May 14, 1853; *Cleveland Daily Herald,* July 22, 1854.
11. *NYH,* January 5, 1860.
12. Philip S. Foner, *Business and Slavery: The New York Merchants and the Irrepressible Conflict* (Chapel Hill, 1941), 1–6; Linda K. Kerber, "Abolitionists and Amalgamators: The New York City Race Riots of 1834," *New York History,* 48 (January 1967), 28–39.
13. William Still, *The Underground Railroad* (rev. ed.: Philadelphia, 1878), 674–75.
14. Record of Fugitives, GP. A transcription of this document will be published, with annotations, in *Secret Lives of the Underground Railroad in New York City,* a forthcoming book by Don Papson and Tom Calarco.

15. Wilbur H. Siebert, *The Underground Railroad from Slavery to Freedom* (New York, 1898), 10–11; Robert Purvis to Wilbur H. Siebert, December 23, 1895, SC.
16. The New York State Vigilance Committee, successor of the New York Committee of Vigilance, claimed in 1849 that the earlier organization had helped 2,000 fugitives gain "personal liberty." Subsequent reports by the second committee claim a total for the two of 3,200 to the year 1856. *NS*, May 18, 1849; Tom Calarco, *Places of the Underground Railroad* (Santa Barbara, 2011), xxi. Sydney Howard Gay's group assisted more than 200 fugitives in 1855 and 1856 and an unknown number in other years.
17. Julie Roy Jeffrey, *Abolitionists Remember: Antislavery Autobiographies and the Unfinished Work of Emancipation* (Chapel Hill, 2008); [Levi Coffin], *Reminiscences of Levi Coffin, the Reputed President of the Underground Railroad* (Cincinnati, 1876); Homer U. Johnson, *From Dixie to Canada; Romance and Realities of the Underground Railroad* (Orwell, Ohio, 1894), 13.
18. Still, *Underground Railroad*; Stephen G. Hall, "To Render the Private Public: William Still and the Selling of 'The Underground Railroad,' " *Pennsylvania Magazine of History and Biography*, 127 (January 2003), 41; R. C. Smedley, *History of the Underground Railroad in Chester and the Neighboring Counties of Pennsylvania* (Lancaster, Pa., 1883). The original records Still used to compile his book are now available online at the website of the HSPa as Journal C of Station No. 2.
19. Siebert, *Underground Railroad*, esp. 62, 67–68, 71, 120; Stephen Kantrowitz, *More than Freedom: Fighting for Black Citizenship in a White Republic, 1829–1889* (New York, 2012), 421; David W. Blight, "Why the Underground Railroad, and Why Now? A Long View," in David W. Blight, ed., *Passages to Freedom: The Underground Railroad in History and Memory* (Washington, D.C., 2004), 233–47.
20. Larry Gara, *The Liberty Line: The Legend of the Underground Railroad* (Lexington, Ky., 1961), esp. vii, 92–95.
21. Stanley Harrold, "Freeing the Weems Family: Another Look at the Underground Railroad," *Civil War History*, 42 (December 1996), 290–92; Franklin and Schweninger, *Runaway Slaves*, 98–101.
22. Kate C. Larson, "Racing for Freedom: Harriet Tubman's Underground Railroad Network through New York," *Afro-Americans in New York Life and History*, 36 (January 2012), 8–9. Judith Wellman, *Uncovering the Freedom Trail in Auburn and Cayuga County, New York* (Auburn, N.Y., 2005), and Cheryl Janifer LaRoche, *The Geography of Resistance: Free Black Communities and the Underground Railroad* (Urbana, Ill., 2014), offer examples of the kind of in-depth local research

that has yielded important new information about fugitives and those who aided them.

23. Hodges, *David Ruggles*; Margaret Hope Bacon, *But One Race: The Life of Robert Purvis* (Albany, 2007); Carol M. Hunter, *To Set the Captives Free: Reverend Jermain Wesley Loguen and the Struggle for Freedom in Central New York, 1835–1872* (New York, 1993); Stanley Harrold, *Subversives: Antislavery Community in Washington, D.C., 1828–1865* (Baton Rouge, 2003); T. Stephen Whitman, *Challenging Slavery in the Chesapeake: Black and White Resistance to Human Bondage, 1775–1865* (Baltimore, 2007); Bordewich, *Bound for Canaan.*
24. Blight, "Why the Underground Railroad?," 233–47.
25. Franklin and Schweninger, *Runaway Slaves*, 97–113; Irwin D. S. Winsboro and Joe Knetsch, "Florida Slaves, the 'Saltwater Railroad' to the Bahamas, and Anglo-American Diplomacy," *Journal of Southern History*, 79 (February 2013), 51–78; Sylviane A. Diouf, *Slavery's Exiles: The Story of the American Maroons* (New York, 2013).
26. Bordewich, *Bound for Canaan*, 115; Harrold, *Border War*, xii; *Wilmington Chicken* in *BS*, January 7, 1850.
27. Christopher Phillips, *Freedom's Port: The African American Community of Baltimore, 1790–1860* (Urbana, Ill., 1997), 15–33, 66–68, 78–80; Richard Newman and James Mueller, eds., *Antislavery and Abolition in Philadelphia: Emancipation and the Long Struggle for Racial Justice in the City of Brotherly Love* (Baton Rouge, 2011), 6–7.
28. Phillips, *Freedom's Port*, 194; Thomas, *Iron Way*, 17–20; *CA*, September 26, 1840.
29. *FDP*, April 6, 1855.
30. For the Lower North, see Eric Foner, *Free Soil, Free Labor, Free Men: The Ideology of the Republican Party before the Civil War* (New York, 1970), 186.
31. Clare Taylor, ed., *British and American Abolitionists: An Episode in Transatlantic Understanding* (Edinburgh, 1974), 341–42.
32. Austin Bearse, *Reminiscences of Fugitive-Slave Law Days in Boston* (Boston, 1880), 33; Siebert, *Underground Railroad*, 104–8; William Lloyd Garrison to James Miller McKim, March 19, 1853, MC; Milton Meltzer and Patricia G. Holland, eds., *Lydia Maria Child: Selected Letters, 1817–1880* (Amherst, Mass., 1982), 244; Wellman, *Uncovering the Freedom Trail*, 24–26; Benjamin Quarles, *Black Abolitionists* (New York, 1969), 148–49.
33. *Life and Times of Frederick Douglass*, 328–29; Webber, *American to the Backbone*, 110–11, 151.
34. Hodges, *David Ruggles*, 4; *Emancipator*, December 1, 1836; Henry Grew, Letter of Introduction for William Still, September 10, 1855, ANHS.

35. Matthew Pinsker, "Vigilance in Pennsylvania: Underground Railroad Activities in the Keystone State, 1837–1861," Report Presented at the Pennsylvania Historical and Museum Commission Annual Conference on Black History, Harrisburg, 2000, 17–18; Bordewich, *Bound for Canaan,* 4–5; *The Works of Charles Sumner* (15 vols.; Boston, 1870–83), 4: 10–11.
36. Mark K. Ricks, "The 1848 *Pearl* Escape from Washington, D.C.," in Paul Finkelman and Donald R. Kennon, eds., *In the Shadow of Freedom: The Politics of Slavery in the National Capital* (Athens, Ohio, 2011), 204–5; Siebert, *Underground Railroad,* 275–79; *Annual Report of the American Anti-Slavery Society . . . for the Year Ending May 1, 1859* (New York, 1860), 100; James B. Stewart, "From Moral Suasion to Political Confrontation: American Abolitionists and the Problem of Resistance," in Blight, ed., *Passages to Freedom,* 86; John Niven, *Salmon P. Chase: A Biography* (New York, 1995), 76–83; *Autobiography of Dr. William Henry Johnson* (Albany, 1900), 17.
37. *FDP,* October 1, 1852; *NAS,* June 29, 1843.
38. *PF,* April 21, 1855; Richard M. Blackett, *Making Freedom: The Underground Railroad and the Politics of Slavery* (Chapel Hill, 2013), 15. See also James Oakes, "The Political Significance of Slave Resistance," *History Workshop,* 22 (Autumn 1986), 89–107.
39. John Ashworth, *Slavery, Capitalism, and Politics in the Antebellum Republic* (2 vols.; New York, 1995–2007), 2: 41; Bordewich, *Bound for Canaan,* 108; Theodore D. Weld, *American Slavery as It Is* (New York, 1839), 77–82.
40. *NAS,* October 21, 1841; Quarles, *Black Abolitionists,* 61; W. Caleb McDaniel, *The Problem of Democracy in the Age of Slavery: Garrisonian Abolitionists and Transatlantic Reform* (Baton Rouge, 2013), 190–207; Robert L. Hall, "Massachusetts Abolitionists Document the Slave Experience," in Donald M. Jacobs, ed., *Courage and Conscience: Black and White Abolitionists in Boston* (Boston, 1993), 80–90.
41. Don E. Fehrenbacher, *The Slaveholding Republic: An Account of the United States Government's Relations to Slavery* (New York, 2001), 92–103, 206–14; Sarah E. Cornell, "Citizens of Nowhere: Fugitive Slaves and Free African Americans in Mexico, 1833–1857," *Journal of American History,* 100 (September 2013), 351–75; *Proceedings of the New York Anti-Slavery Convention Held at Utica, October 21, and New York State Anti-Slavery Society Held at Peterboro, October 22, 1835* (Utica, 1835), 31.
42. *NYT,* November 30, 1855; Ashworth, *Slavery, Capitalism, and Politics,* 2: 41; William W. Freehling, *The Road to Disunion* (2 vols.; New York, 1990–2007), 1: 95; David F. Ericson, *Slavery in the American Republic: Developing the Federal Government, 1791–1861* (Lawrence, Kans., 2011), 91, 103; Barbara J. Fields, *Slavery and Freedom on the Middle Ground* (New Haven, 1985), 16.

43. *FOM*, September 9, 1840; Roy P. Basler, ed., *The Collected Works of Abraham Lincoln* (8 vols.; New Brunswick, N.J., 1953–55), 2: 320; 3: 317; 4: 263–69; Eric Foner, *The Fiery Trial: Abraham Lincoln and American Slavery* (New York, 2010), 46–47; *Chicago Tribune*, August 5, 1857; David Brion Davis, *The Problem of Slavery in the Age of Emancipation* (New York, 2014), 233.
44. *Life and Times of Frederick Douglass*, 329.
45. *Fifth Annual Report of the New York Committee of Vigilance* (New York, 1842), 11; J. Miller McKim to David Lee Child, November 22, n.y. [1850s], AC; *NAS*, February 3, 1855.

2. Slavery and Freedom in New York

1. Christopher Moore, "A World of Possibilities: Slavery and Freedom in Dutch New Amsterdam," in Ira Berlin and Leslie M. Harris, eds., *Slavery in New York* (New York, 2005), 31–46; Graham R. Hodges, *Root and Branch: African Americans in New York and East Jersey, 1613–1863* (Chapel Hill, 1999), 8–13, 26–31; Thelma Foote, *Black and White Manhattan: The History of Racial Formation in Colonial New York City* (New York, 2004), 36–40; Ira Berlin, *Many Thousands Gone: The First Two Centuries of Slavery in North America* (Cambridge, Mass., 1998), 50–53; Edgar J. McManus, *A History of Negro Slavery in New York* (Syracuse, 1966), 4–17.
2. Edwin G. Burrows and Mike Wallace, *Gotham: A History of New York City to 1898* (New York, 1999), 120–29; Foote, *Black and White Manhattan*, 71–77; Vivienne L. Kruger, "Born to Run: The Slave Family in Early New York, 1626 to 1827" (Ph.D. diss., Columbia University, 1985), 128–31.
3. Shane White, *Stories of Freedom in Black New York* (Cambridge, Mass., 2002), 19; Thelma W. Foote, " 'Some Hard Usage': The New York City Slave Revolt of 1712," *New York Folklore*, 18 (2000), 147–60; Foote, *Black and White Manhattan*, 133; Rhoda G. Freeman, *The Free Negro in New York City in the Era before the Civil War* (New York, 1994), 9; Leslie M. Harris, *In the Shadow of Slavery: African Americans in New York City, 1626–1863* (Chicago, 2003), 29, 43–47; Berlin, *Many Thousands Gone*, 180.
4. McManus, *History of Negro Slavery*, 21; Moore, "World of Possibilities," 46–47.
5. Hodges, *Root and Branch*, 51–52; Arthur Zilversmit, *The First Emancipation: The Abolition of Slavery in the North* (Chicago, 1967), 12; Jill Lepore, "The Tightening Vise: Slavery and Freedom in British New York," in Berlin and Harris, eds., *Slavery in New York*, 72–78; Graham Russell Gao Hodges, "Liberty and Constraint: The Limits of Revolution," in Berlin and Harris, eds., *Slavery in New York*, 95;

McManus, *History of Negro Slavery*, 104–5; Charles R. Foy, "Seeking Freedom in the Atlantic World, 1713–1783," *Early American Studies*, 4 (Spring 2006), 46–47.

6. Jonathan Prude, "To Look upon the 'Lower Sort': Runaway Ads and the Appearance of Unfree Laborers in America, 1750–1800," *Journal of American History*, 78 (June 1991), 124–42; Graham R. Hodges and Alan E. Brown, eds., *"Pretends to Be Free": Runaway Slave Advertisements from Colonial and Revolutionary New York and New Jersey* (New York, 1994), xiv–xvi, 313; *New-York Gazette*, February 16, 1761; Foote, *Black and White Manhattan*, 181, 190–91; Kruger, "Born to Run," 227–33; McManus, *History of Negro Slavery*, 109–13.
7. McManus, *History of Negro Slavery*, 115–16; Foote, *Black and White Manhattan*, 180; Don E. Fehrenbacher, *The Slaveholding Republic: An Account of the United States Government's Relations to Slavery* (New York, 2001), 206; William Blackstone, *Commentaries on the Laws of England* (4th ed.: 4 vols.; Dublin, 1771), 3: 4–5.
8. J. William Frost, "Why Quakers and Slavery? Why Not More Quakers?" in Brycchan Carey and Geoffrey Plank, eds., *Quakers and Abolition* (Urbana, Ill., 2014), 30–36; Harris, *In the Shadow of Slavery*, 48–51.
9. Foote, *Black and White Manhattan*, 213–15; Hodges, *Root and Branch*, 141; Eric Foner, *The Story of American Freedom* (New York, 1998), 29–34.
10. Hodges, *Root and Branch*, 144; Cassandra Pybus, *Epic Journeys of Freedom: Runaway Slaves of the American Revolution and Their Global Quest for Liberty* (Boston, 2006), 25–28.
11. Ira Berlin and Leslie M. Harris, "Introduction," in Berlin and Harris, eds., *Slavery in New York*, 13–14; Pybus, *Epic Journeys*, 26–30; Burrows and Wallace, *Gotham*, 248–49.
12. Hodges, "Liberty and Constraint," 95; Pybus, *Epic Journeys*, 28; Foote, *Black and White Manhattan*, 215.
13. Kruger, "Born to Run," 636–41; "Memoirs of the Life of Boston King, a Black Preacher," *Methodist Magazine*, 21 (March 1798), 106–7 (April 1798), 5; Pybus, *Epic Journeys*, 62; Daniel E. Meaders, *Dead or Alive: Fugitive Slaves and White Indentured Servants before 1830* (New York, 1993), 218.
14. Christopher Brown, *Moral Capital: Foundations of British Abolitionism* (Chapel Hill, 2006), 312; Simon Schama, *Rough Crossings: Britain, the Slaves and the American Revolution* (London, 2005), 146–48; Meaders, *Dead or Alive*, 218–23; William R. Riddell, "Interesting Notes on Great Britain and Canada with Respect to the Negro: Jay's Treaty and the Negro," *Journal of Negro History*, 13 (April 1928), 187–91. Graham Hodges, ed., *The Black Loyalist Directory: African Americans in Exile after the American Revolution* (New York, 1996), reproduces and analyzes the Book of Negroes.

15. Zilversmit, *First Emancipation*; Paul Finkelman, "The Kidnapping of John Davis and the Adoption of the Fugitive Slave Law of 1793," *Journal of Southern History*, 56 (August 1990), 398.
16. David F. Ericson, *Slavery in the American Republic: Developing the Federal Government, 1791–1861* (Lawrence, Kans., 2011), 83, 206–8; Max Farrand, ed., *The Records of the Federal Convention of 1787* (3 vols.; New Haven, 1911), 2: 443–53.
17. Farrand, ed., *Records*, 3: 254–55, 325; H. Robert Baker, *Prigg v. Pennsylvania: Slavery, the Supreme Court, and the Ambivalent Constitution* (Lawrence, Kans., 2012), 41–44.
18. T. K. Hunter, "Transatlantic Negotiations: Lord Mansfield, Liberty and Somerset," *Texas Wesleyan Law Review*, 13 (Symposium 2007), 711–27; H. Robert Baker, "The Fugitive Slave Clause and the Antebellum Constitution," *Law and History Review*, 30 (November 2012), 1133–37; Fehrenbacher, *Slaveholding Republic*, 240–41.
19. Ericson, *Slavery in the American Republic*, 206–9; Finkelman, "Kidnapping," 397–422.
20. Baker, "Fugitive Slave Clause," 1136–40; Fehrenbacher, *Slaveholding Republic*, 211–14.
21. Zilversmit, *First Emancipation*, 139–51; David Gellman, *Emancipating New York: The Politics of Slavery and Freedom, 1777–1827* (Baton Rouge, 2006), 33–34, 46; Kruger, "Born to Run," 725–29.
22. Thomas R. Moseley, "A History of the New York Manumission Society, 1785–1849" (Ph.D. diss., University of Michigan, 1963), 1–2, 26–38; *Constitution of the New-York Society for Promoting the Manumission of Slaves, and Protecting Such of Them as Have Been, or May Be Liberated* (New York, 1796); Richard S. Newman, *The Transformation of American Abolitionism: Fighting Slavery in the Early Republic* (Chapel Hill, 2002), 88; Zilversmit, *First Emancipation*, 163, 224.
23. Shane White, *Somewhat More Independent: The End of Slavery in New York City, 1770–1810* (Athens, Ga., 1991), 86–87; William Jay, *Life of John Jay* (2 vols.; New York, 1833), 1: 335; Hodges, *Root and Branch*, 166–67; Gellman, *Emancipating New York*, 161–63; Harris, *In the Shadow of Slavery*, 49–64, 208; Moseley, "History of the New York Manumission Society," 1–2, 33–35, 92–94.
24. Zilversmit, *First Emancipation*, 149–51; White, *Stories of Freedom*, 12-13; White, *Somewhat More Independent*, 5–9.
25. White, *Stories of Freedom*, 13; Burrows and Wallace, *Gotham*, 286, 348; Kruger, "Born to Run," 819; Patrick Rael, "The Long Death of Slavery," in Berlin and Harris, eds., *Slavery in New York*, 124–25; Zilversmit, *First Emancipation*, 176.

26. Gellman, *Emancipating New York*, 160; White, *Somewhat More Independent*, 32–36, 46, 141, 148; Harris, *In the Shadow of Slavery*, 68.
27. Zilversmit, *First Emancipation*, 176–82, 208, 213–14; Hodges, *Root and Branch*, 163–64; Rael, "Long Death," 126–44; Craig Wilder, *A Covenant with Color: Race and Social Power in Brooklyn* (New York, 2000), 39; Freeman, *Free Negro*, 6.
28. Philip S. Foner, *Business and Slavery: The New York Merchants and the Irrepressible Conflict* (Chapel Hill, 1941), 1–6; David Quigley, "Southern Slavery in a Free City: Economy, Politics, and Culture," in Berlin and Harris, eds., *Slavery in New York*, 266–78; *Anti-Slavery Record* (July 1837); J. D. B. De Bow, *The Interest in Slavery of the Southern Non-Slaveholder* (Charleston, 1860), 5; Wilder, *Covenant with Color*, 55–58.
29. Foner, *Business and Slavery*, 1–6; A. K. Sandoval-Strausz, *Hotel: An American History* (New Haven, 2007), 286; John Hope Franklin, *A Southern Odyssey: Travelers in the Antebellum North* (Baton Rouge, 1976), 21, 42, 69, 89.
30. *MOL*, August 1840; James S. Gibbons to Abby Hopper Gibbons, August 7, 1840, Abby Hopper Gibbons Papers, FHL.
31. White, *Stories of Freedom*, 29; Harris, *In the Shadow of Slavery*, 73–82; Daniel Perlman, "Organizations of the Free Negro in New York City, 1800–1860," *Journal of Negro History*, 36 (July 1971), 181–97; Margaret Washington, *Sojourner Truth's America* (Urbana, Ill., 2009), 130; Richard S. Newman and James Mueller, eds., *Antislavery and Abolition in Philadelphia: Emancipation and the Long Struggle for Racial Justice in the City of Brotherly Love* (Baton Rouge, 2011), 6–7.
32. Harris, *In the Shadow of Slavery*, 119; Tyler Anbinder, *Five Points* (New York, 2001), 1–2; *NYT*, August 11, 1853; Leonard P. Curry, *The Free Black in Urban America, 1800–1850* (Chicago, 1981), 260; Berlin and Harris, "Introduction," 17–20, 23–24; Hodges, *Root and Branch*, 232–33; Leslie M. Alexander, *African or American? Black Identity and Political Activism in New York City, 1784–1861* (Urbana, Ill., 2008), 31–32.
33. Craig Wilder, *In the Company of Black Men: The African Influence on African American Culture in New York City* (New York, 2001), 73; Carla Peterson, "Black Life in Freedom: Creating an Elite Culture," in Berlin and Harris, eds., *Slavery in New York*, 184–204.
34. *FJ*, April 20, July 6, 1827.
35. White, *Stories of Freedom*, 26–30; Paul A. Gilje, *The Road to Mobocracy: Popular Disorder in New York City, 1763–1834* (Chapel Hill, 1987), 147–52.
36. *MOL*, January 1839; *CA*, July 3, 1841; Margaret Bacon, *Freedom's Journal: The First African-American Newspaper* (Lanham, Md., 2007), 236–37; *FJ*, October 31, November 7, 14, December 5, 1828; *A Narrative of the Adventures and*

Escape of Moses Roper, from American Slavery (Philadelphia, 1838), 59–63; Gilbert H. Barnes and Dwight L. Dumond, eds., *Letters of Theodore Dwight Weld, Angelina Grimké and Sarah Grimké, 1822–1844* (2 vols.: New York, 1934), 1: 481.

37. Carol Wilson, *Freedom at Risk: The Kidnapping of Free Blacks in America, 1780–1865* (Lexington, Ky., 1994), 10–34; Julie Winch, "Philadelphia and the Other Underground Railroad," *Pennsylvania Magazine of History and Biography*, 111 (January 1987), 3–25; Stanley Harrold, *Border War: Fighting over Slavery before the Civil War* (Chapel Hill, 2010), 53–54; *FJ*, June 22, 1827, February 15, July 6, 25, November 7, 1828, January 31, 1829; *Pennsylvania Freeman*, May 9, 1844; Peter P. Hinks, " 'Frequently Plunged into Slavery': Free Blacks and Kidnapping in Antebellum Boston," *Historical Journal of Massachusetts*, 20 (Winter 1992), 16–31.

38. Gellman, *Emancipating New York*, 47; Charles C. Andrews, *The History of the New York African Free Schools* (New York, 1830), 8–9; Moseley, "History of the New York Manumission Society," 21, 144–47; Freeman, *Free Negro*, 53; Wilson, *Freedom at Risk*, 113; *FJ*, March 7, 1829.

39. Baker, "Fugitive Slave Clause," 1142–51; Baker, *Prigg v. Pennsylvania*, 73–77; Thomas D. Morris, *Free Men All: The Personal Liberty Laws of the North, 1780–1861* (Baltimore, 1974), 45–60; Ericson, *Slavery in the American Republic*, 215–16; John L. Dorsey, *Documentary History of Slavery in the United States* (Washington, D.C., 1851), 54–55.

40. Harris, *In the Shadow of Slavery*, 207–9; *BAP*, 3: 180; *MOL*, January 1839; *Weekly Advocate*, January 14, 1837.

41. Isaac V. Brown, *Biography of the Rev. Robert Finley* (2nd ed.: Philadelphia, 1857), 103–15; Douglas R. Egerton, "Averting a Crisis: The Proslavery Critique of the American Colonization Society," *Civil War History*, 43 (June 1997), 143–47; Daniel W. Howe, *The Political Culture of the American Whigs* (Chicago, 1979), 136; Rael, "Long Death," 143.

42. Hugh Davis, "Northern Colonizationists and Free Blacks, 1823–1837: The Case of Leonard Bacon," *Journal of the Early Republic*, 17 (Winter 1997), 651–75; Paul Goodman, *Of One Blood: Abolitionism and the Origins of Racial Equality* (Berkeley, 1998), xv–2; *BAP*, 3: 80; William M. Brewer, "John Brown Russwurm," *Journal of Negro History*, 13 (October 1928), 413–22; *FJ*, February 14, 21, 1829.

43. Newman, *Transformation*, 96–97; Newman and Mueller, eds., *Antislavery and Abolition*, 6–7; Harris, *In the Shadow of Slavery*, 121–40; David E. Swift, *Black Prophets of Justice: Activist Clergy before the Civil War* (Baton Rouge, 1989), 27–34; *FJ*, March 16, 1827.

44. Manisha Sinha, "Black Abolitionism: The Assault on Southern Slavery and the Struggle for Racial Equality," in Berlin and Harris, eds., *Slavery in New York*, 243–45; *CA*, May 9, 1840.
45. William Lloyd Garrison, *Thoughts on African Colonization* (Boston, 1832), 5; Sinha, "Black Abolitionism," 245–46; Paul Starr, *The Creation of the Media* (New York, 2004), 86–88; Newman, *Transformation*, 131–32, 158–59.
46. Aileen S. Kraditor, *Means and Ends in American Abolitionism* (New York, 1969), 4–6; *Declaration of Sentiments and Constitution of the American Anti-Slavery Society* (New York, 1835).
47. Swift, *Black Prophets*, 43; Alexander, *African or American?*, 84–85; Goodman, *Of One Blood*, 249.
48. Sean Wilentz, *The Rise of American Democracy: Jefferson to Lincoln* (New York, 2005), 423–32; Alice H. Henderson, "The History of the New York State Anti-Slavery Society" (Ph.D. diss., University of Michigan, 1963), 2–4, 43, 203; Hugh Davis, *Joshua Leavitt: Evangelical Abolitionist* (Baton Rouge, 1990), 101; Bertram Wyatt-Brown, *Lewis Tappan and the Evangelical War against Slavery* (Cleveland, 1969), 104–5.
49. Gerald Sorin, *The New York Abolitionists: A Case Study of Political Radicalism* (Westport, Conn., 1971), 71–75; Henderson, "History of the New York State Anti-Slavery Society," 6–11; Wyatt-Brown, *Lewis Tappan*, 102–9, 145; William Still, *The Underground Railroad* (rev. ed.: Philadelphia, 1878), 676; *NYS*, November 9, 1835.
50. Lewis Tappan, *The Life of Arthur Tappan* (New York, 1870), 182, 313; Barnes and Dumond, eds., *Letters*, 2: 512–13; Still, *Underground Railroad*, 678.
51. William Jay to J. C. Hornblower, July 17, 1851, JP; Stephen P. Budney, *William Jay: Abolitionist and Anticolonialist* (Westport, Conn., 2005), 40–41; William Jay to S. S. Jocelyn, August 21, 1833; Will of William Jay, May 15, 1858, JJH; Joseph Sturge, *A Visit to the United States in 1841* (London, 1842), 55.
52. Fergus M. Bordewich, *Bound for Canaan: The Epic Story of the Underground Railroad, America's First Civil Rights Movement* (New York, 2005), 50–59; Margaret Hope Bacon, *Abby Hopper Gibbons: Prison Reformer and Social Activist* (Albany, 2000), 1–30, 70; *NS*, May 19, 1854; *Liberator*, October 22, 1858; Graham Russell Gao Hodges, *David Ruggles: A Radical Black Abolitionist and the Underground Railroad in New York City* (Chapel Hill, 2010), 50, 87. Daniel E. Meaders, *Kidnappers in Philadelphia: Isaac Hopper's Tales of Oppression, 1780–1843* (New York, 1994), reproduces Hopper's articles.
53. James B. Stewart, "From Moral Suasion to Political Confrontation: American

Abolitionists and the Problem of Resistance," in David W. Blight, ed., *Passages to Freedom: The Underground Railroad in History and Memory* (Washington, D.C., 2004), 82–83; *CA*, November 18, 1837; Benjamin Quarles, *Black Abolitionists* (New York, 1969), 30–34.

54. Michael Feldberg, *The Turbulent Era: Riot and Disorder in Jacksonian America* (New York, 1980), 93–94; Burrows and Wallace, *Gotham*, 440; Leonard P. Richards, *"Gentlemen of Property and Standing": Anti-Abolition Mobs in Jacksonian America* (New York, 1970), 77; Linda K. Kerber, "Abolitionists and Amalgamators: The New York City Race Riots of 1834," *New York History*, 48 (January 1967), 30; Wyatt-Brown, *Lewis Tappan*, 115; Anbinder, *Five Points*, 7–9.
55. Glije, *Road to Mobocracy*, 153–68; Anbinder, *Five Points*, 9–12; Harris, *In the Shadow of Slavery*, 197; Hodges, *David Ruggles*, 66; Alexander, *African or American?*, 85–86.
56. Tappan, *Life of Arthur Tappan*, 215–16; *Address to the People of Color of the City of New York* (New York, 1834); Burrows and Wallace, *Gotham*, 557–59; Wyatt-Brown, *Lewis Tappan*, 115–21; Budney, *William Jay*, 33–35.
57. Lawrence B. Goodheart, "The Chronicles of Kidnapping in New York: Resistance to the Fugitive Slave Law, 1834–1835," *Afro-Americans in New York Life and History*, 8 (January 1984), 7–17; *Emancipator*, April 1, 22, June 17, 1834; *Emancipator* in *American Anti-Slavery Reporter*, June 1, 1834.
58. Goodheart, "Chronicles," 7–17; *First Annual Report of the American Anti-Slavery Society* (New York, 1834), 56.
59. *FJ*, April 25, December 5, 1828; *Emancipator*, December 1, 1836; Hodges, *David Ruggles*, 10–80; Sinha, "Black Abolitionism," 248–50; Hodges, *Root and Branch*, 243.
60. *First Annual Report of the NY Committee of Vigilance for the Year 1837* (New York, 1837), 3–5.

3. The New York Vigilance Committee

1. *BAP*, 3: 171–72, 178–79; Graham Russell Gao Hodges, *David Ruggles: A Radical Black Abolitionist and the Underground Railroad in New York City* (Chapel Hill, 2010), 86; *CA*, October 28, 1837; *First Annual Report of the New York Committee of Vigilance for the Year 1837* (New York, 1837), 3, 83.
2. Tom Calarco, *The Underground Railroad in the Adirondack Region* (Jefferson, N.C., 2004), 177–78; Hodges, *David Ruggles*, 90–91, 153; Leslie M. Harris, *In the*

Shadow of Slavery: African Americans in New York City, 1626–1863 (Chicago, 2003), 173, 206; *First Annual Report*; *FOM*, December 22, 1836; *Emancipator*, December 1, 1836, June 1, 1837.

3. *Emancipator*, June 1, 1837; *Liberator*, May 18, 1837; *First Annual Report*, 5, 47.
4. *BAP*, 3: 171–72.
5. *Emancipator*, June 1, July 20, 1837, March 1, 1838; *CA*, December 23, 1837, January 20, 1838, June 8, 1839; *First Annual Report*, 84; *MOL*, July 1838, January 1839; *NS*, May 18, 1849.
6. *Emancipator*, November 2, 1837, March 1, 1838; *NAS*, August 20, 1840.
7. *CA*, July 7, August 25, 1838; *MOL*, July, August 1838.
8. *MOL*, July 1838; Hodges, *David Ruggles*, 128–30, 143–44; *Liberator*, August 17, 1838; *CA*, June 23, July 7, July 28, 1838; *Emancipator*, June 21, 1838.
9. Rhoda G. Freeman, *The Free Negro in New York City in the Era before the Civil War* (New York, 1994), 29–30; *New York Sun* in *National Enquirer and Constitutional Advocate of Universal Liberty* (Philadelphia), January 14, 1837; *CA*, May 20, 1837, June 16, 1838, November 2, 1839.
10. *Emancipator*, May 24, 1838; *MOL*, July 1838; *CA*, September 16, December 2, 1837, July 11, 1840.
11. *Appleton's Cyclopedia of American Biography* (6 vols.; New York, 1888–89), 2: 231; *NYT*, January 29, 1877; *CA*, April 4, May 9, 1840; *Emancipator*, March 1, 1838.
12. *First Annual Report*, 19–29; *NYO*, September 12, 1836.
13. *NAS*, May 23, 1844; *New-York Commercial Advertiser*, April 19, 1837; Daniel E. Meaders, *Kidnappers in Philadelphia: Isaac Hopper's Tales of Oppression, 1780–1843* (New York, 1994), 6.
14. *CA*, April 22, 29, 1837; *New-York Commercial Advertiser*, April 13, 1837.
15. *CA*, July 15, October 28, 1837, January 20, July 28, 1838; *MOL*, August 1838; *Emancipator*, May 24, 1838; *Life and Times of Frederick Douglass Written by Himself* (rev. ed.: Boston, 1892), 251.
16. Case of Nat, RG 21; *MOL*, July 1838; *CA*, April 18, 1840; *NYS*, October 15, 1837; *NYEP*, September 13, 1836.
17. *Narrative of Events in the Life of William Green, (Formerly a Slave) Written by Himself* (Springfield, Mass., 1853), 20–21; *Autobiography of James L. Smith* (Norwich, Conn., 1881), 50; Hodges, *David Ruggles*, 124–27.
18. Hodges, *David Ruggles*, 98; *Liberator*, October 5, 1838; Lydia Maria Child, *Isaac T. Hopper: A True Life* (Boston, 1853), 340–56.
19. *Emancipator*, July 28, 1836; *CA*, April 15, 29, 1837.
20. Harris, *In the Shadow of Slavery*, 213; *Emancipator*, September 1, 1836; Lewis

Perry, *Radical Abolitionism: Anarchy and the Government of God in Antislavery Thought* (Ithaca, 1973), 53, 83; *CA*, December 9, 1837.

21. *CA*, November 17, 1838, January 26, 1839; Samuel E. Cornish to William Jay, November 3, 1838, JP.
22. *CA*, November 17, 1838, July 27, September 7, November 23, 1839; Bertram Wyatt-Brown, *Lewis Tappan and the Evangelical War against Slavery* (Cleveland, 1969), 180; *NAS*, August 20, 1840; David Ruggles, *Plea for "A Man and a Brother"* (New York, 1839), 3–11; *Emancipator*, February 12, November 21, 1839; *MOL*, January 1839, August 1840; Hodges, *David Ruggles*, 162.
23. *NAS*, July 29, 1841; Hodges, *David Ruggles*, 170–94.
24. *NYE*, April 25, 1842; *CA*, August 22, 1840; *Emancipator*, December 15, 1836, July 1, 1837.
25. *Emancipator*, July 20, 1837, May 3, 1838, August 30, 1840; *FOM*, September 9, 1840; *Liberator*, October 4, 1839; *MOL*, January 1839.
26. *MOL*, July 1838, August 1840; Paul Finkelman, "The Protection of Black Rights in Seward's New York," *Civil War History*, 34 (September 1988), 211–34; *CA*, May 23, 1840; *NAS*, July 1, 1841; *Fifth Annual Report of the New York Committee of Vigilance* (New York, 1842), 35–36 .
27. *Liberator*, November 25, 1842; *CA*, April 4, September 26, 1840; *Elevator* (San Francisco), January 11, 1873; *Fifth Annual Report*, 14.
28. Joseph A. Boromé, "The Vigilant Committee of Philadelphia," *Pennsylvania Magazine of History and Biography*, (July 1968), 320–52; Margaret Hope Bacon, *But One Race: The Life of Robert Purvis* (Albany, 2007), 53, 76–81; Robert Purvis to Wilbur H. Siebert, December 23, 1895, SC; *Fifth Annual Report*, 29; *Liberator*, May 24, 1844.
29. *Liberator*, May 18, 1838; *NAS*, August 11, 1842.
30. James B. Stewart, *Holy Warriors: The Abolitionists and American Slavery* (rev. ed.: New York, 1996), 88–93; Lewis Tappan to William Jay, August 18, 1834, JJH; Gerald Sorin, *The New York Abolitionists: A Case Study of Political Radicalism* (Westport, Conn., 1971), 33; *CA*, November 2, 1839; Benjamin Quarles, *Black Abolitionists* (New York, 1969), 26–27.
31. Carolyn L. Karcher, *The First Woman in the Republic: A Cultural Biography of Lydia Maria Child* (Durham, N.C., 1994), 260; Lewis Tappan to William Jay, October 5, 1835, JJH; Oliver Johnson, *William Lloyd Garrison and His Times* (Boston, 1880), 289–92; *CA*, May 23, 1840.
32. Margaret Hope Bacon, *Abby Hopper Gibbons: Prison Reformer and Social Activist* (Albany, 2000), 36–39; Johnson, *William Lloyd Garrison*, 282–96, 322; Alice

H. Henderson, "The History of the New York State Anti-Slavery Society" (Ph.D. diss., University of Michigan, 1963), 328–45; Jane H. Pease and William H. Pease, *Bound With Them in Chains* (Westport, Conn., 1972), 14; James B. Stewart, "From Moral Suasion to Political Confrontation: American Abolitionists and the Problem of Resistance," in David W. Blight, ed., *Passages to Freedom: The Underground Railroad in History and Memory* (Washington, D.C., 2004), 79–80; Sigmund Freud, *Civilization and Its Discontent*, trans. James Strachey (New York, 2002), 51.

33. *CA*, May 30, 1840; Stephen Kantrowitz, *More than Freedom: Fighting for Black Citizenship in a White Republic, 1829–1889* (New York, 2012), 101–13; *BAP*, 3: 22–23; Quarles, *Black Abolitionists*, 18; David E. Swift, *Black Prophets of Justice: Activist Clergy before the Civil War* (Baton Rouge, 1989), 165–69.
34. *Liberator*, March 17, 1843; Florence T. Ray and H. C. Ray, *Sketch of the Life of Rev. Charles B. Ray* (New York, 1887), 35.
35. *NYTrib*, May 14, 1846; *CA*, August 20, 1840, May 22, August 21, 1841; Beth A. Salerno, *Sister Societies: Women's Antislavery Societies in Antebellum America* (DeKalb, Ill., 2005), 138–39; *Fifth Annual Report* (New York, 1842), 8, 11; *NYE*, August 25, 1842, May 8, 1845.
36. *Fifth Annual Report*, 12–29.
37. *Fifth Annual Report*, 5; *BAP*, 1: 90; Steven M. Raffo, *A Biography of Oliver Johnson, Abolitionist and Reformer, 1809–1889* (Lewiston, N.Y., 2002), 74–75; Johnson, *William Lloyd Garrison*, 295–98; *Liberator*, December 4, 1846.
38. Circular Letter, *Outline of Effort, American and Foreign Anti-Slavery Society*, November 1845, AMA; Annie H. Abel and Frank J. Klingberg, *A Side-Light on Anglo-American Relations, 1839–1858* (New York, 1927), 335; Clara M. DeBoer, *Be Jubilant My Feet: African American Abolitionists in the American Missionary Association, 1839–1861* (New York, 1993), xii, 81–83; *BAP*, 3: 36.
39. *Fifth Annual Report*, 3; *BAP*, 2: 117; William Still, *The Underground Railroad* (rev. ed.: Philadelphia, 1878), 674–77; *The Vigilance Committee Appeal*, broadside, New York, June 1844, NYHS; Richard D. Webb, *The National Anti-Slavery Societies in England and the United States* (Dublin, 1852), 14, 53. Tappan's biographer significantly understates the degree of Tappan's involvement with aiding fugitive slaves. Bertram Wyatt-Brown, *Lewis Tappan and the Evangelical War against Slavery* (Cleveland, 1969), 329–30.
40. Sorin, *New York Abolitionists*, 81; Tom Calarco, *People of the Underground Railroad* (Westport, Conn., 2008), 330–32; Reinhard O. Johnson, *The Liberty Party, 1840–1848: Antislavery Third-Party Politics in the United States* (Baton Rouge, 2009), 382.

41. Ray and Ray, *Sketch of the Life*, 7–13, 24–28, 35–36; Charles B. Ray, Petition, March 12, 1850, AMA; Johnson, *Liberty Party*, 367; *BAP*, 2: 79–80; Calarco, *People of the Underground Railroad*, 250–51. By the late 1850s, the Bethesda church was located at 155 Sullivan Street, and the Shiloh at 61 Prince Street. Henry Wilson, *Trow's New York City Directory for the Year Ending May 1, 1858* (New York, 1857), appendix, 34, 36.
42. Bill for Painting, March 24, 1849, AMA; *Elevator* (San Francisco), September 6, 1867; Christopher Phillips, *Freedom's Port: The African American Community of Baltimore, 1790–1860* (Urbana, Ill., 1997), 215–20; *Liberator*, October 16, 1840; Stanley Harrold, "On the Borders of Slavery and Race: Charles T. Torrey and the Underground Railroad," *Journal of the Early Republic*, 20 (Summer 2000), 273–92; T. Stephen Whitman, *Challenging Slavery in the Chesapeake: Black and White Resistance to Human Bondage, 1775–1865* (Baltimore, 2007), 186; *A Narrative of Thomas Smallwood* (Toronto, 1851), 28–30, 40; Louis A. Chamerovzow, *The Slave's Underground Railroad to Freedom* (Edinburgh, n.d.), 2. The 1850 Manuscript U.S. Census for New York City (accessed via AncestryLibrary.com) includes the Gibbs family with two daughters ages nine and six, and a son, age five, with the younger two having been born in New York.
43. *Liberator*, May 24, 1844; *Liberty Almanac for 1849* (New York, 1848), 38; *NS*, May 18, July 13, October 12, 1849; *Circular of the New-York State Vigilance Committee* [ca. 1850], NYHS; Johnson, *Liberty Party*, 356; *Autobiography of the Rev. Luther Lee* (New York, 1882); Calarco, *People of the Underground Railroad*, 134–35, 211–12; *BS*, May 12, 1848.
44. *Circular of the New-York State Vigilance Committee* [ca. 1850]; *NYE*, May 24, 1849; George E. Walker, *The Afro-American in New York City, 1827–1860* (New York, 1993), 101; *NYTrib*, May 10, 1848; *Independent*, May 10, 1849; *NYE*, May 24, 1849, May 16, 1850; *BAP*, 2: 118; Manuscript Circular, 1849, New York State Vigilance Committee, Haverford College; *Doggett's New-York City Directory, for . . . 1848/1849* (New York, 1848), 24; appendix, 13; Still, *Underground Railroad*, 676.
45. *Circular Letter of the New York State Vigilance Committee*, 1850, Miscellaneous Manuscripts, Library of Congress; Manuscript Circular Letter, 1849, New York State Vigilance Committee, Onondaga Historical Association; Gerrit Smith to William Harned, Charles B. Ray and Andrew Lester, March 14, 1849, SP; Seth Barton, *The Randolph Epistles* (Washington, D.C., 1850), 3–4.
46. *NYTrib*, May 10, 1849; MB, November 1, 1848; Manuscript Circular Letter, 1849.
47. *Special Report of the Bristol and Clifton Ladies' Anti-slavery Society: During Eighteen Months, from January 1851 to June, 1852* (London, 1852), 29.

4. A Patchwork System

1. There is no published biography of Gay. See Raimund E. Goerler, "Family, Self and Anti-Slavery: Sydney Howard Gay and the Abolitionist Commitment" (Ph.D. diss., Case Western Reserve University, 1975), 1–78.
2. Goerler, "Family, Self and Anti-Slavery," 105–54, 199–206; Sydney Howard Gay to Thomas Wentworth Higginson, October 28, 1882, Gay to Elizabeth J. Neall, August 26, 1844, Gay to Edmund Quincy, June 28, 1846, Sydney Howard Gay Diary, February 20–March 4, [1844], GP; *BAP*, 3: 416–19; *Liberator*, September 1, 1843, January 26, March 15, April 26, 1844.
3. Goerler, "Family, Self and Anti-Slavery," 210; Christopher Densmore, "The Tarring and Feathering of Daniel Neall at Smyrna, February 29, 1840," paper delivered at Delaware Underground Railroad Coalition, October 26, 2009; "The Tarring and Feathering of Daniel Neall," manuscript, GP; Mary Otis Gay Wilcox, "A Gay Life," typescript, GP; Elizabeth J. Neall to ?, n.d., 1840, GP; Dorothy Sterling, *Ahead of Her Time: Abby Kelley and the Politics of Antislavery* (New York, 1991), 166.
4. *NAS*, April 10, 1845; *Liberator*, May 17, 1850; Steven M. Raffo, *A Biography of Oliver Johnson, Abolitionist and Reformer, 1809–1889* (Lewiston, N.Y., 2002), 79; Gay to Richard D. Webb, July 17, 1844, GP.
5. Annie H. Abel and Frank J. Klingberg, *A Side-Light on Anglo-American Relations, 1839–1858* (New York, 1927), 174; Minute Book of the Vigilant Committee of Philadelphia, May 31, 1839, HSPa; *Life and Adventures of James Williams, a Fugitive Slave, with a Full Description of the Underground Railroad* (San Francisco, 1873), 98–99; Benjamin Quarles, *Black Abolitionists* (New York, 1969), 72; Margaret Hope Bacon, *But One Race: The Life of Robert Purvis* (Albany, 2007), 105; Jean Soderlund, *Quakers and Slavery: A Divided Spirit* (Princeton, 1985), 185–87; *MOL*, August 1838.
6. Sarah H. Emerson, ed., *Life of Abby Hopper Gibbons Told Chiefly through Her Correspondence* (2 vols.; New York, 1897), 1: 91, 99, 114–15; 2: 351; Charles L. Blockson, "The Underground Railroad: The Quaker Connection," in Eliza Cope Harrison, ed., *For Emancipation and Education: Some Black and Quaker Efforts, 1680–1900* (Philadelphia, 1997), 40; Minute Book, New York Association of Friends for the Relief of Those Held in Slavery and the Improvement of the Free People of Color, September 14, December 12, 1840, May 26, November 11, 1841, January 3, 1842, FHL; Circular, 1843, Massachusetts Anti-Slavery Society Records, NYHS; Kathryn Grover, *The Fugitive's Gibraltar: Escaping Slaves and Abolitionism in New Bedford, Massachusetts* (Amherst, Mass., 2001), 32.
7. *NAS*, June 11, 1840, June 9, 1842, May 4, 1843; Carolyn L. Karcher, *The First Woman in the Republic: A Cultural Biography of Lydia Maria Child* (Durham,

N.C., 1994), 273–76; Milton Meltzer and Patricia G. Holland, eds., *Lydia Maria Child: Selected Letters, 1817–1880* (Amherst, Mass., 1982), 139, 186; Deborah P. Clifford, *Crusader for Freedom: A Life of Lydia Maria Child* (Boston, 1992), 162; Sydney Howard Gay to James Miller McKim, February 10, 1846, MAC.

8. *NAS*, September 16, 30, December 30, 1841, June 9, 1842; Karcher, *First Woman*, 264, 273–76, 291–93; Meltzer and Holland, eds., *Lydia Maria Child*, 157, 174, 186–90, 193; James B. Stewart, *Wendell Phillips: Liberty's Hero* (Baton Rouge, 1986), 127; Sydney Howard Gay to Caroline Weston, September 23, 1847 [misdated 1843], GP; James S. Gibbons to Richard D. Webb, February 25, 1844, AC.
9. Sydney Howard Gay to Wendell Phillips, January 19, 1848, Gay to Francis Jackson, February 22, 1849, PP; Gay to Edmund Quincy, July 2, 1844, Gay to Maria Weston Chapman, September 3, 1844, Gay to Quincy, October 15, 1844, GP.
10. Sydney Howard Gay to Wendell Phillips, July 10, 1846, August 26, 1846, April 2, 1847, PP; Phillips to Gay, May 26, August 26, 1846, April 5, 1847, Phillips to W. Chapman, June 21, 1846 (copy), GP; Stewart, *Wendell Phillips*, 130–31.
11. *NAS*, May 30, June 6, 1844; *Liberator*, May 31, 1844; Sydney Howard Gay to Richard D. Webb, July 17, 1844, GP; Gay to Wendell Phillips, July 9, 1848, August 28, 1849, PP; Anne Warren Weston to Maria Weston Chapman, August 22, 1848, AC; Gay to James Miller McKim, February 10, 1846, MAC.
12. Sydney Howard Gay to Thomas Wentworth Higginson, October 28, 1882, GP; Abel and Klingberg, *Side-Light*, 121, 211–12, 220; Donald Yacovone, *Samuel Joseph May and the Dilemmas of the Liberal Persuasion, 1797–1871* (Philadelphia, 1991), 134–36; *NAS*, November 8, 22, 29, 1849, January 10, 24, 1850.
13. *NAS*, March 7, 21, December 26, 1844.
14. *NAS*, December 26, 1844; Sydney Howard Gay to "Friend Woodworth," March 18, n.y., GP; Wilcox, "Gay Life" GP; *NYT*, October 12, 1875; *NYTrib*, March 30, 1881; *New York Sun*, March 31, 1881; *Pacific Appeal* (San Francisco), May 30, 1863. The 1850, 1860, and 1870 Manuscript U.S. Censuses (all available at Ancestry Library.com), Napoleon's marriage record from 1855, and his death certificate from 1881 (the latter two at the New York City Municipal Archives) all list New York City as Napoleon's birthplace. The marriage record gives his year of birth as 1803; the death certificate, 1800. For Napoleon's occupations and residences, see the 1850 Manuscript U.S. Census; John Doggett, *The New York City Directory for 1842 and 1843* (New York, 1842), 240; *Doggett's New York City Directory for 1850–1851* (New York, 1850), 370; Henry Wilson, *Trow's New York City Directory for the Year Ending May 1, 1860* (New York, 1859).
15. *NAS*, October 9, 1845.
16. William Still, *The Underground Railroad* (rev. ed.: Philadelphia, 1878), 675–76;

Manuscript Circular, 1849, New York State Vigilance Committee, Haverford College; Lewis Tappan to Sydney Howard Gay, September 3, 1849, GP.

17. Florence T. Ray and H. C. Ray, *Sketch of the Life of Rev. Charles B. Ray* (New York, 1887), 73; Reinhard O. Johnson, *The Liberty Party, 1840–1848: Antislavery Third-Party Politics in the United States* (Baton Rouge, 2009), 293; R. J. M. Blackett, *Building an Antislavery Wall: Black Americans in the Atlantic Abolitionist Movement, 1830–1860* (Baton Rouge, 1983), 42–43, 110–11; Clare Taylor, ed., *British and American Abolitionists: An Episode in Transatlantic Understanding* (Edinburgh, 1974), 277; *NYTrib*, May 10, 1849.

18. R. C. Smedley, *History of the Underground Railroad in Chester and the Neighboring Counties of Pennsylvania* (Lancaster, Pa., 1883); *NYTrib*, June 17, 1841.

19. Bacon, *But One Race*, 41–42, 48, 84; Smedley, *History of the Underground Railroad*, 353–55; Julie Winch, *Philadelphia's Black Elite: Activism, Accommodation, and the Struggle for Autonomy, 1787–1848* (Philadelphia, 1988), 70, 84–89; Matthew Pinsker, "Vigilance in Pennsylvania: Underground Railroad Activities in the Keystone State, 1837–1861," report presented at Pennsylvania Historical and Museum Commission Annual Conference on Black History, Harrisburg, 2000, 64; Joseph A. Boromé, "The Vigilant Committee of Philadelphia," *Pennsylvania Magazine of History and Biography*, 92 (July 1968), 331–351; William Parker, "The Freedman's Story," *Atlantic Monthly*, 17 (March 1866), 295; Minute Book, Vigilant Committee of Philadelphia, December 27, 1843, March 11, 1844.

20. [Harriet A. Jacobs], *Incidents in the Life of a Slave Girl, Written by Herself*, ed. L. Maria Child (Boston, 1861); Jean Fagan Yellin, ed., *The Harriet Jacobs Family Papers* (2 vols.; Chapel Hill, 2008), 1: 55.

21. John S. Jacobs to Sydney Howard Gay, September 7, June 4, 1845, Robert Purvis to Gay, September 13, 1858, GP; Account Book, May 16, 1854, Sydney Howard Gay Papers, NYPL.

22. Calvin Schermerhorn, *Money over Mastery: Family over Freedom: Slavery in the Antebellum Upper South* (Baltimore, 2011), 160; Jeffrey Ruggles, *The Unboxing of Henry Brown* (Richmond, Va., 2003), 22–27; *Commemoration of the Fiftieth Anniversary of the Organization of the American Anti-Slavery Society* (Philadelphia, 1884), 40; Anna D. Hallowell, *James and Lucretia Mott: Life and Letters* (Boston, 1884), 310–11; James Miller McKim to "Dear Friend," March 28, 1849, MAC; Joseph Ricketson Jr. to Sydney Howard Gay, March 30, 1849, McKim to Gay, March 26, 1849, GP.

23. James Miller McKim to Sydney Howard Gay, March 26, April 3, 1849, Joseph Ricketson Jr. to Gay, March 30, 1849, GP; McKim to Samuel Rhoads, March 29,

1849, MC; Grover, *Fugitive's Gibraltar*, 138, 229; Ricketson to Deborah Weston, April 29, 1849, AC.

24. James Miller McKim to Sydney Howard Gay, March 26, 1849, GP; *NYTrib*, April 17, 24, 1849; *Liberty Almanac for 1851* (New York, 1850), 15; Schermerhorn, *Money over Mastery*, 160; Ruggles, *Unboxing*, 47–110; *Narrative of Henry Box Brown . . .* (Boston, 1849), 64; Richard D. Webb to Maria Weston Chapman, November 12, 1850, AC. In the British edition of his autobiography, Brown did mention briefly having passed through New York City. *Narrative of the Life of Henry Box Brown, Written by Himself* (Manchester, 1851), 59.

25. *Liberator*, July 24, 1857; *PF*, February 7, 1857; Richard M. Blackett, *Making Freedom: The Underground Railroad and the Politics of Slavery* (Chapel Hill, 2013), 68; Still, *Underground Railroad*, 75–76.

26. Laura E. Richards, ed., *Letters and Journal of Samuel Gridley Howe* (2 vols.; Boston, 1909), 2: 239–46; W. P. Garrison to Wilbur H. Siebert, October 30, 1893, SC; Irving H. Bartlett, "Abolitionists, Fugitives, and Impostors in Boston, 1846–1847," *New England Quarterly*, 55 (March 1982), 97.

27. *Liberator*, November 12, 1847; Bartlett, "Abolitionists," 100–104; John W. Browne to Sydney Howard Gay, December 3, 1846, Gay to Browne, December 15, 1846, January 3, 1847, GP; Elias Smith to John Jay II, December 11, 1846, JFP.

28. Bartlett, "Abolitionists," 105–9; John W. Browne to Sydney Howard Gay, March 27, 1847, Gay to Caroline Weston, July 30, 1846, Gay to Browne, January 3, 1847, GP.

29. *National Era*, July 15, 22, September 23, 1847; *NYTrib*, August 5, 6, 1847; *Elevator* (San Francisco), December 19, 1874; Henry Wilson, *History of the Rise and Fall of the Slave Power in America* (3 vols., Boston, 1874), 2: 53–54; *NYE*, August 23, 1847.

30. H. Robert Baker, *Prigg v. Pennsylvania: Slavery, the Supreme Court, and the Ambivalent Constitution* (Lawrence, Kans., 2012), 14–17, 129–44; H. Robert Baker, "The Fugitive Slave Clause and the Antebellum Constitution," *Law and History Review*, 30 (November 2012), 1157–58; William M. Wiecek, "Slavery and Abolition before the United States Supreme Court, 1820–1860," *Journal of American History*, 65 (June 1978), 44–46; Don E. Fehrenbacher, *The Slaveholding Republic: An Account of the United States Government's Relations to Slavery* (New York, 2001), 219–21; Paul Finkelman, "*Prigg v. Pennsylvania* and Northern State Courts: Anti-Slavery Use of a Pro-Slavery Decision," *Civil War History*, 25 (March 1979), 9–13.

31. *NYTrib*, March 5, 9, 1842; *Fifth Annual Report of the New York Committee of*

Vigilance (New York, 1842), 37; Jamal Greene, "The Anticanon," *Harvard Law Review* (December 2011), 428.

32. Beverly W. Palmer, ed., *The Selected Letters of Charles Sumner* (2 vols.; Boston, 1990), 1: 175; Finkelman, *"Prigg v. Pennsylvania,"* 14–27; Stephen Kantrowitz, *More than Freedom: Fighting for Black Citizenship in a White Republic, 1829–1889* (New York, 2012) , 70–74.
33. Paul Finkelman, *An Imperfect Union: Slavery, Federalism, and Comity* (Chapel Hill, 1981), 43, 103–27; *NYTrib*, May 14, 1846.
34. *NYT*, April 7, 1874; Sydney Howard Gay to John Jay II, April 22, 1848, Lewis Tappan to John Jay II, April 22, 1848, JFP; Gay to Maria Weston Chapman, September 2, 1851, John Jay II to Gay, June 2, 1853 [misdated 1833], GP; Johnson, *Liberty Party*, 352; William Jay to J. C. Hornblower, July 17, 1851, JP.
35. *NYT*, January 1, 1880. The Gay Papers, Columbia University, contains three receipts issued in 1856 to the abolitionist Rowland Johnson for money to assist fugitives, each signed with an "X" by Napoleon. (Box 75, Folder "Rowland Johnson.") The 1860 Manuscript and 1880 Manuscript U.S. Census list Napoleon as being unable to read or write.
36. *NYE*, November 10, 1846; *NYTrib*, October 23, 28, 1846; Sydney Howard Gay to John Jay II, April 22, 1848, JFP; *Supplement to the New-York Legal Observer, Containing the Report of the Case in the Matter of George Kirk . . .* (New York, 1847), 456–69, 16–20 [pagination begins again from page one midway in document]; John Jay II, "Notes of Slave Cases," typescript, JJH; *Liberator*, January 13, July 14, 1843; *NAS*, October 29, 1846; *NYO*, October 18, 1846.
37. *NYTrib*, October 30, 31, November 3, 1846; Jay, "Notes of Slave Cases"; Wilson, *History of the Rise and Fall*, 2: 53; *NAS*, November 5, 1846; *NYT*, October 12, 1875.
38. Sydney Howard Gay to Wendell Phillips, November 6, [1846], PP; *NYTrib*, November 3, 1846; *Boston Christian World* in *Liberator*, November 6, 1846; *Richmond Whig*, November 6, 1846.
39. *NAS*, December 28, 1848, January 4, 1849; *NYTrib*, December 25, 28, 1848; *BE*, December 27, 1848, January 18, 1849; Finkelman, *"Prigg v. Pennsylvania,"* 31.
40. *NAS*, April 5, 12, 1849.
41. *Annual Report of the American and Foreign Anti-Slavery Society* (New York, 1849), 65.
42. Josephine F. Pacheco, *The Pearl: A Failed Slave Escape on the Potomac* (Chapel Hill, 2005); Alice H. Henderson, "The History of the New York State Anti-Slavery Society" (Ph.D. diss., University of Michigan, 1963), 121; Excerpt of letter from George W. Clark, vol. 19, William Henry Siebert Collection, Houghton Library, Harvard University; Kenneth Winkle, *Lincoln's Citadel: The Civil War in Washington, D.C.*

(New York, 2013), 36–42, 58–59; Frank Decker, *Brooklyn's Plymouth Church in the Civil War Era: A Ministry of Freedom* (Charleston, 2013), 42, 81–82; *NYTrib*, December 30, 1851; Manuscript Circular, 1849, New York State Vigilance Committee.

43. David F. Ericson, *Slavery in the American Republic: Developing the Federal Government, 1791–1861* (Lawrence, Kans., 2011), 85; Fehrenbacher, *Slaveholding Republic*, 225; Richard K. Crallé, *The Works of John C. Calhoun* (6 vols.; New York, 1863–64), 6: 291–96; Stanley Harrold, *Border War: Fighting over Slavery before the Civil War* (Chapel Hill, 2010), xiii, 139–40.

5. The Fugitive Slave Law and the Crisis of the Black Community

1. *CG*, 31st Congress, 1st Session, 1604–13, appendix, 115–26; *NAS*, November 11, 1847; Stephen Kantrowitz, *More than Freedom: Fighting for Black Citizenship in a White Republic, 1829–1889* (New York, 2012), 90, 117–18; James F. Hopkins, ed., *The Papers of Henry Clay* (10 vols.; Lexington, Ky., 1959–91), 10: 614–20. Levi again returned to Clay a few weeks later.
2. David M. Potter, *The Impending Crisis, 1848–1861* (New York, 1976), 100–102; *CG*, 31st Congress, 1st Session, 1111, appendix, 263–65, 274.
3. Potter, *Impending Crisis*, 108–10; William W. Freehling, *The Road to Disunion* (2 vols.; New York, 1990–2007), 1: 502–3; *CG*, 31st Congress, 1st Session, 1005.
4. Potter, *Impending Crisis*, 113; Freehling, *Road to Disunion*, 1: 504–5; *CG*, 31st Congress, 1st Session, Appendix, 1588, 1597–98, 1608, 1614.
5. *CG*, 31st Congress, 1st Session, appendix, 1583–84, 1601, 1603; Ralph A. Keller, "Extraterritoriality and the Fugitive Slave Debate," *Illinois Historical Journal*, 78 (Summer 1985), 117–23.
6. *NYTrib*, July 9, 1850; Stanley Harrold, *Subversives: Antislavery Community in Washington, D.C., 1828–1865* (Baton Rouge, 2003), 146–63; Norman Dann, *Practical Dreamer: Gerrit Smith and the Crusade for Social Reform* (Hamilton, N.Y., 2009), 483–85; *NAS*, September 12, 1850.
7. *NAS*, August 29, 1850; Stanley Harrold, *Border War: Fighting over Slavery before the Civil War* (Chapel Hill, 2010), 150–51; Dann, *Practical Dreamer*, 477–80; Milton C. Sernett, *North Star Country: Upstate New York and the Crusade for African American Freedom* (Syracuse, 2002), 129–32; *Washington Daily National Intelligencer*, August 13, 1850; Philip S. Foner and George E. Walker, eds., *Proceedings of the Black State Conventions, 1840–1865* (2 vols.; Philadelphia, 1979–80), 1: 44–47.
8. Sernett, *North Star Country*, 480; *CG*, 31st Congress, 1st Session, appendix,

1622; Carol Faulkner, *Lucretia Mott's Heresy: Abolition and Women's Rights in Nineteenth-Century America* (Philadelphia, 2011), 162–63.

9. Fergus M. Bordewich, *America's Great Debate: Henry Clay, Stephen A. Douglas, and the Compromise That Preserved the Union* (New York, 2012), 355; H. Robert Baker, "The Fugitive Slave Clause and the Antebellum Constitution," *Law and History Review*, 30 (November 2012), 1163; Don E. Fehrenbacher, *The Slaveholding Republic: An Account of the United States Government's Relations to Slavery* (New York, 2001), 231; Robert Kaczorowski, "The Supreme Court and Congress's Power to Enforce Constitutional Rights: An Overlooked Moral Anomaly," *Fordham Law Review*, 73 (October 2004), 154–243.
10. Steven Lubet, *Fugitive Justice: Runaways, Rescuers, and Slavery on Trial* (Cambridge, Mass., 2010), 42–44.
11. John Ashworth, *Slavery, Capitalism, and Politics in the Antebellum Republic* (2 vols.: New York, 1995–2007), 2: 36–37; Stanley W. Campbell, *The Slave Catchers: Enforcement of the Fugitive Slave Law, 1850–1860* (Chapel Hill, 1968), 5; Harrold, *Border War*, 144; *CG*, 31st Congress, 1st Session, 233.
12. *Annual Report of the American and Foreign Anti-Slavery Society* (New York, 1850), 10.
13. *NAS*, October 3, 1850; *BS*, September 30, 1850; Prithi Kanakamedala, "In Pursuit of Freedom," manuscript, 2012, Brooklyn Historical Society.
14. *NYTrib*, September 28, 30, 1850; *BS*, September 30, 1850; Lewis Tappan, *The Fugitive Slave Bill: Its History and Unconstitutionality* (3rd ed.: New York, 1850), 3–5; Case of James Hamlet, RG 21.
15. *NYEP*, October 2, 1850; *NAS*, October 10, 1850; *NYTrib*, October 4, 1850; *NS*, October 24, 1850.
16. *NYT*, October 5, 1850; *NS*, October 24, 1850; Kanakamedala, "In Pursuit," 108–11; *NYTrib*, October 7, 1850; *NAS*, October 10, 1850; Tappan, *Fugitive Slave Bill*, 36; Craig Wilder, *In the Company of Black Men: The African Influence on African American Culture in New York City* (New York, 2001), 171–72.
17. MB, October 8, November 6, 1850, January 21, 1851; *Annual Report of the American and Foreign Anti-Slavery Society* (New York, 1851), 12–13, 24.
18. Annie H. Abel and Frank J. Klingberg, *A Side-Light on Anglo-American Relations, 1839–1858* (New York, 1927), 256–57; Philip S. Foner, *Business and Slavery: The New York Merchants and the Irrepressible Conflict* (Chapel Hill, 1941), 35–36, 41–45, 55–61; Sven Beckert, *The Monied Metropolis: New York City and the Consolidation of the American Bourgeoisie, 1850–1896* (New York, 2001), 85–86, *Elevator* (San Francisco), January 11, 1873.
19. Kathryn Grover, *The Fugitive's Gibraltar: Escaping Slaves and Abolitionism in*

New Bedford, Massachusetts (Amherst, Mass., 2001), 244; Henry C. Wright to Sydney Howard Gay, September 13, 1850, Gay to Richard D. Webb, August 5, 1853, GP; *NS*, May 16, 1850; *FDP*, April 29, 1852; Steven M. Raffo, *A Biography of Oliver Johnson, Abolitionist and Reformer, 1809–1889* (Lewiston, N.Y., 2002), 160–61; Walter M. Merrill and Louis Ruchames, eds., *The Letters of William Lloyd Garrison* (6 vols.; Cambridge, Mass., 1971–81), 4: 53, 200.

20. *NYTrib*, December 24, 25, 1850; *NAS*, January 9, 1851.
21. *NYTrib*, December 24, 25, 27, 28, 30, 1850, January 1, 7, 1851; Foner, *Business and Slavery*, 60–61; *Raleigh Daily Register*, January 12, 1851; *BS*, December 25, 27, 30, 1850, January 8, 10, 1851; *Life and Adventures of James Williams, a Fugitive Slave, with a Full Description of the Underground Railroad* (San Francisco, 1873), 19.
22. Foner, *Business and Slavery*, 50–51; *Raleigh Daily Register*, January 12, 1851.
23. *Richmond Enquirer*, January 20, 1851; *NYEP*, January 21, 1851; *NYTrib*, January 21, 1851; *Augusta Chronicle*, February 1, 1851; *BS*, August 5, 1851.
24. *Alexandria Gazette*, January 22, 1851; *Jackson Mississippian and State Gazette*, January 31, 1851; *NAS*, September 4, 1851; *NYTrib*, February 12, 1851; *BS*, February 13, 1851.
25. *NAS*, September 11, 1851; *NYT*, April 2, 1852; *NYTrib*, April 2, 5, 1852.
26. *NYTrib*, April 2, 3, 1852; *NYT*, April 5, 1852; *NYEP*, April 5, 1852; *FDP*, June 3, 1852.
27. Fergus M. Bordewich, *Bound for Canaan: The Epic Story of the Underground Railroad, America's First Civil Rights Movement* (New York, 2005), 323–24; Roy E. Finkenbine, "Boston's Black Churches: Institutional Centers of the Antislavery Movement," in Donald M. Jacobs, ed., *Courage and Conscience: Black and White Abolitionists in Boston* (Boston, 1993), 182; Clare Taylor, ed., *British and American Abolitionists: An Episode in Transatlantic Understanding* (Edinburgh, 1974), 368; *Liberator*, October 25, 1850; *BE*, February 22, 1851; Sernett, *North Star Country*, 147–49.
28. Campbell, *Slave Catchers*, 199–207; *Liberator*, December 23, 1853.
29. [Harriet A. Jacobs], *Incidents in the Life of a Slave Girl, Written by Herself*, ed. L. Maria Child (Boston, 1861), 286–301; *NS*, October 24, 1850; William M. Mitchell, *The Underground Railroad* (London, 1860), 74–75.
30. *Liberator*, January 3, 1851; *NAS*, January 9, 1851; Rhoda G. Freeman, *The Free Negro in New York City in the Era before the Civil War* (New York, 1994), xlv, 34–35, 336.
31. Jane Rhodes, *Mary Ann Shadd Cary: The Black Press and Protest in the Nineteenth Century* (Bloomington, Ind., 1998), 30–36; Robin W. Winks, *The Blacks*

in Canada (New Haven, 1971), 178–214; Michael Wayne, "The Black Population of Canada West on the Eve of the American Civil War: A Reassessment Based on the Manuscript Census of 1861," *Histoire Sociale/Social History*, 56 (November 1995), 465–86; *PF*, May 31, 1856.

32. Michael Hembree, "The Question of 'Begging': Fugitive Slave Relief in Canada, 1830–1865," *Civil War History*, 37 (December 1991), 314; Samuel J. May to ?, August 3, 1852, AMA; *NAS*, December 28, 1848; Benjamin Drew, *A North-Side View of Slavery: The Refugee, or, The Narratives of Fugitive Slaves in Canada* (Boston, 1856), v–vi; Bordewich, *Bound for Canaan*, 246–47; Daniel G. Hill, *The Freedom-Seekers: Blacks in Early Canada* (Agincourt, Canada, 1981), 42–43; Winks, *Blacks in Canada*, 142–44, 248; Alexander L. Murray, "The Extradition of Fugitive Slaves from Canada: A Re-evaluation," *Canadian Historical Review*, 43 (December 1962), 298–314; John R. McKivigan and Jason H. Silverman, "Monarchial Liberty and Republican Slavery: West Indies Emancipation Celebrations in Upstate New York and Canada West," *Afro-Americans in New York Life and History*, 10 (January 1986), 7–18.
33. *NYTrib*, January 14, 31, 1851; Jermain Loguen to George Whipple, March 21, 1851, AMA.
34. *Liberator*, June 25, 1852; *FDP*, May 27, 1852; *NYTrib*, May 25, 1852; Tom Calarco, *People of the Underground Railroad* (Westport, Conn., 2008), 88–89.
35. *Thirteenth Annual Report of the American and Foreign Anti-Slavery Society* (New York, 1853), 197–207; *BE*, May 21, 27, June 7, 9, 1853; *FDP*, June 24, 1853; Lewis Tappan Journal, May 9, 10, 25, 28, 30, June 7, 13, 20, 1853, TP.
36. Benjamin Quarles, *Black Abolitionists* (New York, 1969), 154; Thomas J. Davis, "*Napoleon v. Lemmon*: Antebellum Black New Yorkers, Antislavery, and Law," *Afro-Americans in New York Life and History*, 33 (January 2009), 27–96; *NYT*, November 8, 9, 15, 18, 1852; *Hartford Courant*, May 8, 1874; *NYH*, November 7, 1852; *NYTrib*, November 8, 1852.
37. *NYT*, November 15, 19, 1852; *NYTrib*, November 15, 1852; David E. Swift, *Black Prophets of Justice: Activist Clergy before the Civil War* (Baton Rouge, 1989), 263; Lewis Tappan to John Jay II, December 11, 1852, JFP; *Chicago Inter-Ocean*, December 30, 1900.
38. *FDP*, December 31, 1852; *NYTrib*, November 17, 23, 1852; *NYT*, November 22, 23, 1852; Erastus D. Culver to Lewis Tappan, November 23, 1852, JFP.
39. *Savannah Morning News*, November 30, 1852; *NYTrib*, July 24, 1855, October 5, 1857; *NYT*, March 19, December 24, 1853, June 14, 1854, October 21, 1857.
40. *NYT*, March 7, December 8, 1857, April 16, 1860; N.Y. Court of Appeals, *Report*

of the Lemmon Slave Case (New York, 1860); *Jackson Daily Mississippian*, February 9, 1860; Marie Tyler-McGraw and Dwight T. Pitcaithley, "The Lemmon Slave Case: Courtroom Drama, Constitutional Crisis, and the Southern Quest to Nationalize Slavery," *Common-Place*, 14 (Fall 2013) www.common-place.org; Roy P. Basler, ed., *The Collected Works of Abraham Lincoln* (8 vols.; New Brunswick, N.J., 1953–55), 3: 423, 548–49.

41. Record of Fugitives, October 2, 1855, GP.

42. Nat Brandt, *In the Shadow of the Civil War: Passmore Williamson and the Rescue of Jane Johnson* (Columbia, S.C., 2007); William Still, *The Underground Railroad* (rev. ed.: Philadelphia, 1878), 77–88; John Hill Wheeler Diary, August 3, 1855, John Hill Wheeler Papers, Library of Congress; Record of Fugitives, July 31, September 6, 7, 1855; *NYT*, August 1, 1855; *NYTrib*, August 31, 1855; *NAS*, September 8, 1855.

43. Account Book, November 1855, March 10, 1861, Henry Wadsworth Longfellow Papers, Houghton Library, Harvard University; Jill Lepore, "How Longfellow Woke the Dead," *American Scholar*, 80 (Spring 2011), 33–46; William S. Powell, ed., *Dictionary of North Carolina Biography* (6 vols.; Chapel Hill, 1979–96), 6: 167–68; Henry Louis Gates Jr. and Hollis Robbins, eds., *In Search of Hannah Crafts* (New York, 2004). Crafts's novel was not published until a century and a half had passed: Henry Louis Gates Jr., ed., *The Bondwoman's Narrative* (New York, 2002).

44. Kellie Carter Jackson, "Force and Freedom: Black Abolitionists and the Politics of Violence, 1850–1860," (Ph.D., diss., Columbia University, 2010), 66–78; Gordon S. Barker, *Fugitive Slaves and the Unfinished American Revolution: Eight Cases, 1848–1856* (Jefferson, N.C., 2013), 10–13; Grover, *Fugitive's Gibraltar*, 247; *NAS*, October 10, 1850; *BE*, October 2, 1850.

45. Campbell, *Slave Catchers*, 115; Lois E. Horton, "Kidnapping and Resistance: Antislavery Direct Action in the 1850s," in David W. Blight, ed., *Passages to Freedom: The Underground Railroad in History and Memory* (Washington, D.C., 2004), 166; Steven Lubet, *Fugitive Justice* (Cambridge, Mass., 2010), 51–129; Thomas P. Slaughter, *Bloody Dawn: The Christiana Riot and Racial Violence in the Antebellum North* (New York, 1991).

46. Paula J. Priebe, "Central and Western New York and the Fugitive Slave Law of 1850," *Afro-Americans in New York Life and History*, 16 (January 1992), 19–29; *The Rev. J. W. Loguen, As a Slave and as a Freeman: A Narrative of Real Life* (Syracuse, 1859), 398–442; Donald Yacovone, *Samuel Joseph May and the Dilemmas of the Liberal Persuasion, 1797–1871* (Philadelphia, 1991), 140–50; Jayne Sokolow, "The Jerry McHenry Rescue and the Growth of Northern Antislavery

Sentiment during the 1850s," *Journal of American Studies*, 16 (December 1982), 440–41; Dorothy Sterling, *Ahead of Her Time: Abby Kelley and the Politics of Antislavery* (New York, 1991), 281; Samuel J. May to Wendell Phillips, September 1, 1852, PP.

47. Francis G. Shaw to Sydney Howard Gay, November 1, 1850, GP; Austin Bearse, *Reminiscences of Fugitive-Slave Law Days in Boston* (Boston, 1880), 3–6, 15, 34–37; Sidney Kaplan, "The *Moby Dick* in the Service of the Underground Railroad," *Phylon*, 12 (2nd quarter, 1951), 173–76; Finkenbine, "Boston's Black Churches," 181; Gary L. Collison, "The Boston Vigilance Committee," *Historical Journal of Western Massachusetts*, 12 (October 1984), 111; Robert L. Hall, "Massachusetts Abolitionists Document the Slave Experience," in Jacobs, ed., *Courage and Conscience*, 92–93; "Fugitive Slaves Aided by the Vigilance Committee since the Passage of the Fugitive Slave Bill 1850," manuscript, Massachusetts Anti-Slavery Society Records, NYHS.

48. Barker, *Fugitive Slaves*, 22–32; Lubet, *Fugitive Justice*, 134–45; Gary L. Collison, *Shadrach Minkins: From Fugitive Slave to Citizen* (Cambridge, Mass., 1997).

49. Lubet, *Fugitive Justice*, 145–55; Barker, *Fugitive Slaves*, 54–71; Bearse, *Reminiscences*, 27; Campbell, *Slave Catchers*, 120.

50. Lubet, *Fugitive Justice*, 160–228; Earl M. Maltz, *Fugitive Slave on Trial: The Anthony Burns Case and Abolitionist Outrage* (Lawrence, Kans., 2010), 40–51, 55–64, 95, 101; David F. Ericson, *Slavery in the American Republic: Developing the Federal Government, 1791–1861* (Lawrence, Kans., 2011), 125; Campbell, *Slave Catchers*, 130–32; Sydney Howard Gay to Elizabeth Gay, June 2, 1854, GP.

51. *Liberator*, June 9, 1854; Gordon S. Barker, *The Imperfect Revolution: Anthony Burns and the Landscape of Race in Antebellum America* (Kent, Ohio, 2010), 30–33; Campbell, *Slave Catchers*, 130–32; Maltz, *Fugitive Slave on Trial*, 1–3; Fehrenbacher, *Slaveholding Republic*, 228.

52. George Rogers Taylor, *The Transportation Revolution, 1815–1860* (New York, 1951), 79. The New York State Vigilance Committee claimed to have assisted 648 fugitives between 1851 and 1853 and between 300 and 400 in 1854. As will be related in chapter 7, Sydney Howard Gay's office aided over 200 fugitives in 1855 and 1856. No figures exist for the remainder of the 1850s or for Gay's operation before 1855. *Letter from Mrs. H. B. Stowe to the Ladies' New Anti-Slavery Society of Glasgow*... (Glasgow, 1853); *FDP*, March 23, 1855.

6. The Metropolitan Corridor

1. *NYTrib*, July 14, 1858.
2. Larry Gara, "William Still and the Underground Railroad," *Pennsylvania History*, 28 (January 1961), 33–36; Margaret Hope Bacon, *But One Race: The Life of Robert Purvis* (Albany, 2007), 114; Nat Brandt, *In the Shadow of the Civil War: Passmore Williamson and the Rescue of Jane Johnson* (Columbia, S.C., 2007), 3–12; William Still, *The Underground Railroad* (rev. ed.: Philadelphia, 1878); *Pennsylvania Freeman*, December 8, 1853; Journal C of Station No. 2, HSPa.
3. *Elevator* (San Francisco), September 15, 1865; Robert G. Albion, *The Rise of New York Port, 1815–1860* (New York, 1939), 122–40; Alex Roland, W. Jeffrey Bolster, and Alexender Keyssar, *The Way of the Ship: America's Maritime History Reenvisioned, 1600–2000* (New York, 2008), 171–72; David Cecelski, *The Waterman's Song: Slavery and Freedom in Maritime North Carolina* (Chapel Hill, 2001), 121–46.
4. Larry Gara, *The Liberty Line: The Legend of the Underground Railroad* (Lexington, Ky., 1961), 51–52; Tommy L. Bogger, *Free Blacks in Norfolk, Virginia, 1790–1860* (Charlottesville, 1997), 165–67; Record of Fugitives, May 16, July 8, 1856, GP; Still, *Underground Railroad*, 560; *PF*, April 21, 1855; *Richmond Whig*, November 27, 1855; *Charleston Mercury*, September 9, 1857; *Norfolk Herald* in *PF*, December 22, 1855.
5. *NYH*, July 26, 1856; *NAS*, June 12, 1858; *Liberator*, June 25, 1858; *Richmond Whig*, March 21, 1856.
6. Gary Collison, *Shadrach Minkins: From Fugitive Slave to Citizen* (Cambridge, Mass., 1997), 49–50; Still, *Underground Railroad*, 159–62, 333; Tom Calarco, *Places of the Underground Railroad* (Santa Barbara, 2011), 374; Note on Major Latham, November 10, 1856, GP.
7. Hilary Russell, "Underground Railroad Activists in Washington, D.C.," *Washington History*, 13 (Fall/Winter 2001–2), 35; Stanley Harrold, *Subversives: Antislavery Community in Washington, D.C., 1828–1865* (Baton Rouge, 2003), 96, 149–53, 213; Still, *Underground Railroad*, 173–74, 182–85.
8. *The Wilmington Directory for the Year 1853* (Wilmington, Del., 1853), 26; James A. McGowan, *Station Master on the Underground Railroad: The Life and Letters of Thomas Garrett* (rev. ed.: Jefferson, N.C., 2005), 41–43, 115, 158; Thomas Garrett to Joseph A. Dugdale, November 29, 1856, Joseph A. and Ruth Dugdale Correspondence, FHL; Sarah Pugh to ?, June 6, n.y., AC.
9. Thomas Garrett to Eliza Wighman, October 27, 1856, Cope Family Papers, Quaker and Special Collections, Haverford College; Calarco, *Places of the*

Underground Railroad, 370–73; *Wilmington Chicken* in *BS*, October 22, 1849; Walter H. Williams, *Slavery and Freedom in Delaware, 1639–1865* (Wilmington, Del., 1996), 165–67; William J. Switala, *Underground Railroad in Delaware, Maryland, and West Virginia* (Mechanicsburg, Pa., 2004), 52–58; John Hunn to Wilbur H. Siebert, August 16, 1893, SC.

10. Williams, *Slavery and Freedom*, 249–50; Priscilla Thompson, "Harriet Tubman, Thomas Garrett, and the Underground Railroad," *Delaware History*, 22 (Spring-Summer 1986), 7–9; McGowan, *Station Master*, 33, 53–65; *Easton Gazette*, September 5, 1857.
11. McGowan, *Station Master*, 166; Still, *Underground Railroad*, 560; Record of Fugitives, April 4, June 16, 24, July 8, 1856.
12. Record of Fugitives, September 7, October 13, December 19, 1855, January 18, 31, July 9, 1856; Note on Henry Johnson, November 24, 1856, GP.
13. Record of Fugitives, September 1, 1855, April 4, June 5, 16, 24, 1856; Note on Andrew Jackson, December 29, 1856, GP; Journal C, June 3, 1856.
14. *NAS*, September 16, 1854; William Kashatus, *Just over the Line: Chester County and the Underground Railroad* (West Chester, Pa., 2002), 19–60; McGowan, *Station Master*, 41–43; Frances C. Taylor, *The Trackless Trail* (Kennett Square, Pa., 1976), 3–21; Calarco, *Places of the Underground Railroad*, 144–49, 312; "Branches of the Underground Railroad from Wilmington, Delaware to Philadelphia," typescript, SC; Christopher Densmore, "Aim for a Free State and Settle among Quakers," in Brycchan Carey and Geoffrey Plank eds., *Quakers and Abolition* (Urbana, Ill., 2014), 123–24; *Pennsylvania Freeman*, January 2, 1851; Oliver Johnson to ?, April 2, 1857, JL.
15. Deborah J. Warner, *Graceanna Lewis: Scientist and Humanitarian* (Washington, D.C., 1979); Graceanna Lewis, "Underground Railroad Memoirs," 1912, Lewis-Fussell Papers, FHL; Graceanna Lewis, *An Appeal to Those Members of the Society of Friends Who, Knowing the Principles of the Abolitionists, Stand Aloof from the Anti-Slavery Enterprise* (N.p., n.d. [1840s]); David G. Smith, *On the Edge of Freedom: The Fugitive Slave Issue in South Central Pennsylvania, 1820–1870* (New York, 2012), 6–9, 29–37; Still, *Underground Railroad*, 683; William Still to Elijah Pennypacker, November 24, 1855, PL; R. C. Smedley, *History of the Underground Railroad in Chester and the Neighboring Counties of Pennsylvania* (Lancaster, Pa., 1883), 206–9; William J. Switala, *Underground Railroad in Pennsylvania* (Mechanicsburg, Pa., 2001), 122–24, 174–77; Kashatus, *Just over the Line*, 59.
16. Record of Fugitives, May 28, June 23, October 3, December 3, 5, 6, 1855, April 4, May 25, 1856.

17. Record of Fugitives, November 10, 1855; Journal C, November 8, December 1, 3, 1855; Still, *Underground Railroad*, 24–26, 300–301, 339; Judith Bentley, *"Dear Friend": Thomas Garrett and William Still, Collaborators on the Underground Railroad* (New York, 1997), 60–66.
18. "Branches of the Underground Railroad"; Lewis, "Underground Railroad Memoirs": Calarco, *Places of the Underground Railroad*, 311; William Still to James M. McKim, November 2, 1857, PL.
19. *Pennsylvania Freeman*, December 9, 1852; "Resolutions, Philadelphia, April 27, 1853," manuscript, MC; Elizabeth Varon, " 'Beautiful Providences': William Still, the Vigilance Committee, and Abolitionists in the Age of Sectionalism," in Richard Newman and James Mueller, eds., *Antislavery and Abolition in Philadelphia: Emancipation and the Long Struggle for Racial Justice in the City of Brotherly Love* (Baton Rouge, 2011), 230–32; Vigilance Committee of Philadelphia, Accounts, 1854–57, HSPa.
20. Journal C, October 24, 1854; *Pennsylvania Freeman* in *PF*, July 8, 1854; *PF*, November 11, 1854; Robert B. Toplin, "Peter Still versus the Peculiar Institution," *Civil War History*, 13 (December 1967), 340–49; Kate E. R. Pickard, *The Kidnapped and the Ransomed* (3rd ed.: Syracuse, 1856).
21. *PF* in *Anti-Slavery Reporter* (London), May 1, 1856, 103–4; *PF*, June 10, 1854, March 28, 1857.
22. Still, *Underground Railroad*, 217–18; Stanley Campbell, *The Slave Catchers: Enforcement of the Fugitive Slave Law, 1850–1860* (Chapel Hill, 1968), 199–206; *Philadelphia Morning Times*, January 21, 1857.
23. Still, *Underground Railroad*, 27–28, 583.
24. Journal C, April 19, July 20, September 23, October 25, November 25, 1853; Vigilance Committee of Philadelphia Accounts, November 5, 6, 1855; Still, *Underground Railroad*, 129–30, 187–93.
25. *Sunshine and Shadow of Slave Life. Reminiscences as Told by Isaac D. Williams to "Tege"* (East Saginaw, Mich., 1885), 47.
26. *NYTrib*, April 19, 1852; *NYT*, May 12, 1853; Lewis Tappan to John Smith, March 3, 1857, Letterbooks, TP.
27. Leslie M. Harris, *In the Shadow of Slavery: African Americans in New York City, 1626–1863* (Chicago, 2003), 238–39, 272; Craig Wilder, *In the Company of Black Men: The African Influence on African American Culture in New York City* (New York, 2001), 171; *FDP*, December 25, 1851; Judith Wellman, *Brooklyn's Promised Land: The Free Black Community of Weeksville, New York* (New York, 2014).
28. *NAS*, December 18, 1851, January 22, December 16, 1852; *FDP*, February 5, April

29, 1852; Rhoda G. Freeman, *The Free Negro in New York City in the Era before the Civil War* (New York, 1994), 32.

29. Circular Letter of the New York State Vigilance Committee, November 6, 1850, Miscellaneous Manuscripts, Library of Congress; *Letter from Mrs. H. B. Stowe to the Ladies' New Anti-Slavery Society of Glasgow*... (Glasgow, 1853); Freeman, *Free Negro*, 65; *FDP*, May 20, 1852; Charles B. Ray to Gerrit Smith, April 29, 1856, SP; *NYH*, January 5, 1860; Still, *Underground Railroad*, 674–75; Lewis Tappan to Eliza Wighman, February 6, 1857, Tappan to "Dear Sir," July 4, 1857, Letterbooks, TP.

30. Harrold, *Subversives*, 203–20; Still, *Underground Railroad*, 150–51, 170–71, 181; *Anti-Slavery Reporter*, December 1, 1852, 182; *BAP*, 1: 328; Frank Decker, *Brooklyn's Plymouth Church in the Civil War Era: A Ministry of Freedom* (Charleston, 2013), 44; Lewis Tappan Journal, November 30, December 3, 1855, TP; Tappan to E. L. Stevens, February 6, 1857, Tappan to Henry Richardson, February 6, 1857, Letterbooks, TP.

31. *FDP*, January 22, 1852; *NYE*, January 8, March 29, 1855; *NS*, January 23, April 3, 1854; *Independent* in *American and Foreign Anti-Slavery Reporter*, May 1, 1851, 116; Lewis Tappan to J. Smith, March 3, 1857, Letterbooks, TP; *Rochester Anti-Slavery Bazaar* (Halifax, N.S., 1857).

32. "Capture, Trial and Return of the Fugitives, Stephen Pembroke and His Two Sons, to Slavery," manuscript, n.d., African-American Records Collection, Lancaster County Historical Society, Pa.; Still, *Underground Railroad*, 166–69; Journal C, May 24, 1854; *NYT*, May 27, 1854; *NAS*, June 3, 1854; Christopher Webber, *American to the Backbone: The Life of James W. C. Pennington, the Fugitive Slave Who Became One of the First Black Abolitionists* (New York, 2011), 344; Case of Stephen Pembroke, RG 21.

33. *NYTrib*, May 27, July 4, 18, 1854; *PF*, June 10, 1854; Still, *Underground Railroad*, 167–70.

34. Annie H. Abel and Frank J. Klingberg, *A Side-Light on Anglo-American Relations, 1839–1858* (New York, 1927), 347–48, 358–60; MB, March 16, May 18, 1854; Oliver Johnson, *William Lloyd Garrison and His Times* (Boston, 1880), 296; *NAS*, April 21, 1855; Lewis Tappan Journal, July 19, 1855, TP; Prithi Kanakamedala, "In Pursuit of Freedom," manuscript, Brooklyn Historical Society, 2012, 121.

35. *NYH*, January 5, 1860; *Sixth Annual Report of the Glasgow New Association for the Abolition of Slavery* (Glasgow, 1857), 6.

36. Wendell Phillips to Sydney Howard Gay, September 6, 1852, Henry I. Bowditch to Gay, November 12, 1850, William Jay to Gay, September, n.d., 1854, GP; *NAS*, August 4, November 4, 1854.

37. Sydney Howard Gay to Elizabeth Gay, June 2, 1854, GP.

38. Henry Wilson, *History of the Rise and Fall of the Slave Power in America* (3 vols.; Boston, 1874), 2: 51–52; Still, *Underground Railroad*, 119–20; Anti-Slavery Standard Account Book, February 3, September 14, December 30, 1854, March 24, August, November, December 1855, Sydney Howard Gay Papers, NYPL. Record of Fugitives at the end of 1855 lists twenty-three payments to Napoleon over two years. Gay's name does not appear in the index of many books on the underground railroad.
39. Record of Fugitives, July 24, August 10, 14, 1855.
40. Record of Fugitives, September 5, October 13, 1855, July 9, 1856; Note on Elizabeth Anderson, undated, GP.
41. James McCune Smith to Gerrit Smith, October 6, 1855, SP; Record of Fugitives, February 9, 20, 1855; Account Current 1855–1856, GP; Elizabeth Neall Gay to Mrs. H. G. Chapman, June 11, 1857, Francis Jackson to Sydney Howard Gay, July 9, 1855, May 1, 1856, GP.
42. Abigail H. Gibbons to Rowland Johnson, April n.d., 1856, GP; William H. Leonard to Johnson, July 23, 1856; Louis Napoleon, receipt, June 2, 1856, GP; Record of Fugitives, January 25, 1856.
43. *NAS*, May 17, 1856; Sydney Howard Gay to Weston, February 6, 1853, Weston to Gay, May 18, 1853, Edmund Quincy to Gay, May 23, 1853, GP.
44. Still, *Underground Railroad*, 27–28; William H. Leonard to William Still, November 24, 1856, ANHS.
45. Henry Wilson, *Trow's New York City Directory for the Year Ending May 1, 1856* (New York, 1855), 320; Still, *Underground Railroad*, 27–28; Jacob R. Gibbs to Timothy R. Hudson, October 18, 1857, Anti-Slavery Collection, Oberlin College; Sydney Howard Gay to James Miller McKim, September 11, 1858, MAC; Marriage Record, Louis Napoleon and Elizabeth Seaman, December 4, 1855, Municipal Archives, New York City; Henry Wilson, *Trow's New York City Directory for the Year Ending May 1, 1860* (New York, 1859), 629; Manuscript U.S. Census, 1860, accessed via AncestryLibrary.com.
46. Agents of the U. G. R. R., n.d., March 1856?, Record of Fugitives; *NYT*, March 30, 1857.
47. Calarco, *Places of the Underground Railroad*, 8–10; Marcy S. Sacks, "'We Rise or Fall Together': Separatism and the Demand for Equality by Albany's Black Citizens, 1827–1860," *Afro-Americans in New York Life and History*, 20 (July 1996), 7–34; Stephen Myers to Gerrit Smith, March 22, 1856, SP; Manuscript U.S. Census, 1860.
48. Stephen Myers to Francis Jackson, May n.d., 1858, AC; Stephen Myers, broadside, January 1, 1860, JJH; *Journal of Commerce* in *Charleston Mercury*, February 15, 1858; *PF*, July 19, 1856.

49. *Northern Star and Freeman's Advocate* (Albany), December 8, 1842; Stephen Myers, *Circular to the Friends of Freedom* (Albany, 1858); *NYT*, February 2, 1860; Stephen Myers to John Jay II, December 17, 1858, JFP; Myers to John Jay II, January 2, December 17, 1860, JJH; *Weekly Anglo-African*, November 5, 1859; Stephen Myers, broadside, January 1, 1860.

50. *Weekly Anglo-African*, May 5, November 24, 1860; Manuscript U.S. Census, 1860; Carol M. Hunter, *To Set the Captives Free: Reverend Jermain Wesley Loguen and the Struggle for Freedom in Central New York, 1835–1872* (New York, 1993), 18, 31–43, 60; *The Rev. J. W. Loguen, as a Slave and as a Freeman: A Narrative of Real Life* (Syracuse, 1859), ii–vi, 444, 451–55; Samuel J. May, *Some Recollections of Our Antislavery Conflict* (Boston, 1869), 290–92; *Elevator* (San Francisco), October 5, 1872.

51. Hunter, *To Set the Captives Free*, 153–67; *FDP*, April 6, 1855, January 21, 1856; *PF*, February 2, 1856; Angela Murphy, " 'It Outlaws Me, and I Outlaw It!' Resistance to the Fugitive Slave Law in Syracuse, New York," *Afro-Americans in New York Life and History*, 28 (January 2004), 43–72; *Syracuse Daily Standard*, November 25, 1854; *NAS*, October 3, 1857; *Douglass' Monthly*, March 1857.

52. *Liberator*, March 17, May 5, 1854; Reinhard O. Johnson, *The Liberty Party, 1840–1848: Antislavery Third-Party Politics in the United States* (Baton Rouge, 2009), 357; Clara M. DeBoer, *Be Jubilant My Feet: African American Abolitionists in the American Missionary Association, 1839–1861* (New York, 1994), 16; Donald Yacovone, *Samuel Joseph May and the Dilemmas of the Liberal Persuasion, 1797–1871* (Philadelphia, 1991), 132, 140–41, 159–62; *Circular of the New-York State Vigilance Committee* [ca. 1850], NYHS; Ira H. Cobb to Lewis Tappan, October 27, 1856, AMA.

53. Frederick Douglass to Sydney Howard Gay, January 8, 1848, GP; John Blassingame and John R. McKivigan, eds., *The Frederick Douglass Papers* (New Haven, 1979–), ser. 3, 1: 226–27, 555; *NAS*, August 12, 1847, September 3, 24, December 24, 1853.

54. *FDP*, December 9, 1853, December 29, 1854, October 14, 1859; *NAS*, December 23, 1854, January 13, 1855, April 14, 1860; *BAP*, 4: 180, 259; Thomas Henning to Sydney Howard Gay, April 11, 1855, GP; Frederick Douglass to Wilbur H. Siebert, March 27, 1893, SC; *Life and Times of Frederick Douglass Written by Himself* (rev. ed.: Boston, 1892), 271–72.

55. Alice Taylor, "Selling Abolitionism: The Commercial, Material, and Social World of the Boston Antislavery Fair, 1834–1858" (Ph.D. diss., University of Western Ontario, 2008), 12, 31–35, 240; Beth A. Salerno, *Sister Societies: Women's Antislavery Societies in Antebellum America* (DeKalb, Ill., 2005), 121-32; *NAS*, January 26, 1843.

56. *NAS*, August 18, 1842; *Liberator*, February 7, 1851; Salerno, *Sister Societies*, 117–18; Carol Faulkner, *Lucretia Mott's Heresy: Abolition and Women's Rights in Nineteenth-Century America* (Philadelphia, 2011), 169.
57. Lee Chambers-Schiller, " 'A Good Work among the People': The Political Culture of the Boston Antislavery Fair," in Jean Fagan Yellin and John C. Van Horne, eds., *The Abolitionist Sisterhood: Women's Political Culture in Antebellum America* (Ithaca, 1994), 250–51; *NAS*, January 31, 1857; Taylor, "Selling Abolitionism," 42–43; Horace Scudder, ed., *The Complete Poetical Works of James Russell Lowell* (Boston, 1924), 111.
58. Salerno, *Sister Societies*, 108–12, 130–33; Taylor, "Selling Abolitionism," 55–60, 88–89, 170; *NAS*, January 24, 1850, December 17, 1853; Chambers-Schiller, " 'Good Work,' " 251–53, 267–68; Sarah H. Southwick, *Reminiscences of the Early Anti-Slavery Days* (Cambridge, Mass., 1893), 36.
59. Jean Soderlund, "Priorities and Power: The Philadelphia Female Anti-Slavery Society," in Yellin and Van Horne, eds., *Abolitionist Sisterhood*, 68, 81–85; Lawrence B. Glickman, " 'Buy for the Sake of the Slave': Abolitionism and the Origins of American Consumer Activism," *American Quarterly*, 56 (December 2004), 889–912; Anna D. Hallowell, *James and Lucretia Mott: Life and Letters* (Boston, 1884), 127; Julie Roy Jeffrey, *The Great Silent Army of Abolitionism: Ordinary Women in the Antislavery Movement* (Chapel Hill, 1998), 108–22; Sydney Howard Gay to Richard D. Webb, June 17, 1849 (copy), AC.
60. Webber, *American to the Backbone*, 180; Andrew Paton to Sydney Howard Gay, January 30, March 21, 1851, GP; Richard D. Webb to Anne Warren Weston, November 1, 1850, Paton to Weston, November 15, 1850, AC.
61. Clare Taylor, ed., *British and American Abolitionists: An Episode in Transatlantic Understanding* (Edinburgh, 1974), 342–47, 396–97; *Friend of the Fugitive, and Anti-Slavery Record* (Glasgow), April 1, 1853; *NYTrib*, December 25, 1851; *Report of the Edinburgh Ladies' New Anti-Slavery Association for the Years 1856 and 1857* (Edinburgh, 1858); Glasgow New Association for the Abolition of Slavery, *Anti-Slavery Bazaar*, broadside, Glasgow, 1855; Still, *Underground Railroad*, 675; R. J. M. Blackett, *Building an Antislavery Wall: Black Americans in the Atlantic Abolitionist Movement, 1830–1860* (Baton Rouge, 1983), 132; *NAS*, October 8, 1853; Andrew Paton to Maria Weston Chapman, November 20, 1857, AC; Paton to Sydney Howard Gay, January 30, February 14, 1851, GP; Webber, *American to the Backbone*, 342; DeBoer, *Be Jubilant My Feet*, 93; Calarco, *Places of the Underground Railroad*, 217.
62. *FDP*, December 11, 1851; *NAS*, October 22, 1840, February 24, 1842.
63. John B. Estlin, *Reply to a Circular Issued by the Glasgow Association for the Abolition*

of Slavery (Paris, n.d.), 2–6; *Liberator*, May 22, 1857; *Weekly Anglo-African*, October 15, 1859.

64. Elizabeth Gay to Caroline Weston, December 15, 1847, Gay to Mrs. H. G. Chapman [Maria Weston Chapman], June 11, July 25, October 31, December 16, 1857, Chapman to Gay, June 15, 1857, Gay to Sarah Pugh, July 2, 1857, GP; *NYT*, December 9, 10, 1857.

65. Taylor, "Selling Abolitionism," 267–73; Taylor, *British and American Abolitionists*, 431; Chambers-Schiller, " 'Good Work,' " 271–73; *NAS*, June 28, 1858; *Report of the Twenty-Fourth National Anti-Slavery Festival* (Boston, 1858), 19–21.

7. The Record of Fugitives

1. Kate C. Larson, *Bound for the Promised Land: Harriet Tubman, Portrait of an American Hero* (New York, 2004), xvi–xviii, 83–93, 105–37; Kate C. Larson, "Racing for Freedom: Harriet Tubman's Underground Railroad Network through New York," *Afro-Americans in New York Life and History*, 36 (January 2012), 7–33; Milton C. Sernett, *Harriet Tubman: Myth, Memory, and History* (Durham, 2007), 321–33; Catherine Clinton, " 'Slavery Is War': Harriet Tubman and the Underground Railroad," in David W. Blight, ed., *Passages to Freedom: The Underground Railroad in History and Memory* (Washington, D.C., 2004), 195–96.

2. Larson, "Racing for Freedom," 9–10; Lewis Tappan to Anthony Lane, November 16, 1855, Letterbooks, TP; Alan Singer, "We May Never Know the Real Harriet Tubman," *Afro-Americans in New York Life and History*, 36 (January 2012), 70–71; Larson, *Bound for the Promised Land*, 105–7, 137.

3. William Still, *The Underground Railroad* (rev. ed.: Philadelphia, 1878), 295; Lewis Tappan to Anthony Lane, November 16, 1855, Letterbooks, TP; Nicholas M. Young et al., "Even Superheroes Need a Network: Harriet Tubman and the Rise of Insurgency in the New York State Underground Railroad," *Du Bois Review*, 6 (2009), 397–429; James A. McGowan, *Station Master on the Underground Railroad: The Life and Letters of Thomas Garrett* (rev. ed.: Jefferson, N.C., 2005), 98, 167–87.

4. Record of Fugitives, May 14, 1856, GP; Still, *Underground Railroad*, 295–95; Dorchester (Md.) *American Eagle*, May 14, 1856; Journal C of Station No. 2, HSPa; Canada Census, 1861, accessed via AncestryLibrary.com.

5. Larson, *Bound for the Promised Land*, 133–36; Larson, "Racing for Freedom," 17–21; Statement by William Bailey, November 26, 1856, Note on Eliza Manokey, November 27, 1856, GP; Journal C, November 26, 1856; Still,

Underground Railroad, 272–74; Thomas Garrett to Joseph Dugdale, November 29, 1856, Joseph A. and Ruth Dugdale Correspondence, FHL; Sernett, *Harriet Tubman*, 55.

6. John Brown, who met Harriet Tubman in Canada in 1858, referred to her as "General Tubman." Sernett, *Harriet Tubman*, 77.
7. Patience Essah, *A House Divided: Slavery and Emancipation in Delaware, 1638–1865* (Charlottesville, 1996), 80; Elwood L. Bridner Jr., "The Fugitive Slaves of Maryland," *Maryland Historical Magazine*, 66 (March 1971), 36–39; John Hope Franklin and Loren Schweninger, *Runaway Slaves: Rebels on the Plantation* (New York, 1999), 210.
8. Still, *Underground Railroad*, 162.
9. Record of Fugitives, February 9, December 5, 21, 26, 1855, January 4, June 4, 5, November 10, 1856; Note on Albert McCealee and John Edward Dayton, December 30, 1856, GP; William S. Powell, ed., *Dictionary of North Carolina Biography* (6 vols.; Chapel Hill, 1979–96), 1: 210; Manuscript U.S. Census, 1850, 1860, accessed via AncestryLibrary.com; Midori Takagi, *"Reading Wolves to Our Own Destruction": Slavery in Richmond, Virginia, 1782–1865* (Charlottesville, 1999), 73; Templeman and Goodwin Account Book, 1849–1851, Special Collections, University of Virginia Library.
10. *NAS*, October 8, 1853; Record of Fugitives, October 13, 26, 1855, April 4, 30, July 9, December 30, 1856; Still, *Underground Railroad*, 335–36, 380–81; Journal C, April 10, 1856.
11. Record of Fugitives, June 24, 1856; Still, *Underground Railroad*, 293; Journal C, June 23, August 31, September 7, November 15, 1855, January 3, 1856.
12. Record of Fugitives, October 26, 1855, April 18, July 11, 1856; Statement of James Morris, undated, GP; Still, *Underground Railroad*, 119–20, 314–15.
13. Record of Fugitives, October 26, December 21, 1855, July 23, 1856; Journal C, November 29, 1855.
14. Record of Fugitives, January 4, April 9, 1856; Still, *Underground Railroad*, 114–15; *Baltimore Sun*, November 26, 27, 28, 29, 30, December 1, 1855, March 26, 27, 1856.
15. Record of Fugitives, August 17, December 5, 1855, June 5, 1856.
16. Record of Fugitives, January 17, July 22, 23, 28, September 17, November 10, 1856; Journal C, December 20, 1855, January 3, 1856.
17. Note on Elizabeth Harris, December 8, 1856, GP; Record of Fugitives, August 31, 1855, April 2, 1856; Still, *Underground Railroad*, 285–87, 325–26, 516; Muster Roll of USS *Saranac*, March, May, June, July 1856, Muster Rolls and Payrolls for U.S. Navy Vessels 1798–1860, Miscellaneous Records of the Office of Naval Records and Library, Record Group 45, Entry 68, National Archives.

18. Record of Fugitives, December 26, 1855, March 17, 25, 27, 1856; Canada Census, 1861.
19. Record of Fugitives, November 17, 1855, April 11, September 17, 1856.
20. Record of Fugitives, April 7, September 7, 1856; Still, *Underground Railroad*, 319–22.
21. Record of Fugitives, January 18, August 19, 1856; Still, *Underground Railroad*, 117–22; Journal C, January 16, 1856.
22. *NYTrib*, May 14, 1858; Record of Fugitives, May 16, June 4, 1856; Still, *Underground Railroad*, 163–65, 316, 382–83.
23. Stanley Harrold, *Border War: Fighting over Slavery before the Civil War* (Chapel Hill, 2010), 177; Richard Blackett, *Making Freedom: The Underground Railroad and the Politics of Slavery* (Chapel Hill, 2013), 77; Record of Fugitives, October 3, November 10, 1855; *BS*, July 20, 1858.
24. Record of Fugitives, March 17, 20, 27, April 2, 1856; Note on Albert McCealee and John Edward Dayton, December 30, 1856, GP.
25. Record of Fugitives, September 1, 1855, March 27, May 15, 26, 1856; Still, *Underground Railroad*, 214, 222; *BS*, May 22, 24, 28, 29, 1856.
26. Record of Fugitives, April 3, May 28, December 5, 1855, January 4, June 5, 1856; *PF* in *Anti-Slavery Reporter* (London), May 1, 1856, 103–4; Still, *Underground Railroad*, 114–15, 219; Journal C, January 2, 1856; Canada Census, 1861.
27. Record of Fugitives, August 30, September 5, 7, December 21, 1855, September 17, 1856.
28. Record of Fugitives, October 8, 1855; Still, *Underground Railroad*, 293–94; Journal C, October 7, 1855.
29. Record of Fugitives, June 25, December 21, 1855, May 16, 1856; Journal C, June 23, December 30, 1855; Still, *Underground Railroad*, 122.
30. Record of Fugitives, August 17, 1855, January 4, 28, 1856; Journal C, August 17, 1855, January 29, 1856.
31. *NAS*, March 6, 1858; *NYH*, January 5, 1860; New Account with William H. Leonard, 1859, Record of Fugitives. The Anti-Slavery Standard Account Book in the Gay Papers at the New York Public Library records numerous small payments to Louis Napoleon between 1857 and 1861.
32. Lewis Tappan to John Smith, March 3, 1857, Letterbooks, TP; *NYH*, January 5, 1860; *NYT*, December 3, 4, 1857; *NAS*, December 12, 1857; *Savannah Georgian* in *Charleston Mercury*, December 9, 1857; *BE*, December 2, 1857.
33. *NYH*, April 1, 1860; Oliver Johnson to James Miller McKim, May 2, 1860, MAC; William H. Leonard to William Still, February 6, 1858, October 5, 1860, ANHS; Still, *Underground Railroad*, 555.

34. *NYH*, October 21, 1860; *Liberator*, August 27, 1858; *NYT*, March 25, 26, 1858.
35. James Miller McKim to Maria Weston Chapman, November 19, 1857, AC; Fergus M. Bordewich, *Bound for Canaan: The Epic Story of the Underground Railroad, America's First Civil Rights Movement* (New York, 2005), 408–11; *Liberator*, May 28, 1858; Stephen Myers to John Jay II, January 2, 1860, JJH.
36. Case of Josiah Hoy and Allen Graff, RG 21; *BS*, May 3, 1860.
37. William H. Leonard to James Miller McKim, May 3, 1860; Oliver Johnson to McKim, May 2, 1860, MAC; *NAS*, May 5, 1860; *Liberator*, June 29, 1860.
38. *NYTrib*, December 4, 7, 1860, March 5, 1861; *NAS*, December 1, 1860; *Richmond Dispatch*, November 29, 1860.
39. *Richmond Whig*, May 26, 1857; *Alexandria Gazette*, December 18, 1857.

8. The End of the Underground Railroad

1. Charles Ballance to Lyman Trumbull, May 7, 1860, Lyman Trumbull Papers, Library of Congress; Stanley W. Campbell, *The Slave Catchers: Enforcement of the Fugitive Slave Law, 1850–1860* (Chapel Hill, 1968), 86–87, 171–85; Vroman Mason, "The Fugitive Slave Law in Wisconsin, with Reference to Nullification Sentiment," *Proceedings of the State Historical Society of Wisconsin*, 43 (1895), 117–44; Eric Foner, *Free Soil, Free Labor, Free Men: The Ideology of the Republican Party before the Civil War* (New York, 1970), 76–84, 135; *NYT*, March 9, 1857; George H. Porter, *Ohio Politics during the Civil War Period* (New York, 1911), 20–22.
2. Timothy O. Howe to George Rublee, April 3, 1859, Timothy O. Howe Papers, State Historical Society of Wisconsin; *NYT*, May 29, 1854.
3. Roy P. Basler, ed., *The Collected Works of Abraham Lincoln* (8 vols.; New Brunswick, N.J., 1953–55), 2: 233, 384, 390–91, 394–95; *Liberator*, June 22, July 13, 1860; *NAS*, April 16, 1859.
4. *NYH*, January 5, 1860; Stanley Harrold, *The Abolitionists and the South* (Lexington, Ky., 1995), 161.
5. John A. May and Joan R. Faunt, *South Carolina Secedes* (Columbia, S.C., 1960), 76–81; Constitution of the Confederate States of America, Article IV, Section 2.
6. Howard C. Perkins, *Northern Editorials on Secession* (2 vols.; New York, 1942), 1: 101–2; Jerome Mushkat, *Fernando Wood: A Political Biography* (Kent, Ohio, 1990), 111–13; Philip S. Foner, *Business and Slavery: The New York Merchants and the Irrepressible Conflict* (Chapel Hill, 1941), 248–51, 287–88; Eric Foner, *The Fiery Trial: Abraham Lincoln and American Slavery* (New York, 2010), 146–47.
7. David E. Kyvig, *Explicit and Authentic Acts: Amending the U.S. Constitution,*

1776–1995 (Lawrence, Kans., 1996), 146–49; *CG*, 36th Congress, 2d Session, 11, 25; James A. Rawley, *Edwin D. Morgan, 1811–1883: Merchant in Politics* (New York, 1955), 124; Lyman Trumbull to Richard Yates, [December 1860], Richard Yates Papers, Rare Book and Manuscript Library, Columbia University.

8. Basler, ed., *Collected Works*, 4: 154–57, 263–64; Russell McClintock, *Lincoln and the Decision for War: The Northern Response to Secession* (Chapel Hill, 2008), 92–95; *Douglass' Monthly*, April 1861; *Liberator*, March 8, 1861.
9. Stephen Myers to John Jay II, December 17, 1860, JJH; *NYTrib*, April 15, 1861; *Harrisburgh Telegraph* in *NAS*, August 10, 1861; *NAS*, December 28, 1861.
10. Foner, *Fiery Trial*, 166–67, 191–92, 201–2; Barbara J. Fields, *Slavery and Freedom on the Middle Ground* (New Haven, 1985), 100; Campbell, *Slave Catchers*, 192–93.
11. Oliver Johnson to James Miller McKim, October 11, 1860, MAC; Foner, *Fiery Trial*, 166–67, 173, 187, 194–95.
12. *NYH*, December 4, 1861; Fergus M. Bordewich, *Bound for Canaan: The Epic Story of the Underground Railroad, America's First Civil Rights Movement* (New York, 2005), 430; *Liberator*, October 17, 1862; *NAS*, December 14, 1861; *Principia* (New York), October 29, 1863; Adam Arrenson, "Experience Rather than Imagination: Researching the Return Migration of African North Americans during the American Civil War and Reconstruction," *Journal of American Ethnic History*, 32 (Winter 2013), 73–77.
13. Foner, *Fiery Trial*, 295; Robert Kaczorowski, "The Supreme Court and Congress's Power to Enforce Constitutional Rights: An Overlooked Moral Anomaly," *Fordham Law Review*, 73 (October 2004), 154–243; *CG*, 39th Congress, 1st Session, 475, 1117–18.
14. James A. McGowan, *Station Master on the Underground Railroad: The Life and Letters of Thomas Garrett* (rev. ed.: Jefferson, N.C., 2005), 80, 152–53; Kate Larson, *Bound for the Promised Land: Harriet Tubman, Portrait of an American Hero* (New York, 2004), 271–78.
15. *BAP*, 5: 140–41; Stephen G. Hall, "To Render the Private Public: William Still and the Selling of 'The Underground Railroad,' " *Pennsylvania Magazine of History and Biography*, 127 (January 2003), 35–55; Allen W. Turnage to William H. Still, August 9, 1902, ANHC.
16. Ira V. Brown, "Miller McKim and Pennsylvania Abolitionism," *Pennsylvania History*, 30 (January 1963), 69–72; Margaret Hope Bacon, *But One Race: The Life of Robert Purvis* (Albany, 2007), 2, 202.
17. *Autobiography of Dr. William Henry Johnson* (Albany, 1900), 61; *Albany Evening Times*, February 14, 1870; Carol M. Hunter, *To Set the Captives Free: Reverend*

Jermain Wesley Loguen and the Struggle for Freedom in Central New York, 1835–1872 (New York, 1993), 225–28.

18. Bertram Wyatt-Brown, *Lewis Tappan and the Evangelical War against Slavery* (Cleveland, 1969), 339; *BAP*, 2: 80; 3: 478; Margaret Hope Bacon, *Abby Hopper Gibbons: Prison Reformer and Social Activist* (Albany, 2000), 100, 114–15, 170–71.
19. Sydney Howard Gay to Thomas Wentworth Higginson, October 28, 1882, GP; Gregory M. Pfitzer, *Popular History and the Literary Marketplace, 1840–1920* (Amherst, Mass., 2008), 75–121; Gilbert H. Muller, *William Cullen Bryant: Author of America* (Albany, 2008), 323–24.
20. Sydney Howard Gay to Thomas Wentworth Higginson, October 28, 1882, GP; William Cullen Bryant and Sydney Howard Gay, *A Popular History of the United States* (4 vols.; New York, 1876–80), 4: 316, 324, 335–36, 342, 345, 435, 600.
21. Manuscript U.S. Census, 1870, accessed via AncestryLibrary.com; *NYTrib*, May 20, 1873; *New York Age*, April 25, August 22, 1907.
22. *Brooklyn Daily Union*, June 20, 1871; *Brooklyn Eagle*, November 13, 1872; *NYTrib*, October 12, 1875; *New York Sun*, March 31, 1881; Death Certificate of Louis Napoleon, March 28, 1881, Municipal Archives, New York City.

INDEX

Page numbers in *italics* refer to maps; page numbers beginning with 235 refer to endnotes.